THE IRANIAN REVOLUTION AT FORTY

THE
IRANIAN REVOLUTION
AT FORTY

Edited by
SUZANNE MALONEY

BROOKINGS INSTITUTION PRESS
Washington, D.C.

The Brookings Institution is a private nonprofit organization devoted to research, education, and publication on important issues of domestic and foreign policy. Its principal purpose is to bring the highest quality independent research and analysis to bear on current and emerging policy problems. Interpretations or conclusions in Brookings publications should be understood to be solely those of the authors.

Library of Congress Cataloging-in-Publication Data
Names: Maloney, Suzanne, editor.
Title: The Iranian revolution at forty / edited by Suzanne Maloney.
Description: Washington, D.C. : Brookings Institution Press, 2020.
Identifiers: LCCN 2019048650 (print) | LCCN 2019048651 (ebook) | ISBN
    9780815737933 (paperback) | ISBN 9780815737940 (epub)
Subjects: LCSH: Iran—History—Revolution, 1979. | Iran—History—
    Revolution, 1979—Influence. | Iran—Foreign relations—United States.
    | United States—Foreign relations—Iran. | Iran—Foreign relations—
    Middle East. | Middle East—Foreign relations—Iran. | Iran—Foreign
    relations—1979–1997. | Iran—Foreign relations—1997–
Classification: LCC DS318.81 .I735 2020 (print) | LCC DS318.81 (ebook) |
    DDC 955.05/3—dc23
LC record available at https://lccn.loc.gov/2019048650
LC ebook record available at https://lccn.loc.gov/2019048651

9 8 7 6 5 4 3 2 1

Typeset in Minion Pro

Composition by Elliott Beard

Contents

Acknowledgments   ix

Introduction   xiii

PART I
Iran Recast

1 **A View of the Revolution from the Shah's Palace**   3
STROBE TALBOTT

2 **The Revolution's Broken Promises**   8
ALI FATHOLLAH-NEJAD

3 **Iran's Economy since the Revolution**   18
Populism and Pragmatism
DJAVAD SALEHI-ISFAHANI

4 **Revolution, Reform, and the Future of the Islamic Republic**   27
SUZANNE MALONEY

5 **Poppies and Public Health**   40
1979 and Narcotics in Iran
VANDA FELBAB-BROWN *and* BRADLEY S. PORTER

6 **Girls of Revolution Street** 50
Iranian Women since 1979
SUZANNE MALONEY *and* ELIORA KATZ

PART II

The Revolution and Washington

7 **"We Used to Run This Country"** 69
How the Revolution Upended an American-Iranian Alliance
SUZANNE MALONEY

8 **After 1979, America's Torch Song for Tehran** 80
KENNETH POLLACK

9 **The Iranian Hostage Crisis and Its Effect** 88
on American Politics
ELAINE KAMARCK

10 **Washington, the Shah, and the Problem of Autocratic Allies** 92
TAMARA COFMAN WITTES

11 **The Revolution and Washington's Reliance** 96
on Economic Pressure
KATE HEWITT *and* RICHARD NEPHEW

12 **The Rules of the Game** 103
International Law and Iranian-American Relations
SCOTT R. ANDERSON

13 **1979 and the World's Second Oil Shock** 115
SAMANTHA GROSS

PART III

The Ripple Effect of Iran's Revolution
across the Middle East

14 How 1979 Transformed the Regional Balance of Power   123
    ITAMAR RABINOVICH

15 The Iranian Revolution's Legacy of Terrorism   129
    DANIEL BYMAN

16 Iraq and the "First Islamic Revolution"   135
    RANJ ALAALDIN

17 Saddam's Monumental Mistakes   140
    BRUCE RIEDEL

18 Hezbollah: Revolutionary Iran's Most Successful Export   143
    JEFFREY FELTMAN

19 The Origins of the Saudi-Iranian Battle   156
    for the Broader Middle East
    SUZANNE MALONEY *and* BRUCE RIEDEL

20 Coexistence and Convergence in Turkish-Iranian Relations   168
    KEMAL KIRIŞCI

21 Israel's Reverse Periphery Doctrine   174
    NATAN SACHS

22 Emboldened and Then Constrained   181
    Repercussions of Iran's Revolution for Sunni Islamists
    SHADI HAMID *and* SHARAN GREWAL

23 In Pakistan, Another Embassy Under Siege   188
    MADIHA AFZAL

24 Bad Judgment and a Chain of Blunders   192
Soviet Responses to the Iranian Revolution
PAVEL BAEV

APPENDIX A
Iranian Revolution Timeline of Events   197
SUZANNE MALONEY *and* KEIAN RAZIPOUR

APPENDIX B
What to Read to Understand the 1979 Iranian Revolution   203
SUZANNE MALONEY, ELIORA KATZ,
and KEIAN RAZIPOUR

Contributors   211

Index   219

Acknowledgments

This volume emerged from a fortuitous conversation while waiting in the buffet line for a lunch among colleagues in the Brookings Foreign Policy program. The inimitable Bruce Riedel, whose depth of knowledge and range of experience in the Middle East and beyond transcend that of almost anyone in Washington, remarked about the long shadow cast by the events of 1979, which he experienced at the early stages of his career in the intelligence community. As we surveyed the catering options, we began to imagine an effort to engage our colleagues from across Brookings and beyond, to offer their perspectives on Iran's revolution and its reverberations around the broader Middle East and the world, as well as its implications for American domestic politics.

That conversation might have remained just an interesting diversion were it not for the energetic and entrepreneurial leadership of the Brookings Center for Middle East Policy (CMEP). With his uncommon collegiality and thoughtful expertise, CMEP director Natan Sachs transformed a casual exchange into an initiative that engaged more than two dozen scholars in and around Brookings. All of the center's work, including this book, has greatly benefitted from the support of Nicki Sullivan and Kristen Belle-Isle.

The Brookings Institution's leadership has long recognized the centrality of Iran in shaping the dynamics of the broader Middle East and the security of American interests and allies in the region. Driven by their own deep engagement with these questions during their government service, President John Allen and his predecessor, Strobe Talbott, have nurtured scholarship and programming dedicated to Iran, as did Martin Indyk in his multiple leadership roles across Brookings. I'm especially grateful to Bruce Jones, vice president and director of Foreign Policy, and Michael O'Hanlon, the program's research director and an incredibly productive scholar, for creating an environment that has drawn the top-notch experts in this volume and encouraged their collaboration on project such as this one.

My recent intern, Keian Razipour, and my current research assistant, Eliora Katz, appear in these pages, and they follow in the tradition of their predecessors, especially Mehrun Etebari, Hanif Zarrabi-Kashani, and Emma Borden, in their diligence, intellectual curiosity, and exceptional writing skills. I am profoundly grateful to them all, and to the other Brookings researchers, such as Kevin Huggard, Israa Saber, and Maggie Tennis, who contributed to individual chapters in this volume.

All the contributors to this volume owe a huge debt of gratitude to the exceptional Brookings Communications staff, past and present, including Sadie Jonath, Suzanne Schaeffer, and Anthony Yazaki. Rachel Slattery applied her gifted design skills to the online publication and promotion of each essay; Fred Dews and Gaston Reboredo produced an elegant and evocative episode of the Brookings Cafeteria podcast that drew on the insights of various contributors, with support from Camilo Ramirez, Chris McKenna, and Adrianna Pita; and George Burroughs and Ian McAllister crafted a superb video to amplify the ideas in this series.

Spearheading all this work, and literally every other publication, podcast, and multimedia output from our Foreign Policy program, was Anna Newby, our brilliant and supernaturally efficient managing editor and communications director. Every piece in this book was improved by Anna's skillful editing, and she has been a vital sounding board as the project moved from an internet platform to a book. Similarly, all the authors in this volume owe a huge debt to Bill Finan, Cecilia González, and the entire team at the Brookings Institution Press, whose encouragement, professionalism, and flexibility guided this project into print. Special thanks are due to Carla Huelsenbeck, whose exquisite copyediting greatly improved the text.

The work of all the thinkers, writers, researchers, editors, and designers who contributed to this book requires generous resources, sustained over time. The Brookings Foreign Policy Development team—especially Michele Swain and Patrick Cole—under the guidance of dedicated leadership, both present (Miguel Vieira) and past (Elisa Glazer), has made this book and everything that we do at Brookings possible. Equally essential are the senior administrators of the Foreign Policy program, especially Margaret Humenay, Andrew Moffatt, and Kevin Scott.

We are deeply grateful for the ongoing support from the MacArthur Foundation and the Carnegie Corporation of New York for Brookings' work on Iran and U.S. policy responses to the challenges posed by Iran's government since the 1979 revolution.

Introduction

SUZANNE MALONEY

In July 2019, as tensions between the United States and Iran escalated, an Iranian politician delivered a thinly veiled warning to Washington via Twitter, the favorite mode of communication of President Donald Trump. "We have unseated an American president in the past," pronounced Hesameddin Ashena, an adviser to Iranian President Hassan Rouhani, adding "We can do it again."[1]

Ashena was taunting Trump by invoking the indelible memories of 1979, when upheaval within Iran helped undermine the domestic and foreign policy agendas of President Jimmy Carter and ultimately wrecked his reelection prospects. In the first days of 2020, the simmering frictions between the two countries racheted up even further with a U.S. drone strike that killed Qassem Soleimani, an infamous Iranian military commander who was the architect of Iran's expanding regional influence. As Washington and Tehran exchanged epithets in the days that followed, Trump warned that the United States had developed a target list for retaliatory strikes ("52 Iranian sites (representing the 52 American hostages taken by Iran many years ago), some at a very high level & important to Iran & the Iranian culture"[2]).

Such is the enduring consequence of the revolution that ousted Iran's monarchy and yielded a unique and disruptive Islamic Republic in its wake. Even after four decades, 1979 remains a vivid touchstone, a watershed moment for Iran, the United States, and the world.

Few events in the modern era have proven as powerfully transformative as the 1979 Iranian Revolution, and the legacy of those epic developments continues to resonate forty years later within Iran, the broader Middle East, and America's engagement in that region. That revolution supplanted not just the prevailing system of government in Iran but also reconfigured much of what had defined the Iranian state and social order for half a century. It ensconced a leadership determined to refashion Iran's politics, economy, and society and to spurn the country's existing allies as well as the conventions that governed the international order. Iran's transformation from pro-Western monarchy to revolutionary theocracy confirmed the primacy of political Islam as an ideological force to be reckoned with and an enduring security challenge.

The world has experienced stunning changes over the four decades since 1979: the demise of the Soviet Union and the attenuation of the Cold War; the rise of China as an economic and strategic rival to the United States; the expansion of market economies and democratic governance into previously inhospitable environments around the globe; and the diffusion of technology and the empowerment of localities and the manifold forces of globalization.

For the moment, however, these considerable changes have not manifestly altered the core consequences of the revolution within Iran and its neighboring states or the challenges posed by Iranian domestic and regional policies. Recent developments have only highlighted the persistence of the dilemmas created in 1979 for today's policymakers. Recent developments suggest some echo of the precariousness and volatility of forty years ago. Inside Iran, an aging revolutionary leadership is deploying brute force to thwart popular frustration; along its borders, Tehran's brash influence is newly vulnerable to the very instability that has expanded its reach; and the United States and Iran dance along the precipice of a dangerous escalation. History will not repeat itself, but the cadences of past crises can be felt within Iran and across the broader Middle East today.

So it is especially timely to consider the lessons and implications of 1979. This volume approaches the implications of the revolution through three distinct lenses: first and foremost the impact on Iran and Iranians; the fallout for Washington, both domestically and in its strategic posture; and the broader consequences for the Middle East and the world. Although the authors represent a variety of backgrounds, and their analyses engage multiple perspectives, what links their contributions together is a rigorous effort to consider the legacy of the dramatic events of forty years ago in light of the challenges facing Washington and the world today. This book does not claim to be either holistic or complete; conceived and executed from the United States, its contributions cannot speak authoritatively to the experience of Iranians today. However, by convening two dozen scholars and analysts, we have attempted to present a thoughtful, wide-ranging appraisal of the 1979 revolution as a critical juncture in the history of Iran, the Middle East, and U.S. foreign policy.

We start with the revolution itself, as seen first-hand through the eyes of a journalist who had been granted an interview with a monarch who was faltering in the face of his own mortality and that of his reign. Strobe Talbott reflects on his September 1978 visit to Tehran as a reporter for *Time* magazine and the sense of despair that shrouded his audience with Mohammad Reza Pahlavi as the revolution entered its most intense and final phase. It is a fitting opening for a study of an historical episode that became intensely personalized around three men: the dying, displaced shah; an agonized U.S. president who had been forced to confront the limits of American influence; and their common nemesis, Ayatollah Ruhollah Khomeini, the charismatic figure who ascended to lead the post-revolutionary state.

The subsequent chapters in Part I address what came in the revolution's wake for Iranians. Ali Fathollah-Nejad analyzes the expectations of social justice, freedom, and independence that emerged during the thrilling success of popular mobilization and how the Islamic Republic has fared in meeting them. Djavad Salehi-Isfahani examines the formulation and implementation of economic policies by a leadership that had not devoted significant prior consideration to these questions. My own contribution surveys the structure of power established in the aftermath of the revolution and its impact on Iran's subsequent political evolution.

Vanda Felbab-Brown and Bradley S. Porter review the impact of the revolution on Iranian drug policies, highlighting the overall consistency in approach even during dramatic political changes. Part I concludes with my appraisal, written with Eliora Katz, of the revolution's repercussions on the rights and status of women and the movement that has recently emerged to challenge the Islamic Republic's imposed dress code.

This volume then moves beyond Iran to examine the bilateral relationship, or lack thereof, between Tehran and Washington. The severing of formal diplomatic relations between the two countries occurred more than a year after the monarchy's ouster, but from the beginning the revolution's passions and purpose had America in its sights as the principal architect and genesis of the adversities facing Iranians. Part II begins with a snapshot of the *status quo ante*, outlining the depth of the official Iranian-American partnership and the social, cultural, and economic linkages that seemed to underpin it. Next, Kenneth Pollack offers a sober view on the prospects for any durable amelioration of the antagonism that evolved in the aftermath of the revolution and argues that anti-Americanism remains an essential component of the Islamic Republic's legitimacy.

Elaine Kamarck looks back on Washington's response to the November 1979 seizure of the U.S. Embassy in Tehran, which precipitated a fifteen-month-long hostage crisis and consumed the final months of the Carter presidency. And Tamara Cofman Wittes widens the perspective, examining the heated debate over Carter's human rights policy that intensified after the fall of the shah and how the U.S. experience in Iran shaped Washington's approach to advancing human rights and democracy with other authoritarian allies.

The application of both pressure and persuasion has formed the framework for American policy toward the Islamic Republic in the immediate aftermath of the revolution and the embassy seizure and has proven curiously durable. Kate Hewitt and Richard Nephew discuss Washington's increasing reliance on economic sanctions as a means of shaping Iranian policies since the 1979 revolution. International law has also featured prominently as a means of regulating the frictions between Washington and Tehran, and Scott R. Anderson dissects the efforts of first Washington and more recently Tehran in using international legal rules to secure relief and to brand one another as a pariah. Finally, Samantha Gross explores the implications of the revolution on energy markets and the wide-ranging changes that were generated by supply disruptions and government policies in 1979.

The final part of this book moves beyond Iran and America to take stock of the revolution's impact across the wider Middle East and beyond. Itamar Rabinovich examines the expansionary impetus of Iran's post-revolutionary leadership, which has helped to transform the Middle Eastern system, investing Tehran in an array of regional crises and a wider confrontation with American influence. Daniel Byman considers Tehran's role in fueling terrorism, the response of its regional adversaries, and the fundamental changes for American counterterrorism institutions and attitudes that were generated by the revolution.

Iran's relationship with Iraq has loomed large in its security posture throughout the past forty years. Ranj Alaaldin provides an insightful look at the reverberations of the Iranian Revolution and the clerical leadership of the new state forged in its aftermath among Iraqi Shia. Bruce Riedel expands on the suspicions and ambitions that shaped the early dynamics between Iran's revolutionaries and Baghdad, which resulted in Saddam Hussein's 1980 invasion of Iran and the devastating eight-year war that followed. The revolution also produced a dramatic shift in Iran's relationship with other Shia partisans, especially in Lebanon, where Tehran's intervention cultivated the establishment of a powerful proxy militia, Hezbollah, and secured an enduring strategic asset for extending Iranian influence to the Mediterranean Sea.

Together with Bruce Riedel, we also examine the roots of the Saudi-Iranian rivalry and the role of the revolution in magnifying the interdependence between Washington and Riyadh and expanding the U.S. military footprint into the Persian Gulf. Kemal Kirişci surveys the patterns of coexistence and convergence that have persisted over the course of the past forty years between Turkey and Iran, driven on both sides by a long-standing pragmatism about the bilateral relationship.

No state in the region experienced a more dramatic disjuncture in its relationship with Tehran as a result of 1979 than did Israel. Natan

Sachs explains Israel's reverse periphery doctrine, which has created an alignment with core Arab states around their shared sense of threat from Iran. Iran's revolution may have sought an ecumenical appeal, but its Shia identity has helped fuel a dramatic and long-lasting sectarian divide. Shadi Hamid and Sharan Grewal consider how Iran's revolution initially emboldened Sunni Islamist groups, only to eventually alienate them through ideological disagreements, sectarian animus, and strategic considerations.

Madiha Afzal reintroduces an important episode that has been dwarfed by other contemporaneous events in the region: the seizure of the U.S. Embassy in Islamabad only weeks after a similar attack in Tehran. Afzal details how the Iranian Revolution coincided with state-led Islamization in Pakistan and helped stoke Sunni-Shia tensions there. Finally, Pavel Baev sheds light on the Russian view of 1979 and how the turmoil in Iran shaped Moscow's decisionmaking on Afghanistan. This volume concludes with appendices that include a timeline of the revolution and suggestions for further reading that were crafted in cooperation with Eliora Katz and Keian Razipour.

It has been said that a revolution is not a secret that can be conclusively revealed, but rather a mystery—a phenomenon that requires unravelling and interpretation. Four decades after the Iranian Revolution reconfigured the strategic landscape of the Middle East, we are still trying to decipher its aftereffects and develop policies that can effectively address the challenges created in the revolution's aftermath. This volume is Brookings's contribution to better inform the persistent policy conundrum of Iran. As the conflict between Washington and Tehran enters its fifth decade in an even more combustible climate than ever, we hope that the reflections in this volume will contribute to enlightening decisionmakers and the wider public.

NOTES

1 Hesameddin Ashena (@hesamodin1) via Twitter: "We have unseated an American President in the past. We can do it again. Trump can listen to Pompeo and we'll make sure he stays a one-term President. Or he could listen to @ TuckerCarlson and we might have a different ball game." July 3, 2019, https:// twitter.com/hesamodin1/status/1146341845833834496.

2 Donald J. Trump (@realDonaldTrump) via Twitter: "...targeted 52 Iranian sites (representing the 52 American hostages taken by Iran many years ago), some at a very high level & important to Iran & the Iranian culture, and those targets, and Iran itself, WILL BE HIT VERY FAST AND VERY HARD. The USA wants no more threats!" January 4, 2020, https://twitter.com/real DonaldTrump/status/1213593975732527112.

PART I

Iran Recast

FROM MONARCHY TO ISLAMIC REPUBLIC

1

A View of the Revolution from the Shah's Palace

STROBE TALBOTT

Mohammad Reza Pahlavi owed an American president and the Cold War for the zenith of his reign. The quagmire in Indochina convinced Richard Nixon that America should delegate the containment of communist expansion to nations situated in vulnerable regions, ruled by Western-leaning leaders, equipped with formidable militaries, and known to have stable regimes.

Iran uniquely qualified in all four of those attributes for the Nixon Doctrine—or so U.S. policymakers believed. They regarded the shah as a reliable deputy marshal who would oversee law and order in the badlands of West Asia for decades to come. As for the shah on the Peacock Throne, he was looking into the distant past as well as the future. With the mightiest superpower in history at his back, he sought to restore the glory and hegemony of the Persian Empire in his own part of the world.

In 1971, two years after Nixon announced his plan, the shah put on the bash of the millennia. Sixty-eight heads of states attended a five-day

gathering in Persepolis, the ancient Persian capital. The caviar and carpets were local, but all the other luxuries seemed to come from abroad. In
his address to the invitees and to his neighbors, the shah insinuated that
he was the modern successor of Cyrus the Great.

I was a roving reporter for *Time* magazine, and the event gave me a
chance for my first visit to Iran. I came early, skipped some of festivities,
and stayed afterward to meet Iranians who were discontented and, in
some cases, seething: students, leftists (some, no doubt, Soviet agents),
and Islamists who were followers of Ayatollah Ruhollah Khomeini.

After the foreign visitors left, Khomeini distributed his own message
to his fellow Iranians via tape recordings from his exile in Iraq:

> Let the voice of the oppressed people of Iran be heard throughout
> the world. . . . Let them ask that this plundering and squandering
> be brought to an end, and that they cease behaving toward our
> people in this way, that huge budget of the government be spent on
> the wretched and hungry people. . . . I tell you plainly that a dark,
> dangerous future lies ahead and that it is your duty to resist and to
> serve Islam and Muslim people.[1]

Seven years later, the shah was on the brink of exile himself, and Khomeini was readying himself to return as Iran's Supreme Leader.

The Interview

The U.S. government was slowly coming out of denial, largely because
the protests and accompanying violence had intensified dramatically in
early September 1978. Washington is rarely the best vantage by which to
assess fast-moving events thousands of miles away, especially if the U.S.
government has a long-standing stake in a policy that has gone awry.

As I was preparing for a trip to see for myself, White House and State
Department sources told me that the shah had the situation under control. On arrival, I joined with two colleagues, Dean Brelis from *Time*'s
Cairo bureau and our local colleague Parvis Raein, who were more real-
istic. The revolution was gathering momentum by the day, if not by the

hour. Several Iranian government ministers we had expected to see had been fired, quit, or fled the country.

One appointment, however, was still on: an audience with the shah. Tanks and armored cars circled the Saadabad Palace in the northern outskirts of Tehran, keeping back angry crowds. Their chants could be heard even from inside.

Our host was a broken man. He told us he had declared martial law the day before because he needed six months of "discipline and calm" so that he could work with the parliament on sweeping democratic reforms. It was hardly a logical political stratagem, and he seemed to not believe it himself.

Some advisors were urging the shah to legalize the underground Communist Party, but he was afraid that the Soviet Union would use it as a pretext for extending "fraternal assistance" to Moscow's Iranian comrades.

We asked his view of President Jimmy Carter's robust human rights policy, especially condemnation of torture by the shah's secret police, known by its acronym SAVAK. He claimed that he had already reined in such abuses before Carter came into office. We asked if the recurring U.S. criticism of government repression was bolstering his political enemies. His answer, through pursed lips: "Well, maybe you should ask them." Other than that, he shied away from questions about U.S. policies.

When the ninety-minute interview was over, he asked me to stay behind. When the others left, he called for an aide who methodically moved around the room deactivating listening devices hidden in the bookcases.

Once we were alone, the shah let down his reserve and self-control. He had one matter on his mind: a conviction that the Central Intelligence Agency (CIA) was plotting to overthrow him. I tried several angles to get him to elaborate: What would possibly be the American motive? Did he think that the Carter administration had given up on him? Was the United States hoping that there were moderate Iranians who would be more effective in blocking Khomeini at the head of a radical theocracy?

He refused to say anything more than that America had turned on him.

As I left the palace and made my way through swarms of protestors and police, I jumped in a cab and went to the U.S. embassy. I knew
Ambassador William Sullivan and asked for an urgent private meeting.
When he took me into his office, I said I had just heard something in
private from the shah to pass on, preferably in the "vault," a window-
less chamber that was believed to be secure from the most sophisticated
eavesdropping. Rolling his eyes, Sullivan said, "Let me guess. He told you
the CIA is out to get him. He's whispering that to anyone who will listen.
Welcome to Tehran."

I felt more than a touch sheepish. I had not gotten a scoop for my editors nor a sensitive piece of information for the U.S. government. In the
article accompanying the interview with the shah, I inserted a sentence:
"There is even talk in high circles of another possible villain [other than
the Kremlin]: the CIA, which is being accused of deliberately infiltrating
the opposition so that its agents would be in place in the new government
if the shah were overthrown."

There was, however, one secret that very few knew: The shah's doc-
tors learned in 1974 that he had a form of leukemia. Not even the patient
knew for some time. During our interview, he answered a question cryp-
tically. "Is this your gravest hour, Your Majesty?" With a grim smile, he
said: "We have had many hours, including some grave ones."

An Ignominious Exit

Five months later, on January 16, 1979, the shah left his realm to the ayatollahs, never to return. In addition to his lethal disease, his ignominious
fate had him flying from country to country, hospital to hospital. The
Carter administration grudgingly accepted him for treatment, which
contributed to the storming of the American embassy in Tehran and the
capture of the staff as hostages on November 4 of that year. As a result,
the weakening shah had to leave, initially for Panama and eventually to
Egypt, where he died on July 27, 1980, at the age of 60, in Cairo. Egypt's
president Anwar Sadat gave him a full state funeral.

Fifteen months later, Sadat was gunned down by dissident soldiers
during a parade. Joyous demonstrations broke out in Tehran, and the

ayatollahs renamed a street in honor of Lieutenant Khalid Islambouli, the ringleader of the Egyptian assassination squad. The overthrow of one key leader in the Middle East and the martyrdom of another set back American policy in the region in ways that have yet to be recovered.

NOTES

1 Ayatollah Ruhollah Khomeini's message on October 31, 1971, "The Incompatibility of Monarchy with Islam," from *Khomeini va Junbish*, pp. 36–53, as translated by Hamid Algar in *Islam and Revolution: Writings and Declarations of Imam Khomeini* (Berkeley, CA: Mizan Press, 1980), pp. 203, 206–07.

2

The Revolution's Broken Promises

ALI FATHOLLAH-NEJAD

If Iran were to hold a referendum on the Islamic Republic today, over 70 percent would clearly oppose it—among them the wealthy, academics, clerics, and village and city dwellers. This remarkable hypothetical was not declared by an exiled Iranian dissident, but by the well-known Tehrani political science professor Sadegh Zibakalam, in an interview during the upheaval that took place in late 2017 and early 2018.[1]

But how is it that even a formerly enthusiastic supporter of the Islamic Revolution has delivered such a devastating verdict? To understand this radical shift and the frustration behind it, we must revisit the promises that the revolution made four decades ago. The 1979 Iranian Revolution promised three goals: social justice, freedom and democracy, and independence from great power tutelage.

Iran's Paradoxical Quest for Social Justice

Framed in a Marxist–Islamist mindset, the revolution was made on behalf of the *mostazafin*—the downtrodden—who were left behind by the monarchy's uneven development model. In the following four decades, intense controversy has erupted over the Islamic Republic's socioeconomic performance. While some claim that remarkable progress has been made under the Islamist regime,[2] others depict an entire country mired in misery. More nuance and contextualization are needed.

Iran has indeed experienced progress over the last forty years. Whether these successes have been a result of post-revolutionary policies, societal pressures, or the foundations laid by the shah remains hotly debated.

The shift from the shah's pro-urban, elite-centered policies to a pro-rural and pro-poor (populist) approach under the Islamic Republic included expanding infrastructure and basic services—such as electricity and clean water—from cities to the countryside. In short, the revolution sought to eliminate the rural–urban divide. In rural Iran, the expansion of health and education led to a clear reduction in poverty: The 1970s poverty rate of 25 percent dropped to less than 10 percent by 2014. These social policies, biased in favor of the poor, help to explain why Iran's Human Development Index (HDI) has been relatively positive.

Unlike before the revolution, most Iranians today enjoy access to basic services and infrastructure, while the population has almost doubled and most of the country is urbanized. Other measures of social development have similarly improved. Literacy has more than doubled, especially among women, and now encompasses almost all the population.[3] Meanwhile, female students have outnumbered their male counterparts at universities for more than a decade.

However, while statistics indicate that absolute poverty has declined sharply, a majority of Iranians continue to suffer from socioeconomic precarity. Official sources state that 12 million live below the absolute poverty line and another 25 million to 30 million live below the poverty line.[4] Estimates suggest that one-third of Iranians, as well as 50 to 70 percent of workers, are in danger of falling into poverty.[5] Fourteen percent of Iranians live in tents, according to the Statistical Center of Iran, and one-third of the urban population lives in slums.[6] The living conditions of what anthropologist Shahram Khosravi calls Iran's "other half," or working-class poor, are striking: a seventeen-fold increase in the number of Iranians living in slums; 50 percent of the work force have only irregular employment; approximately 10 million to 13 million Iranians "entirely excluded from health, work or unemployment insurance."[7]

And Iran's socioeconomic challenges cannot be separated from its political economy that favors regime loyalists and is marked by mismanagement, cronyism, nepotism, corruption, and the absence of much-needed structural reforms.[8] Although U.S. sanctions have undoubtedly had negative repercussions, their overall impact on Iran's economic situation is often overstated. For instance, in the summer of 2018, Hossein Raghfar, an economist at Tehran's Allameh Tabataba'i University, has suggested that as low as 15 percent of Iran's economic problems can be attributed to sanctions.[9] The "illiberal neoliberalization"[10] in various Iranian economic policies since the 1990s, featuring clientelistic privatizations and deregulated labor market, has helped form *nouveaux riches* on one hand and precarious social strata on the other.

A chief failure of the Islamic Republic has been the lack of job creation, with jobless growth even increasing during oil booms. Unemployment rates remain high, especially among the youth, university graduates, and women. Officially, every eighth Iranian is unemployed. According to the Iranian parliament's research center, the unemployment rate will reach 16 percent by 2021 in an optimistic scenario, 26 percent if conditions are less auspicious.[11] Among the youth, one in four is unemployed, but some estimates go as high as 40 percent. These figures rank Iran's youth unemployment rate as among the highest worldwide.

Iran's Gini index of income inequality has remained consistently high, at above 0.40, pointing to the lack of inclusive economic growth. Studying levels of inequality in pre- and post-revolutionary Iran, Djavad Salehi-Isfahani found that inequality in 2002 was about the same as in 1972, adding

The findings on inequality raise important questions about the nature of the Islamic Revolution. Did it significantly affect the power structure as a social revolution of its magnitude should have? This is particularly relevant in the case of Iran because, in addition to changes in the distribution of productivity, the distribution of access to oil rents also affects inequality. Since access is directly related to political power, inequality may reflect the distribution of power. Thus, the finding that inequality in 2002 was about the same as in 1972 raises questions about the significance of the Islamic Revolution as a social and political revolution.[12]

In other words, the class character of Iranian society has remained unchanged, with one ruling class replaced by another, only with another social composition.[13] In political cartoons, this was reflected in pictures of the shah's crown merely being replaced by the mullahs' turban. Such continuity led some scholars to interpret the 1979 revolution as merely a "passive revolution, a revolution without change" in class relations.[14] Today, there is a strong public perception of high income inequality, given the ostentatious display of wealth and nepotism by the offspring of regime affiliates, the so-called âghâzâdeh, that Iranians observe on the streets of Tehran or on their smartphones through Instagram accounts like "Rich Kids of Tehran."[15]

The Islamic Republic's relative achievements in the fields of rural infrastructure, education, and literacy, along with its failure to create jobs, have produced a socioeconomic paradox that is politically explosive. Iran's job market simply cannot absorb the hundreds of thousands of university graduates. This paradox has produced a stratum of "middle-class poor," as described by sociologist Asef Bayat.[16] Defined as those with middle-class qualifications and aspirations but suffering from socioeconomic precarity, this group was considered the social base of the 2017–2018 uprising and is widely expected to continue to voice its anger and frustration.

On the situation of Iran's youth under the Islamic Republic, Bayat explained in a 2016 interview:

The youth not only want a secure future—that is reasonable jobs, a place to live, get married, and form a family in the future—they also want to reclaim their "youthfulness," a desire to live the life of youth, to pursue their interests, their individuality, free from the watchful eyes of their elders, from moral and political authority. This dimension of young people's lives adds to the existing social tensions in Iran.[17]

As alluded to before, Iranians face another structural impediment to socioeconomic opportunities. Regime "insiders" (khodi), or those with access to state resources and privileges, also enjoy privileged access to jobs.[18] These frustrations have led many young Iranians to vote with their feet. Even under President Hassan Rouhani, Iran has continued to experience world record-breaking levels of brain drain, losing an estimated $150 billion per year.[19]

Political Freedom and Democracy

In addition to social justice, the architects of the 1979 revolution contended that the ouster of the monarchy would usher in greater freedom. However, the brief post-revolutionary euphoria and sense of liberation quickly gave way to the new rulers' systemic Islamization of state and society. That one dictatorship was replaced by another, and by an even more brutal one, became apparent in the Islamic Republic's first decade. Between 1981 and 1985, nearly 8,000 people were executed, and similar numbers were killed during what many Iranians call "the great massacre" in the final year of the 1980–1988 war with Iraq. By contrast, in the eight years preceding the revolution (1971–1979), fewer than 100 political prisoners were executed.[20] The Islamic Republic became one of the most repressive systems on the globe, more recently with the world's highest execution rate.

In this process, modern Iran's three dominant politico-ideological formations, or political cultures—namely nationalism, socialism, and Islamism—were narrowed to heavy emphasis on Islamism, which managed to incorporate elements of the others.[21] Although there is some variety, the new political elite is largely limited to various stripes of Islamism. The revolutionary movement's political pluralism has been suppressed, with no veritable opposition party allowed by the state.

Likewise, Iranian civil society's constitutive movements—women, students, and labor—have faced systemic repression, undermining their organizational capacities and leaving Iran's dynamic civil society weak compared with the state. State repression has also targeted dissidents of various ideological persuasions, non-Persian minorities, and journalists. Iran today is one of the world's leading jailers of journalists, ranked 170th among 180 by Reporters Without Borders.[22] While the Islamic Republic's press landscape displays a remarkable degree of vibrancy and openness within the system's redlines, the hard-line-dominated judiciary has regularly banned publications and imprisoned journalists.

Overturning the existing monarchical order, the Islamic Republic established a peculiar political system that is conventionally understood to be based on two pillars: theocratic (with the Supreme Leader at the top as the head of state) and republican (with an elected parliament and president). However, the latter is at best semi-republican, as the Guardian Council only allows candidates deemed loyal to the Islamic Republic to run for office.[23] This unique configuration has been a key impediment for the creation of democracy: non-elected institutions still dominate, while elected ones have remained faithful to the system. Most importantly, the Islamic Republic's hybrid authoritarianism has shown remarkable resilience against meaningful political change, leading to widespread popular frustration today with both regime wings—the so-called moderates as well as the hard-liners.

Independence Inseparable from Freedom

The revolution's fervent opposition to both Cold War superpowers, the United States and the Soviet Union, was encapsulated in the revolutionary slogan "Neither West, nor East, [only] the Islamic Republic." But it was the revolution's animosity toward Washington that has dominated Iran's international relations. And while Iran has found itself in a geopolitical confrontation with the West, it was never geopolitically integrated into the East. Instead, as the policies of Russia, China, and India during heightened U.S. sanctions have demonstrated, Iran has found itself forced to give concessions to Asian great powers that have consistently prioritized their ties with Washington over those with Tehran. As a result, Iran has experienced new patterns of dependency on those Eastern great powers, since confronting them is not an option so long as Tehran is at loggerheads with the international system's most powerful state.

Against this backdrop, how can Iranians safeguard their long-standing desire for independence in a twenty-first century, interdependent world? Ruhollah Ramazani, the late doyen of Iranian foreign policy studies, rightly emphasized that in an interdependent world, there is no such thing as absolute independence, but rather degrees of dependence.[24] In other words, Iran's national development will suffer if today it tries to maintain a fervent, ideological adherence to an abstract notion of absolute independence.

Iran's domestic authoritarian context poses another formidable challenge for safeguarding independence, as it favors close ties with authoritarian rather than democratic states. The hard-line custodians of the Islamic Republic need not fear that like-minded authoritarian regimes, such as China and Russia, will introduce issues like human rights and democracy in bilateral relations. The result is a geopolitical preference for a "Look to the East" policy, mostly favored by those forces who stand to benefit politically and economically from such an orientation. The shadow of Iran's antagonism with the United States has sustained its conflictual relationship with the Western world. This has not only prevented Iran from developing its full potential by building robust ties with both the West and the East, but also pushed the country into the hands of the latter powers, who have abused Iran's isolation from the West and its need of the East. For this reason, Ramazani aptly noted that a democratic polity is a necessary precondition to prevent dependency, noting that "the breakdown of the rule of law and politicized judiciary will ultimately undercut Iran's ability to maintain its independence in world politics."[25] He also emphasized that freedom and independence are inseparable.

A more open political climate, as in India, for example, would allow for domestic debates about foreign policy choices and the stakes involved for the population. Hence, democratization would significantly improve Iran's international image and potentially improve its bargaining power vis-à-vis great powers, especially given Western powers' tendency toward instrumentalizing human rights in order to generate political pressure.

Conclusion

So, did the Iranian Revolution eventually deliver on its promises? Despite some achievements, the overall picture looks bleak, particularly when it comes to promises of democracy. Whether that is reversible is another difficult question. The acute triple crisis—socioeconomic, political, and ecological—the Islamic Republic faces in its fortieth year,[26] a growing sense of popular disillusionment and frustration that forcefully erupted during the 2017–2018 upheaval, and the ongoing confrontation with the world's most powerful state leaves little hope that the same system that failed to deliver on these promises for decades will succeed in the future.

NOTES

1 Interview audio file posted by Farnaz Fassihi, *Wall Street Journal*, January 5, 2018 (https://twitter.com/farnazfassihi/status/949285948021526528). On the 2017–2018 revolt, see Ali Fathollah-Nejad, "Causes behind Iran's Protests: A Preliminary Account," *Al Jazeera English*, January 6, 2018; Fathollah-Nejad, "There's More to Iran's Protests than You've Been Told," *PBS NewsHour*, April 3, 2018.

2 See, for example, Elaheh Rostami-Povey, *Iran's Influence: A Religious-Political State and Society in Its Region* (London: Zed Books, 2013).

3 Zahra Mila Elmi, "Educational Attainment in Iran," Middle East Institute, January 2009 (www.mei.edu/publications/educational-attainment-iran).

4 Sepehr Lorestani, "Das neue iranische Jahr: Das Jahr des Absturzes und der Flucht?" [The New Iranian Year: The year of Collapse and Flight?], translated from Persian into German by Iman Aslani, *Iran Journal*, March 29, 2018 (http://iranjournal.org/politik/iran-proteste-98/2).

5 Ibid.

6 "Bread, Jobs, and Freedom: A Conversation with Arang Keshavarzian about the Street Protests in Iran," *Jadaliyya*, January 8, 2018 (www.jadaliyya.com/Details/34978/Bread,-Jobs,-and-Freedom-A-Conversation-with-Arang-Keshavarzian-about-the-Street-Protests-in-Iran).

7 Shahram Khosravi, "How the Other Half Lives in Iran," *New York Times*,

January 14, 2018 (www.nytimes.com/2018/01/14/opinion/iran-protests-inequa
lity.html).

8 See, for example, Nadereh Chamlou, "Iran's Economic Performance Since
the 1979 Revolution," Atlantic Council *IranSource*, February 1, 2019 (www
.atlanticcouncil.org/blogs/iransource/iran-s-economic-performance-since-
the-1979-revolution).

9 Cited in Natalie Amiri, "US-Sanktionen: Wirtschaftliche Lage im Iran
wird schwieriger" [U.S. Sanctions: Economic Situation in Iran Gets More
Difficult], *Tagesschau*, August 6, 2018 (www.tagesschau.de/multimedia/video/
video-433791.html).

10 Kamran Matin, "Rojhelat Rises: Reflections on the General Strike in
Iranian Kurdistan," *The Region*, December 9, 2018 (https://theregion.org/
article/13107-rojhelat-rises-reflections-on-general-strike-iranian-kurdistan).

11 Lorestani, op. cit.

12 Djavad Salehi-Isfahani, "Poverty, Inequality, and Populist Politics in
Iran," *Journal of Economic Inequality*, vol. 7, no. 1 (March 2009), pp. 24–25.

13 See Sohrab Behdad and Farhad Nomani, "What a Revolution! Thirty
Years of Social Class Reshuffling in Iran," *Comparative Studies on South Asia,
Africa and the Middle East*, vol. 29, no. 1 (2009), pp. 84–104.

14 Gholam Khiabany, "Religion and Media in Iran: The Imperative of the
Market and the Straightjacket of Islamism," *Westminster Papers in Communication and Culture* (WPCC), vol. 3, no. 2 (2006), p. 14 (www.westminster
papers.org/articles/abstract/10.16997/wpcc.27/).

15 See, for example, Golnaz Esfandiari, "Pics of Posh Iranian Wedding
Renew Criticism of Double Standards," *Radio Free Europe/Radio Liberty* August
2, 2018 (www.rferl.org/a/in-the-haute-seat-glimpse-into-lifestyles-of-iran-s-
elite-kids-spurs-anger/29406785.html); Holly Dagres, "Rage against the Elite:
How Iran's Nouveau Riche Profits [sic] from Sanctions," Atlantic Council
IranSource, August 31, 2018 (www.atlanticcouncil.org/blogs/iransource/rage-
against-the-elite-how-iran-s-nouveau-riche-profits-from-sanctions); Scott Peterson, "Iran: As Economy Stumbles, Tension Grows between Rich and Poor,"
Christian Science Monitor, October 10, 2018 (www.csmonitor.com/World/
Middle-East/2018/1011/Iran-As-economy-stumbles-tension-grows-between-
rich-and-poor).

16 Asef Bayat, "The Fire That Fueled the Iranian Protests," *The Atlantic*,
January 27, 2018 (www.theatlantic.com/international/archive/2018/01/iran-pro
test-mashaad-green-class-labor-economy/551690/).

17 Özgür Gökmen, "Five Years after the Arab Uprisings: An Interview with
Asef Bayat," *Jadaliyya*, April 30, 2016 (www.jadaliyya.com/Details/33222/Five-
Years-After-the-Arab-Uprisings-An-Interview-with-Asef-Bayat).

18 Saeid Jafari, "Talk of 'Good Genes' Provokes Nepotism Outcry in Iran,"

Al-Monitor, August 31, 2017 (www.al-monitor.com/pulse/originals/2017/08/iran-good-genes-aref-mousavi-lari-bahmani-aghazadeh.html); Golnaz Esfandiari, "Firestorm in Iran as Politician's Son Credits 'Good Genes' for his Success," *Radio Free Europe/Radio Liberty,* September 5, 2017 (www.rferl.org/a/iran-aref-son-good-genes-firestorm/28718364.html).

19 "The Shadow of 1979: Four Decades after Its Revolution, Iran Is Still Stuck in the Past," *The Economist,* February 9, 2019 (www.economist.com/middle-east-and-africa/2019/02/09/four-decades-after-its-revolution-iran-is-still-stuck-in-the-past); "Top Cleric Admits 'Brain Drain' Is a Problem," *Radio Farda,* March 11, 2019 (en.radiofarda.com/a/top-cleric-admits-brain-drain-is-a-problem/29815433.html).

20 Ervand Abrahamian, *Tortured Confessions: Prisons and Public Recantations in Modern Iran* (University of California Press, 1999), p. 169.

21 Hamid Dabashi, *Iran: A People Interrupted* (New York: The New Press, 2007).

22 Reporters Without Borders, 2019 World Press Freedom Index (https://rsf.org/en/ranking_table).

23 Pejman Abdolmohammadi and Ali Fathollah-Nejad, "Hybrid Authoritarianism in Post-Revolutionary Iran," in Mehran Kamrava, ed., *The Routledge Handbook on Persian Gulf Politics* (Routledge, 2020).

24 Ruhollah K. Ramazani, "Iran's Foreign Policy: Independence, Freedom and the Islamic Republic," in Anoushiravan Ehteshami and Mahjoob Zweiri, eds., *Iran's Foreign Policy: From Khatamit to Ahmadinejad* (Ithaca, NY: Ithaca Press, 2008).

25 Ibid, p. 12.

26 Ali Fathollah-Nejad, "Swamped in a Triple Crisis," *Cairo Review of Global Affairs,* no. 33 (Spring 2019), pp. 120–25.

3

Iran's Economy since the Revolution
Populism and Pragmatism

DJAVAD SALEHI-ISFAHANI

Unlike the socialist revolutions of the last century, the Islamic Revolution of Iran did not identify itself with the working class or the peasantry and did not bring a well-defined economic strategy to reorganizing the economy. Apart from eliminating the interest rate from the banking system, which was achieved in name only, the revolution put forward few specific economic policies that could be called an Islamic economic development strategy. To be sure, its populist and pro-poor rhetoric was quite distinct from the Pahlavi regime it replaced, but its actual policies could be found in the toolboxes of most developing countries and international organizations.

For the most part, pragmatism and the worldviews of individual leaders who commanded the state machinery—prime ministers in the 1980s and presidents afterward—determined the direction in which the economy moved. The strong anti-market policies of the 1980s, when the government rationed goods and took over banks and large industries, were more the result of circumstances than ideology—the eight-year war with Iraq and the flight of the Pahlavi-era upper class.

In the early 1990s, to the surprise of the visiting teams from the World Bank and International Monetary Fund, the government's rhetoric and policies radically shifted to become pro-market. Without any benefits in terms of loans from these organizations, the administration of President Ali Akbar Hashemi Rafsanjani (1989–1997) implemented structural adjustment. Likewise, the shift from the populist administrations of President Mahmoud Ahmadinejad (2005–2013) to the neoliberal Hassan Rouhani administration starting in 2013 did not amount to a break with the economic ideology of the Islamic Republic.

The main shift in policy after the revolution can be characterized as from urban-biased and elite-centered to rural-biased and populist. Populism in the Islamic Republic has a natural origin—the huge oil boom of the 1970s—which gave Iran a windfall in terms of a large inflow of foreign exchange. Unaware of the vagaries of the world oil market, the revolutionaries believed that the road to a bright economic future was paved with rising oil revenues.

Such thinking immediately after the largest oil windfall in Iran's history is not surprising. In the five years before the revolution, 1974–1979, oil revenues had exceeded one trillion dollars (in 2018 dollars), about $5,000 per person per year. However, within a decade, population growth, falling oil prices, and lower oil production made delivery on populist promises very difficult. During the second oil boom, 2003–2013, oil revenues per person had declined to one-fourth of their value in the 1970s and by 2018 they were one-tenth of their 1970s value.

The Dividends of Populist Policies

The pro-rural and pro-poor approach of the Islamic Revolution did make its mark on Iran's economy and society, by building infrastructure that has all but eliminated the rural-urban divide, a relic of Iran's feudal past. The shah's land reform of the 1960s was the first step in this direction, but his urban-biased economic policies in the 1970s stopped well short of closing the divide.

After the revolution, expansion of basic services, such as electricity and clean water, which had become the norm in pre-revolution urban Iran, accelerated in rural areas.[1] By 2000, these services had become universal, and household amenities—such as washing machines and air conditioners—had expanded significantly (see figure 3-1). In the 1970s, resources had flowed much faster to the more privileged urban neighborhoods. For example, during 1973–1975, when Iran was flush with cash, access to piped water in urban areas increased from 65 to 80 percent, while the gain in the disadvantaged rural areas was less than 1 percentage point, from 7.6 to 8.5 percent.

Expansion of health and education to rural areas sharply reduced poverty. The poverty rate, which had exceeded 25 percent in the 1970s, fell to less than 10 percent in 2014.[2] A major rural health program in the

FIGURE 3-1. **Change in Access to Basic Services and Key Household Amenities**

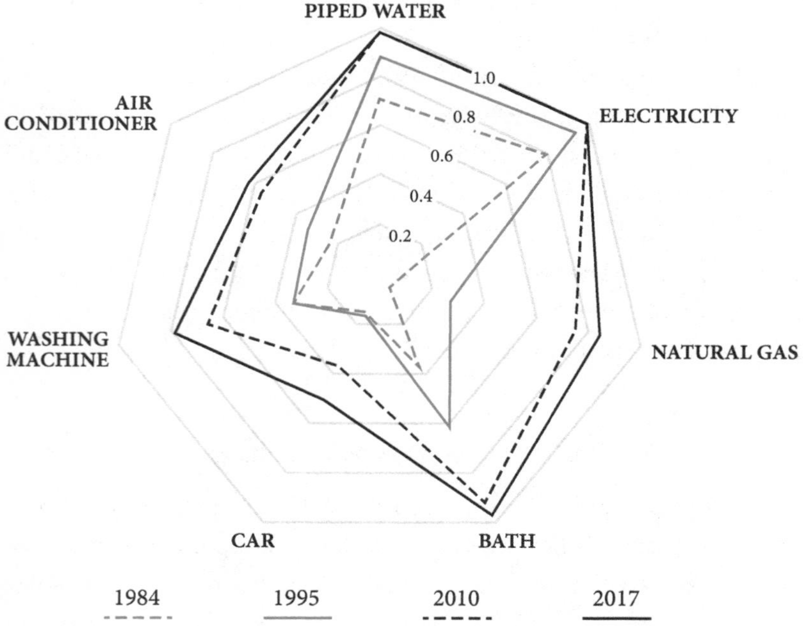

Source: Household Expenditure and Income Surveys, Statistical Center of Iran, various years.

1980s, which expanded to include family planning in the 1990s, revolutionized family life in the countryside, reducing fertility and infant and maternal mortality. As a result of its pro-poor social policies and despite the destruction caused by the war, Iran's Human Development Index (HDI) increased to overtake that of Turkey by 1990 and has remained higher.[3]

Comparison of GDP per capita between Iran and Turkey in figure 3-2 is useful in benchmarking and putting in perspective the overall performance of the economy. The comparison also highlights Iran's disadvantage relative to Turkey in terms of resources available to reach a certain level of HDI. What Iran lacked in terms of resources during this period, it was able to compensate for by shifting attention to rural areas.

Figure 3-2 is also useful in showing the heavy dependence of Iran's economy on oil exports. The economy grew fast under both the shah

FIGURE 3-2. GDP Per Capita in Iran and Turkey,
in Purchasing Power Parity U.S. Dollars

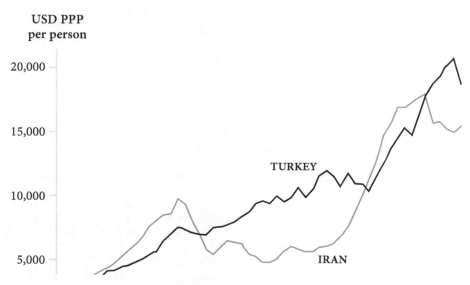

Source: Maddison Project Data 2018.

and the Islamic Republic, when oil revenues were high, and faltered after 2011, when sanctions reduced these revenues.

Finally, to appreciate the extent of social development in the last forty years, consider the changing composition of social classes before and after the revolution. Figure 3-3 shows the proportion of the population in four income groups: the poor, the lower middle class, the middle class, and the upper middle class. The data are derived from the household expenditure and income surveys collected by the Statistical Center of Iran for more than half a century, the microfiles of which since 1984 data are publicly available. The thresholds for these income classes are based on per capita household expenditures, measured in purchasing power parity (PPP) in U.S. dollars, of less than $5.50 (poor), $5.50–$11 (lower middle class), $11–$50 (middle class), and greater than $50 (upper middle class).[4]

FIGURE 3-3. The Share of Income Classes in Iran, 1972–2017

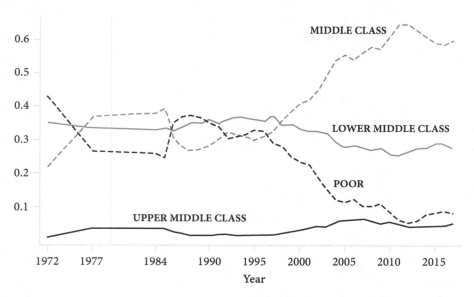

Notes: The poor are defined as living in households with less than $5.50 in expenditures per person per day (in PPP USD), the lower class in the $5.5–$11 range, the middle class $11–$50, and the rest are classified as rich. As with expenditure surveys in other countries, these surveys miss the very rich, which would raise their shares slightly.

Source: Household Expenditure and Income Surveys, Statistical Center of Iran, various years.

In 1972, the poor were the largest group, accounting for over 40 percent of the population, and the middle class comprised less than a quarter of the population. With the first oil boom, the share of the poor dropped to close to a quarter of the population and the middle-class share increased to more than one-third, a little higher than the lower middle-class share. After the revolution, these proportions remained about the same until the late 1990s, when they began to change dramatically in favor of the middle class. By 2011, before sanctions hit, the middle class accounted for about 65 percent of the population and the poor had dropped to less than 10 percent.

Post-Revolutionary Policy Failures

While the Islamic Republic has been relatively successful in the expansion of infrastructure for rural development and poverty reduction, it has failed in two important respects.

First, it has failed in providing job opportunities for its youth. The unemployment rate for college-educated youth is alarmingly high. For men and women ages 25–29, unemployment rates are 34.6 percent and 45.7 percent, respectively, according to the 2016–2017 census. Such high unemployment rates for educated youth, occurring after a decade of robust growth, suggest deeper problems with the Islamic Republic's model of economic growth.

The largest obstacle to job creation is the stifling of the private sector under the combined weight of an interventionist government bureaucracy and omnipresent foundations and state enterprises. The state domination of the commanding heights of the economy—the oil and gas sectors, large industries, and the banking system—discourage the rise of the private sector. Added to these structural impediments is the fact that the flow of oil income encourages corruption as well as anti-growth populist economic policies.

The oil boom of the 2000s was particularly harmful in this regard, especially in failing to prepare the country for the tightening international sanctions and rising tensions with the United States. The boom encouraged imports, rent-seeking, and crony capitalism, as well as hurt

employment. Oil exports enabled the populist Ahmadinejad government to keep the exchange rate low, which encouraged cheap imports,
discouraging domestic production and employment. Similarly, by using
the abundant energy at its disposal for domestic distribution (twice as
much as it exported), various Islamic governments in Iran have kept domestic energy prices low (the lowest in the world after Venezuela). This
policy has not only bankrupted the public purse, but also encouraged the
replacement of workers with energy-intensive machinery. The combined
influence of these policies resulted in jobless growth during the oil boom.
Between 2006 and 2011, census figures reveal that the economy added
only 14,000 jobs each year when, on average, 700,000 young people entered the labor market.

It is no wonder that, at that time, youth flocked to various education
institutions, seeking diplomas. Enrollments in higher education soared,
rising by 80 percent from 2005 to 2015. The result has been a rather peculiar situation in which more education is associated with higher unemployment, as shown in figure 3-4. The social exclusion of women, which
is also depicted in figure 3-4, is a particularly unproductive feature of
Iran's post-revolution labor markets.

A second failure, given the lofty egalitarian goals of the revolution, is
high and persistent inequality.[5] The Gini index of income inequality in
Iran has remained generally above 0.40, no different than that of Turkey,
which has no particular claim to egalitarian development. The only time
when the Gini index fell below this level was following generous cash
transfers that were distributed as part of Ahmadinejad's energy subsidy
reform.[6] Emphasis on equalizing incomes instead of productivities is the
hallmark of petro-populism.

The failure to deliver inclusive economic growth is seen not only in
high income inequality, but also in high degrees of inequality of opportunity. Despite a relatively egalitarian approach to building schools, access
to educational opportunities has remained highly unequal. Iranian children who enter school have a lower probability of reaching secondary
school than their counterparts in Egypt, Jordan, and Tunisia.[7] Furthermore, an Iranian child from a disadvantaged background has about one-
fourth the likelihood of a child from an advantaged background to reach

FIGURE 3-4. **Unemployment and Education**

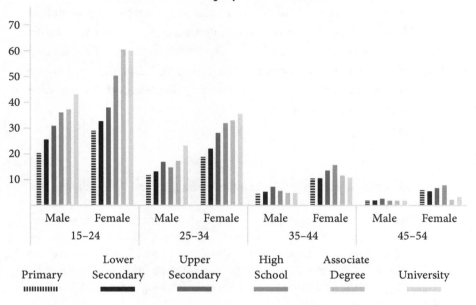

Source: Two-percent Sample of the National Census of Population 2016/2017, Statistical Center of Iran.

secondary school. Similarly, high levels of inequality of opportunity in educational achievement are observed from math and science scores collected by the Trends in International Mathematics and Science Study (TIMSS).[8]

Lessons Learned and Missed

There were two lessons that the revolutionaries could have learned from looking at the Pahlavi-era development strategy. The first, from the 1970s, was about the problems of urban bias and neglecting the rural-urban divide. This lesson helped the Islamic Republic to engage in more inclusive growth and to unleash the productive potential of a much wider spectrum of the Iranian society.

But there was another, equally important lesson that could have been drawn from economic growth before the revolution, this one from the

1960s. During 1962–1972, when oil revenues were very modest, Iran managed to grow its economy by more than 10 percent per year, doubling its GDP per capita in a short period (see figure 3-2). One important lesson from this experience, which has resonated with Iran's middle class and the moderate Rouhani government, is the need for Iran's economy to stay connected to the rest of the world and to pursue policies that emphasize jobs instead of consumption.

NOTES

1 Djavad Salehi-Isfahani, "The Revolution and the Rural Poor," *Radical History Review*, no. 105 (Summer 2009), pp. 139–44.

2 The poverty rate in both periods measures the share of population below the World Bank middle-income poverty line of about $5.50 PPP per person per day. Aziz Atamanov, Mohammad-Hadi Mostafavi, Djavad Salehi-Isfahani, and Tara Vishwanath, "Constructing Robust Poverty Trends in the Islamic Republic of Iran: 2008–2014," World Bank Policy Research working paper, no. WPS 7836, 2016.

3 United Nations Development Programme, Human Development Data, 1990–2017 (http://hdr.undp.org/en/data).

4 Iran's really rich households are poorly represented in income and expenditure surveys, hence the term upper middle class for those above $50 per person per day.

5 Djavad Salehi-Isfahani, "Poverty and Income Inequality in the Islamic Republic of Iran," *Revue Internationale des Etudes du Développement*, special issue, no. 1 (2017), pp. 113–136. Djavad Salehi-Isfahani, "Poverty, Inequality, and Populist Politics in Iran," *Journal of Economic Inequality*, vol. 7, no. 1 (March 2009), pp. 5–24.

6 Djavad Salehi-Isfahani, "Energy Subsidy Reform in Iran," *The Middle East Economies in Transition*, edited by Ahmed Galal and Ishac Diwan (Palgrave Macmillan, International Economic Association Series: 2016), pp. 186–98.

7 Ragui Assaad, Rana Hendy, and Djavad Salehi-Isfahani, "Inequality of Opportunity in Educational Attainment in the Middle East and North Africa: Evidence from Household Surveys," *International Journal of Educational Development*, vol. 66 (2019), pp. 24–43.

8 Djavad Salehi-Isfahani, Nadia Belhaj-Hassine, and Ragui Assaad, "Inequality of Opportunity in Educational Achievement in the Middle East and North Africa," *Journal of Economic Inequality*, vol. 12, no. 4 (2014), pp. 489–515.

4

Revolution, Reform, and the Future of the Islamic Republic

SUZANNE MALONEY

Iranians came to the streets en masse in February 2019 to mark the fortieth anniversary of the revolution that brought their Islamic Republic to power. As always in Iran, the scenes reflected the full panoply of the country's diverse and dynamic society; senior officials and stalwart defenders of the theocratic state mingled alongside those carrying signs denouncing the corruption within the post-revolutionary system.

For Iran's leadership, the annual commemoration offered a reminder of the regime's endurance and an opportunity for reassurance after an *annus horribilis*. The year 2018 opened with an intense spasm of protests across the country, then was punctuated by the American withdrawal from the 2015 nuclear deal and reimposition of economic sanctions, and ended with the demise of yet another mandarin of the revolutionary leadership, Ayatollah Mahmoud Hashemi Shahroudi, who was once seen as a contender for the regime's senior post.

While the epic volley of demonstrations that rocked the country that winter has mostly faded from the headlines, the convergence of pressures from within and without is pushing Iran's post-revolutionary system steadily toward the brink. The tempo may have slowed and the furies seemed to ebb, but the upheaval laid bare public frustrations with the stalemate over Iran's future that lies just beneath the fractious partisanship of its political establishment.

It is an impasse that has confronted Iran since 1979, over how to reconcile the contradictions between the revolution's ideological imperatives and the prerequisites of effective governance and diplomacy. The divergence within Iran's political elites themselves on this question has generated a persistent competition among them, and a succession of attempts to reform the ruling system from within.

The latest iteration began with the 2013 election of President Hassan Rouhani. With his tempered slogan of "hope and prudence," Rouhani promised to swing Iran toward a more responsible center via an agenda of economic reform and international engagement. Still, even before the Trump administration took aim at the 2015 nuclear deal, Rouhani's policies fell short of redressing long-simmering disappointment with a system that staked its legitimacy on social justice. By February 2019, he was not quite halfway through his second and final term as president. But Rouhani's model of moderation was already in ruins, much like every prior attempt to temper and rationalize the state that was forged in the aftermath of the 1979 revolution.

The boisterous celebration of the revolution's anniversary cannot reverse the costs of mismanagement and provocation, nor can it restore Iranians' patience with promises of evolutionary change. The repeated unravelling of gradualist approaches to overhauling a post-revolutionary state highlights the fundamental dilemma facing Iran today: The system cannot be reformed sufficiently or successfully. Instead, the nature of the post-revolutionary state and its relationship with the world must be fundamentally transformed. In the Islamic Republic, that is quite literally heresy—a reality that may help to explain the ferocity of the passions on both sides of the debate that is unfolding inside Iran.

What this heralds for the Islamic Republic in the near term is neither revolution nor collapse, but rather a slow-motion metastasis that is echoing across the political establishment, the economy, and society. The trajectory is uncertain, but the repercussions are expanding the boundaries of Iran's political imagination beyond the personality politics of the clerical state's insular elite: Iranians are no longer asking simply *who* comes next in the forty-year procession of regime troubleshooters; rather, they are increasingly beginning to wonder *what* might come next.

This is an episode of monumental importance, a tectonic shift that is unfolding almost entirely beneath the radar of most of the Western media and under a shadow of uncertainty surrounding Iran's future and its relations with the broader international community. The tumultuous history of Iran's evolution should check any temptation toward easy optimism: Progress is rarely linear and, given the Islamic Republic's survival instincts, the political atmosphere within Iran is bound to get worse before it gets better. And thanks to the Trump administration's decision to dismantle the 2015 nuclear agreement, the prospects for internal change in Iran have become even more inextricably entangled with the fierce passions around the relationship with Washington.

Still, the intense debate over the U.S. approach to Iran should not eclipse the rumblings of upheaval inside the country. Nor should the ham-fisted cheerleading for regime change among some corners of Team Trump short-circuit a necessary deliberation over the role of the international community during this unpredictable period in Iran. In fact, the confrontational U.S. strategy only heightens the need for a clear-eyed assessment of Iran's domestic dynamics and the implications of U.S. policies. For the past four decades, Iran's domestic politics have had an outsized impact on regional security and American policy. What does it mean for Washington and the world if all the assumptions of the past forty years about Iranian politics are beginning to crumble?

A Swing toward Change?

Any forecast of change within Iran invites argument. The annals of Iran analysis are littered with prognostications of doom that ultimately proved premature, at least in part because of the tendency for enthusiasm to overtake common sense. Some critics of the post-revolutionary regime perennially see a course correction just around the corner; for Washington's inveterate regime changers, Iran's Supreme Leader has been on his deathbed for decades. The scent of opportunity has revived the small but rabid personality cults around the former Pahlavi crown prince and the even more discredited left-wing terrorist group, the Mujahideen-e Khalq. In impassioned postings, online activists berate anyone who dares question the imminence of #IranRegimeChange.

The faith is strong, but the proof has been stubbornly absent. Iran has endured every crisis short of the plague—revolution, war, tribal uprisings, terrorism, earthquakes, drought, and routine episodes of internal unrest—but still, the *nezam* (the system) endures. The Islamic Republic's staying power has engrained a considerable skepticism toward the very concept of a revolutionary redux. Indeed, some saw the intense interest in the protests that swept the country in late 2017 and early 2018 as yet another case of wishful thinking, and their apparent dissipation seemed proof that the international media overhyped the upheaval.

But for all the false prophecies inspired by Iran, it is equally important to question the strangely static conventional wisdom that has taken root among academics and policy analysts alike. This assessment emphasizes Iran's internal coherence, the equilibrium among its perennially warring factions, and its citizens' understandable aversion to revolutionary change, borne of four decades of post-revolutionary disillusionment as well as the disastrous outcome of more recent upheaval in neighboring states. By this logic, gradualism remains the preferred approach of most Iranians; to suggest otherwise is to be branded a simpleton, an ideologue, a warmonger, or all three.

Like any dogma, the gospel of the Islamic Republic's durability is vulnerable to the inconvenient forces of reality. The presumption of Iranian stability is always true, until it is not, since it is challenged by recurrent convulsions that are never anticipated by the cognoscenti. Iran's contested internal landscape, with a fractious elite and routine opportunities for limited political voice, may be the Islamic Republic's hidden strength, but the deep challenges to the existing order have never been fully suppressed or satisfied. And just as in the 1970s, Americans tend to overestimate the continuing resilience of the regime.

For this reason, the prospect of meaningful change in Iran forever lies somewhere between unthinkable and inevitable. Some signs suggest that the pendulum may be swinging toward change.

After the Revolution

Over the past forty years, Iran has experienced multiple episodes in which political movements sought to temper the ideological impulses of the revolutionary state, in divergent directions and with a range of outcomes. From the start, Iran's post-revolutionary political landscape has been fraught and contested. The revolution itself was amorphous and shape-shifting, driven by a multiplicity of actors and with a tempo that fluctuated over time. The extraordinary diversity within the coalition that opposed the monarchy helped oust it, but the disparate political constituencies and activists among the opposition shared little beyond their antipathy toward the continuation of the rule of Mohammad Reza Pahlavi.

Ayatollah Ruhollah Khomeini put steel in the opposition's spine, but no sooner had the monarchy collapsed than the inherent tensions among the unruly coalition came to the fore. While Khomeini's vision of clerical rule ultimately prevailed, the state that was forged from the ashes of the upheaval incorporated a wide array of philosophies and power centers. In fact, the new government itself became an arena for political competition, as the chaotic transition created fissures that left authority contested and inspired the establishment of redundant institutions.

Officially, the new order was led by Mehdi Bazargan, a religious intellectual with a technocratic background who was appointed to lead the post-revolutionary provisional government. In reality, the man who appointed him—Khomeini—was already exercising his primacy to imprint his vision on the new state. During the subsequent nine months, the stage was set for the first of the many showdowns that have punctuated Iranian politics ever since, pitting moderates against maximalists, technocrats against theologians, and—eventually—the institutions of the formal state, including an executive branch and parliament subject to semi-competitive elections and some mechanisms of accountability, against the sprawling domain of the Islamic Republic's ultimate arbiter, its supreme religious leader.

During his brief tenure, Bazargan sought to hold the center as the exigencies of state-building and the dynamics of competition among the revolutionary coalition pushed the country toward the extremes. He was determined to reestablish central authority in a chaotic environment, a mission that entailed deliberation, collaboration and moderation. But Bazargan's mission was foiled by his rivals' willingness to utilize informal channels of authority, as well as by their tendency to invoke absolutist rhetoric. From the beginning, Bazargan was outflanked by radicals within Khomeini's Revolutionary Council, waging mostly losing battles on day-to-day decisions while steadily ceding ground in the struggle to shape the state itself. The November 1979 seizure of the U.S. embassy, and its quick endorsement and exploitation by Khomeini, conclusively decided the power struggle in favor of the Islamists, who quickly set about formalizing their interpretation of Islamic state.

Bazargan's resignation and the collapse of the provisional government did not resolve the tensions between the revolution's radicals and its more moderate elements. In fact, Iran has experienced recurrent episodes of efforts to transform its revolutionary system from within—each of which has elevated hopes of durable moderation among Iranians and the world, to mostly disappointing results. During the 1990s, President Ali Akbar Hashemi Rafsanjani embraced pragmatism and internationalism as mechanisms for advancing post-war recovery and economic growth, but he proved unwilling or unable to rein in the Islamic Republic's thuggish ways at home or in the region. Rafsanjani's presidency helped germinate Iran's vaunted reform movement, which sought to rehabilitate the post-revolutionary regime by implementing its original, limited promises of representative government and greater freedom. However, the reformists also found most of their agenda stymied by resistance from orthodox defenders of the *nezam*.

In similar fashion, each of the subsequent turns along Iran's turbulent path has elicited renewed anticipation of positive change with predictably disappointing results, including and especially the reversion to pragmatism under Iran's current president, Hassan Rouhani. Even before the Trump administration's 2018 decision to scuttle the nuclear deal and re-impose crippling economic pressure on Iran, frustrations over dashed public expectations had already begun to erupt. Despite a dynamic society and persistent elite strife, the Islamic Republic has proven more durable than all of its internal challengers. Why?

The Bankruptcy of the Middle Path

The explanation for the Islamic Republic's endurance flows directly from the structure of power. The Islamic Republic is not a typical authoritarian state. The post-revolutionary ruling system biases all outcomes in favor of its own continuation, since the structure of the state creates insurmountable hurdles for efforts to reform its policies or institutions. Any engagement in politics in the Islamic Republic requires obeisance to the unquestioned hegemony of the Supreme Leader, whose self-interest precludes meaningful devolution of the authority of his office or transformation of other essential elements of the theocratic system. Advocates of gradual reform in Iran must play by the rules of the game, including fidelity to *velayet-e faqih-ye motlaq* (absolute guardianship of the jurist). Anything less promises a prison sentence or exile—and effective irrelevance to political outcomes in contemporary Iran.

In practice, however, playing by the rules of the game costs moderates and reformers the entire match. Iran's robust and frenzied elections have tended to focus resources and energies on the discrete objective of securing victory at the ballot box. The forces behind the reform movement, for example, devoted considerable time and energy to strategies aimed at enhancing their control of various electoral institutions, and to strengthening those same institutions: implementing a strategy to avoid disqualifications, honing their messages, preparing a slate of candidates, and seeking legislative remedies for the constraints on the authority of various representative institutions.

Electoral remedies cannot compel outcomes in a system where the ultimate authorities remain beyond the purview of the popular vote. As a result, the utility of elections in determining Iranian policies remains profoundly circumscribed. Coercive power, both legal and extralegal, has remained almost wholly outside the grasp of the elected institutions—meaning that moderates can neither impose penalties on their adversaries within the political system, nor can they insulate their own ranks from the threat or use of intimidation.

Iranian political actors who are interested in reform or moderation have sought to emphasize the art of the possible, both to preserve their access to political activity within the narrow parameters of tolerated discourse and to avoid inflating popular expectations. The politicians who are interested in moderating the system have been selective and focused, targeting their efforts in limited sectors—such as economic policy, for Rafsanjani, or incremental reforms, during the period of reformist ascendancy. Rouhani deliberately kept his campaign pledges modest, branding his administration the "government of hope and prudence." Within these narrow horizons, the men who seek the Islamic Republic's moderation have achieved some results.

However, reforms that are limited in scope and impact have failed to generate momentum that might empower a platform of broader or systemic change; in some cases, reform has helped entrench the existing establishment, thanks to the prevalence of corruption and nepotism. The economic openings championed by successive Iranian presidents have boosted foreign direct investment and trade, but neither economic growth nor economic reform has succeeded in opening up political space or restraining Tehran's regional interventions.

Meanwhile, opponents of change are willing to avail themselves of any means necessary to assert their preeminence and forestall systemic change. They have long experience in provoking crises as a means of reinforcing revolutionary fervor, for example, through the pronouncement of a *fatwa* condemning British writer Salman Rushdie to death for his novel *The Satanic Verses* in 1989; in Mahmoud Ahmadinejad's deliberate demagoguery around Israel and the Holocaust; and with the 2016 torching of the Saudi embassy in Tehran. By reviving ideological furies, these episodes obliged the reflexive reinforcement of the status quo, and in so doing enhanced the advantage of hard-liners at the expense of their factional adversaries.

And if that does not work, defenders of the ruling system have deployed extremist tactics to block meaningful shifts in the political balance of power. Moderates and reformers have been the victims of skillful campaigns of character assassination, political "dirty tricks," impeachment, prosecution, harassment and intimidation, and even deadly violence. Early in his presidency, reformist president Mohammad Khatami lamented the fact that he faced a new crisis every nine days, but he never managed to devise an effective strategy to repel or overcome the proliferation of assaults against his supporters and his agenda.

Iran's agents of change do not lack leverage of their own; however, they tend to flinch at deploying the most formidable tools at their disposal, such as their participation in the system and their considerable base of public support. Bazargan threatened to resign repeatedly during his short tenure as prime minister, beginning within the first weeks of his appointment; however, by the time he finally made good on his threat, his departure and the related collapse of the provisional government only strengthened his rivals' position.

For his part, Khatami wrestled with restraining the more ambitious elements of the reformist front, most notably when student leaders led protests in 1999 against press restrictions. Ultimately, his unwillingness to champion his most ardent constituency splintered the movement and eroded his popular appeal and advantage. Even when reformists tried more confrontational tactics—such as mobilizing the streets to protest the rigged 2009 presidential elections—they found themselves quickly outgunned and outmaneuvered by the overwhelming repressive force and survival skills of the state.

The Future of the Revolution

The durability of the *nezam* is perhaps the most important legacy of Iran's 1979 revolution. None of the extraordinary developments within or around Iran over the course of the past forty years has managed to significantly alter it—not the considerable evolution of Iranian society, nor the country's steady reengagement with the world, nor the incremental reforms advanced by various factions within the establishment. In many respects, the structure of power in the Islamic Republic has become even more firmly embedded today than it was at its precarious creation.

The staying power of Iran's post-revolutionary system lends itself to a certain fatalism; if war, internal upheaval, regional turmoil, natural disasters, crippling economic sanctions, and near-constant infighting among the political establishment have failed to weaken theocratic authority, perhaps any hope for change is simply futile. This conclusion prompted disengagement from politics among some younger Iranians, particularly as the reform movement experienced its early stumbles. A reporter who interviewed young Iranians in 2005 found "an overwhelming picture of a generation lost, disaffected and stained by longing."[1]

However, Iran's "lost generation" is now approaching the age of the revolution itself, and as middle adulthood nears, the absence of a promising political or economic horizon has become painfully acute—and not simply for the urban elites, but for the larger population of Iran's postrevolutionary baby boom. Birth rates in Iran during the first decade of the revolution were among the highest in the world, a trend sharply reversed by official family planning initiatives launched in the late 1980s. This cohort of Iranians has benefited from the revolution's dramatic expansion of educational opportunities and broader social welfare infrastructure, and the populist promises of official rhetoric has shaped its aspirations. The 2015 nuclear deal only supersized those hopes, with Tehran's narrative around the agreement stoking expectations of monumental economic opportunities and more. "This will bring hope to our life," an Iranian man commented in the midst of the jubilant celebrations that greeted the deal's conclusion. "Now we will be able to live normally like the rest of the world," another remarked.[2]

Even before Washington spurned the deal, disenchantment with the deal among ordinary Iranians had surfaced, feeding into a broader sense of letdown. As Ali Fathollah-Nejad chronicles in chapter 2 of this volume, the Islamic Republic's failure to fulfill the promises of the revolution has generated deep disaffection that has manifested itself in frequent, mainly small-scale episodes of organized unrest. This alone is not a useful predictor of change in post-revolutionary Iran. Despite its well-entrenched mechanisms of repression, the Islamic Republic has experienced a vigorous pattern of mostly small-scale unrest since its inception, a legacy of the revolution itself as well as the old Persian tradition of *bast*, or seeking sanctuary as a form of political protest. As the post-revolutionary state slowly began to take form, and a vacuum of both security and authority remained, collective action—both spontaneous and opportunistic—by a wide range of groups and political actors served as a critical instrument for the disparate constituents of the opposition to gain advantage in the chaotic struggle for power.

Most infamously, this led to the seizure of the American embassy in November 1979 by university students, an action that toppled Iran's liberal-leaning provisional government and permanently escalated tensions between Washington and Tehran. Long after the most intense phase of internal upheaval had abated, Iranians' penchant for protest has continued, as has its cynical deployment by the regime itself, whose internal schisms have frequently occasioned official and semi-official groups to use public demonstrations to advance their own agendas.

As a result, Iranians are well familiar with political, social, and economic protest. Over the course of the past forty years, Iran has routinely witnessed all varieties of rallies and riots: sit-ins by families of political prisoners; labor strikes by teachers, truckers, and factory workers; student demonstrations over everything from free speech to dormitory conditions and cafeteria food; soccer riots; and marches and sit-ins sparked by localized grievances. These manifestations have never been limited by geography or class.

Still, the pace and intensity of recent unrest is remarkable. The Iran Human Rights Documentation Center recorded more than 1,200 labor actions related to nonpayment of wages between January 2017 and November 2018.[3] And while the Islamic Republic has overwhelming capabilities to manage or repress discrete demonstrations, the episode that erupted in the final days of 2017 and into the early days of 2018 highlights the dangers posed by the pervasive frustration and alienation. Then, what apparently began as a provincial political stunt intended to undermine Rouhani quickly flared into a spasm of furious demonstrations. Within forty-eight hours, protests were convulsing at least eighty cities, and the refrains of the demonstrators had catapulted from economic grievances to explicit denunciations of the *nezam* and the entirety of its leadership.

The size of the 2017–2018 protests remained quite modest by historical standards—at least an order of magnitude smaller than the million-plus

Iranians who came to the streets to demand fair elections in 2009. And the upheaval was quashed rapidly and with limited violence. However, the episode unnerved the Iranian leadership, and for good reasons: the rapid progression from mundane, localized demands to radical rejection of the system as a whole; the transmission and coordination of protests via social media rather than mediated through the more manageable traditional press; the engagement of the government's core constituency, the rising middle class; and the near-instantaneous dispersion from local to national, without a specific precipitant beyond opportunism. All of these factors highlight the Islamic Republic's vulnerability at a time when, thanks to the Trump administration's application of "maximum pressure," the leadership has severely limited resources to address or preempt the sources of dissatisfaction.

What Next?

Tehran today is facing an epic, interconnected set of crises: the crisis of unmet expectations, which feeds a crisis of legitimacy for a system whose waning ideological legitimacy has been supplanted by reliance on a more prosaic emphasis on state performance and living standards. Iran's predicament is exacerbated by the uncertainties surrounding leadership succession, both with respect to the position of the Supreme Leader, who recently marked his eightieth birthday, and the legions of senior officials from the same generation who helped shape the post-revolutionary state from its inception.

To overcome its internal liabilities, the Islamic Republic can rely on a time-tested playbook of repression and co-optation. At minimum, the pressures from within and without will almost certainly inspire innovation and adaptation, such as the hints from Rouhani and others around utilizing the provision of Iran's constitution that authorizes referendum as a mechanism for important national decisions.[4] The path toward any durable change in Iran is uncertain and unpredictable, and the next phase of Iran's riveting post-revolutionary evolution will almost defy all expectations.

NOTES

1 Megan Stack, "In Clerics' Iran, Children of the Revolution Seek Escape," *Los Angeles Times*, December 26, 2005 (www.latimes.com/archives/la-xpm-2004-dec-26-fg-iranyouth26-story.html).

2 Saeed Kamali Dehgan, "Iranians Celebrate the Nuclear Deal: 'This Will Bring Hope to Our Life,'" *The Guardian*, April 2, 2015 (www.theguardian.com/world/2015/apr/02/iranians-celebrate-nuclear-deal-tehran).

3 "Controlled and Pursued: Labor Activism in Contemporary Iran," Iran Human Rights Documentation Center, December 11, 2018 (https://iranhrdc .org/controlled-and-persued-labor-activism-in-contemporary-iran/).

4 "Rouhani Suggests Holding a Referendum on Nuclear Issue," *Radio Farda*, May 26, 2019 (https://en.radiofarda.com/a/rouhani-suggests-holding-a-refer-endum-on-nuclear-issue/29963481.html); Amir Paivar, "Iranian President Rouhani's Referendum Warning to Hard-liners," BBC, January 6, 2015 (www .bbc.com/news/world-middle-east-30697037).

5

Poppies and Public Health
1979 and Narcotics in Iran

VANDA FELBAB-BROWN *and* BRADLEY S. PORTER

Since its 1979 revolution, Iran has developed a reputation for having some of the world's harshest drug penalties and as an opponent of efforts to reform global drug policy. Overall, however, Iran's drug policies have been highly varied, with some policy experimentation taking place even after the revolution. And certainly long before it, Iran experimented—perhaps more than any other country—with a broad range of policies to respond to widespread drug use and poppy cultivation, alternating between permissive and very harsh.

What is perhaps most surprising is how little the Iranian Revolution actually changed drug policies in Iran. And while the revolution did have pronounced effects on international drug markets, they were, once again, actually less than meets the eye. Importantly, for example, poppy production was bound to increase in Afghanistan regardless.

Iran's Opium before the Revolution

From the nineteenth century up to the 1979 revolution, drug policy in Iran oscillated widely, running the gamut from legalization to harsh prohibition. By the end of the nineteenth century, Iran—then known as Persia—was one of the world's top opium exporters, even as the government did not have effective control over most of the country's territory.

Nonetheless, the state's promotion of opium poppy agriculture was so "successful"[1] that wheat was abandoned for opium poppy, contributing to the Great Famine of 1870–1872, in which some 1.5 million people died. (Iranian narratives blame British machinations.) Opium exports became a key source of Iran's foreign currency and tax revenues. It was for those economic reasons that Iran was loath to control its opium exports to China and elsewhere, although Iran had signed a variety of international commitments to that effect in the early twentieth century. Even as China specifically banned the imports of Persian opium in 1912, Iran encouraged its farmers and businessmen to export it to China.[2]

Following a 1928 law to monopolize opium production under a state agency, Iran's poppy cultivation increased to 25,000 hectares.[3] Exports and tax revenues also increased, as did Iran's reputation as a global drug pariah. Not all of the exports were illegal: By international agreement, Iran was allowed to supply 25 percent of the world's legal opium requirements for medications between 1929 and 1955.

Meanwhile, in the early part of the twentieth century, opium abuse in Iran also dramatically increased. Among Iran's early responses to growing addiction was a program in the 1920s to provide addicts with opium ration coupons.[4] Progressively, however, policies toward use hardened, particularly as widespread mobilization by social activists—such as the Society Against Opium and Alcohol—highlighted addiction's devastating effects. Still, by the 1950s, Iran was estimated to have some 1.5 million drug users, out of a population of, at the time, 20 million.[5]

In 1955, the shah imposed a total ban on cultivation and outlawed the possession and sale of opium. The policy had a devastating effect on Iran's 300,000 poppy farmers. In a country where many rural areas had no medical facilities of any kind and opium was widely used as a universal medicine, the policy also had a severe impact on a broad range of medicinal practices. The economic and social hardships were great, even though use and addiction did not subside. Users and addicts were imprisoned for longer and longer periods: In 1959, even the possession of poppy seeds, such as on bread, was criminalized with up to three years of imprisonment.[6]

Prohibition was systematically undermined by widespread smuggling of opium and heroin from Afghanistan and Turkey—an inevitable outcome, as the ban did not end demand and no treatment facilities and programs were in place. Amounting to some 100 tons yearly, the smuggling from Afghanistan proved particularly violent: Many smugglers risked their lives for as little as $13 per trip, often in bondage to Afghan feudal *khans*.[7] Iran's widespread use of the death penalty for drug trafficking did little to deter smuggling, especially as the Afghan smugglers also faced execution from their Afghan overlords if they returned to Afghanistan empty-handed. Thus, when smugglers lost drugs to interdiction operations, they often looted Iranian rural settlements and dragged off villagers into Afghanistan for ransom.

Frustrated by international trafficking (in the same way that Iran's policies a few decades earlier undermined China's drug policy goals) and facing massive losses of gold and hard currency paid to international drug traffickers, the shah lifted the ban in 1969. Once again under a state monopoly, poppy cultivation swung back to 20,000 hectares. Some 110,000 addicts, those deemed unable to quit because of age or other physical conditions, were given registration cards to obtain state-provided opium.[8] At least 300,000 officially estimated users, however, did not end up on the registration list, and the actual addiction rate was believed to be much higher.[9]

Revolutionary Highs and Lows

After the 1979 revolution, Ayatollah Ruhollah Khomeini declared drug use "un-Islamic," once again seeking to reduce addiction. Although the ayatollah called the shah's drug executions "inhuman," the revolution put in place a "purification" program that extensively jailed and executed drug offenders.

A notorious chief justice of the Revolutionary Tribunals and simultaneously head of the anti-narcotics campaign, Sadegh Khalkhali, previously a minor cleric, sentenced to death at least 582 drug dealers during his eleven-month reign in 1979, along with the hundreds of others whom he had arbitrarily executed for imagined offenses with zero due process.[10] The use of capital punishment for drug crimes intensified after 1988,[11] and some 10,000 people have received the death penalty for drug-related offenses since then.[12]

The revolution also ended domestic experimentation with legal cultivation of poppy. Despite the economic impacts on Iran's farmers, any illicit cultivation was also effectively suppressed. Opium and methadone maintenance were discontinued, but no other treatment for widespread addiction was available.

And once again, outsiders moved to supply the intense demand for drugs. By then, Turkey had effectively legalized its opium production and prevented diversion into the illegal trade, with the United States committing itself to buy a substantial portion of such legal Turkish opium.[13] So, drug smuggling into Iran shifted to Pakistan. Poppy cultivation took off in Pakistan's impoverished tribal areas and thrived there during the 1980s, supplying Iran, Europe, and other markets. By the early 1990s, Pakistan's illegal production dried up as a result of U.S.-sponsored eradication and alternative livelihoods efforts.[14]

Critically, opiate production switched robustly to Afghanistan and—along with Central Intelligence Agency (CIA) money from the mid-1980s on—funded the *mujahideen* who fought the invading Soviet Army. To starve the *mujahideen* and deprive them of food and shelter among the population, the Soviet Army adopted a scorched-earth policy. In order to drive the rural population into cities (which the Soviets controlled), Russian troops burned orchards and fields and destroyed water canals. The consequence was a significant increase in poppy cultivation: Simply no other crop could survive the harsh weather and lack of water and fertilizers. Unlike legal goods that needed to be processed and depended on good roads and legal value-added chains and markets, harvested opium resin would not spoil.

It was of little comfort to the Afghan people that the heroin production flourishing in the destroyed land also got the Soviet Army extensively addicted. The 1990s Taliban policy of taking an already impoverished and devastated country back to the ninth century—with systematic destruction of administration and socioeconomic facilities—had one key outcome: more and more poppy. By 1998, Afghanistan surpassed Myanmar as the world's top producer of opiates. It has remained the dominant supplier of illegal organic opiates since.[15] Seventeen years of U.S. counterinsurgency and state-building efforts in Afghanistan have not managed to mitigate insecurity and other structural drivers of opium poppy cultivation in the country, and opium poppy continues to thrive and be exported to and through Iran.[16]

Drugs and Drug Policy in Iran Today

Despite the dramatic political developments in 1979 and a series of wide policy swings for over a century, drug use in Iran has remained remarkably stubborn.

Addiction and Reforms

Out of a population of 81 million, about 2 million to 3 million Iranians are estimated to be addicts, continually one of the world's highest addiction rates.[17] Prisons abound with users: In 1987, roughly 78,000 people were imprisoned in Iran on drug-related charges; in 2004, the number was 431,430.[18] In the mid-2000s, Iran and the United States shared a similar rate of imprisonment for drug users,[19] some of the highest rates in the world.

The revolution transformed the sociopolitical context: Alcohol was prohibited for all other than religious minorities, severe restrictions were imposed on social interaction among unrelated men and women, and few opportunities existed for personal self-fulfillment. These developments likely exacerbated drug use. However, addiction rates, including by the world's standards, were very high even before the revolution. Perhaps the most significant and detrimental effect of greater penalties and intensified efforts at supply control after the revolution has been the switch to hard drugs. Because it is compact and easier to hide, heroin is easier to smuggle than opium. Thus, although the rate of addiction in

Iran may be half of what it was in the 1950s, the severity of addiction and its associated effects worsened.

The failures of harsh policies periodically resurrect reforms. In the late 1990s, President Mohammad Khatami reduced penalties for drug use, emphasizing instead drug treatment and harm reduction efforts focused particularly on preventing the spread of HIV/AIDS. Methadone maintenance came back into vogue,[20] with some 130,000 receiving methadone in 2009.[21] Such progressive reforms, however, weakened during the Mahmoud Ahmadinejad years, and treatment facilities and harm reduction support systems are still hard to come by, particularly for women, while social stigma and fear of law enforcement persist.[22]

In January 2018, Iran raised the amount of drugs in possession that triggers the death penalty from a mere 30 grams of heroin, morphine, and cocaine, and 5kg of cannabis and opium, to more than 50kg of opium, 2 kg of heroin, and 3 kg of crystal meth.[23] The change allowed around 5,000 people on death row to have their cases reviewed, with the prospect of having their sentences commuted to imprisonment or fines.[24] The death penalty for marijuana possession and trafficking has been completely eliminated. And in the spirit of marijuana-legalizing times, a 2015 proposal even sought to decriminalize opium and marijuana and introduce state-controlled cultivation.[25]

Supply Control and Its Contradictions

With Afghan opium poppy blooming on its doorstep and its own addiction unabating, Iran has sought to prevent trafficking into the country. It has spent more than $800 million on concrete barriers and deep ditches along its borders with Afghanistan and Pakistan.[26] Annually, Iran carries out some 500 to 600 armed interdiction operations.[27] In 2017, it was making three-quarters of the world's opium seizures and one-quarter of the world's heroin seizures, according to the United Nations.[28] Around 4,000 Iranian police officers and border guards have lost their lives in counternarcotics operations.[29]

Through technical and financial support, Iran has also sponsored alternative livelihood efforts in Afghanistan's Herat Province. Amid growing insecurity in Afghanistan and many economic and governance challenges to legal economic development, those efforts fared as well—or poorly—as U.S. and Western efforts at promoting legal livelihoods in Afghanistan.[30] Some one-third of Afghanistan's heroin continues to flow into and through Iran, supplying Iran's own market and other parts of the Middle East and Europe.

But even as Iran has devoted vast resources to supply control, suffered widespread addiction, and railed against Western failures to end poppy cultivation in Afghanistan, a variety of state and Iran-sponsored actors have been implicated in drug trafficking. The U.S. Department of the Treasury designated multiple individuals within the Quds Force of Iran's Islamic Revolutionary Guard Corps as drug traffickers.[31] Iran's sponsored proxy paramilitary forces, such as the Lebanese Hezbollah and various pro-Iranian paramilitary *hashd* groups in Iraq, have also been implicated in drug trafficking. Hezbollah is not only alleged to tax and protect cannabis fields in Lebanon's Bekaa Valley,[32] a charge it denies, but also accused of trafficking cocaine from Latin America,[33] such as from the tri-border region of Argentina, Brazil, and Paraguay.[34] As Felbab-Brown learned during interviews in Iraq in December 2018, Iranian-sponsored paramilitary groups in Iraq are alleged to smuggle heroin from Iran and the narcotic Captagon from Syria into Iraq.[35] Such accusations are eagerly seized upon by Saudi Arabia, which revels in charging its archrival intelligence forces and proxies, such as Lebanon's Hezbollah, with purposefully poisoning and destroying Saudi youth by facilitating drug smuggling to the kingdom.[36]

Overall, the key takeaway in the years before and since Iran's Islamic Revolution is that imperatives and principles of public health at home compete with Iran's economic and geopolitical objectives abroad, as they have for many countries—earth-shaking revolution or not.

NOTES

1 Anthony Richard Neligan, *The Opium Question with Special Reference to Persia* (London: J. Bale, Sons, and Danielson, 1927).

2 Elizabeth Pauline MacCallum, *Twenty Years of Persian Opium, 1908–1928* (New York: Foreign Policy Association, 1928).

3 Thomas Quinn, "Drug Control in Iran: A Legal and Historical Analysis,"

Flash: The Fordham Law Archive of Scholarship and History, 1974 (ir.lawnet. fordham.edu/cgi/viewcontent.cgi?article=1795&context=faculty_scholarship).

4 John Calabrese, "Iran's War on Drugs: Holding the Line?" Middle East Institute, December 1, 2007 (www.mei.edu/publications/irans-war-drugs-hold ing-line).

5 Henry Kamm, "They Shoot Opium Smugglers in Iran, but . . ." *New York Times,* February 11, 1973, (www.nytimes.com/1973/02/11/archives/they-shoot-opium-smugglers-in-iran-but-teherans-swingers-such-stuff.html).

6 Quinn, op. cit., p. 494.

7 Kamm, op. cit.

8 Ibid.

9 Quinn, op. cit., p. 523.

10 Philip Robins, *Middle East Drug Bazaar: Production, Prevention, and Consumption* (London: Hurst, 2016).

11 Golnar Nikpour, "Drugs and Drug Policy in the Islamic Republic of Iran," Middle East Brief 119, Center for Middle East Studies, Brandeis University, June 2018 (www.brandeis.edu/crown/publications/meb/meb119.html).

12 Ramin Mostaghim and Shashank Bengali, "Iran Suspends Death Penalty for Some Drug Crimes, Potentially Sparing Thousands on Death Row," *Los Angeles Times,* January 10, 2018 (www.latimes.com/world/la-fg-iran-drugs-death-penalty-20180110-story.html).

13 Vanda Felbab-Brown, "Opium Licensing in Afghanistan: Its Desirability and Feasibility," *Foreign Policy Studies Policy Paper* 1, Brookings Institution Press, August 2007 (www.brookings.edu/research/opium-licensing-in-afghan istan-its-desirability-and-feasibility/).

14 Vanda Felbab-Brown, "The Drug Economy in Afghanistan and Pakistan, and Security in the Region," in *Narco-jihad: Drug Trafficking in Afghanistan and Pakistan,"* National Bureau of Asian Research, December 2009 (www.nbr.org/ publications/specialreport/pdf/sr20.pdf).

15 Vanda Felbab-Brown, *Shooting Up: Counterinsurgency and the War on Drugs* (Brookings Institution Press, 2010).

16 Vanda Felbab-Brown, *Aspiration and Ambivalence: Strategies and Realities of Counterinsurgency and State-Building in Afghanistan* (Brookings Institution Press, 2013).

17 Ahmad Majidyar, "Iran's Mixed Track Record of Fighting Drugs Trafficking," Middle East Institute, June 29, 2017 (www.mei.edu/publications/ irans-mixed-track-record-fighting-drugs-trafficking).

18 Bill Samii, "Iran: Country's Drug Problems Appear to be Worsening," *Radio Free Europe/Radio Liberty,* June 18, 2005 (www.rferl.org/feature sarticle/2005/07/c7250035-e43c-4a33-a019-a5198ed722c2.html).

19 Lionel Beehner, "Afghanistan's Role in Iran's Drug Problem," Council on

Foreign Relations, September 13, 2006 (www.cfr.org/backgrounder/afghan istans-role-irans-drug-problem).

20 Siavash Jafari, Richard Mathias, Ronald S. Joe, Souzan Baharlou, and Ashkan Nasr, "Effect of Law Enforcement on Drug Abuse: A Comparison of Substance Use in Pakistan, Afghanistan, Iran, and Turkey," *Journal of Substance Use*, vol. 20, no. 4 (August 2015), pp. 295–300.

21 Robins, op. cit.

22 Jason Rezaian, "Women Addicted to Drugs in Iran Begin Seeking Treatment Despite Taboo," *Washington Post*, May 12, 2014 (www.washingtonpost. com/world/middle_east/women-addicted-to-drugs-in-iran-begin-seeking-treatment-despite-taboo/2014/05/11/b11b0c59-cbb4-4f94-a028-00b56f2f4734_ story.html?utm_term=.d9827e7882c9).

23 "Iran Must Not Squander Opportunity to End Executions for Drug-related Offenses," Amnesty International, July 28, 2017 (www.amnesty.org/en/ latest/news/2017/07/iran-must-not-squander-opportunity-to-end-executions-for-drug-related-offences/).

24 Thomas Erdbrink, "Iran Eases Death Penalty for Drug Crimes, Saving Potentially Thousands of Lives," *New York Times*, January 10, 2018 (www .nytimes.com/2018/01/10/world/middleeast/iran-drugs-death-penalty.html).

25 Maziyar Ghiabi, Masoomeh Maarefvand, Hamed Bahari, and Zohreh Alavi, "Islam and Cannabis: Legalisation and Religious Debate in Iran," *International Journal of Drug Policy* Volume 56 (2018), pp. 121-27.

26 Jafari et al., op. cit.

27 Fatemeh Aman, "Traffickers Find Novel Ways of Smuggling Drugs into Iran from Afghanistan," Atlantic Council *IranSource*, April 29, 2016 (www .atlanticcouncil.org/blogs/iransource/traffickers-find-novel-ways-of-smug gling-drugs-into-iran-from-afghanistan).

28 Zein Basravi, "Why Iran Is a Global Hub for Narcotics," *Al Jazeera*, October 23, 2017 (www.aljazeera.com/news/2017/10/iran-global-hub-narcotics -171023150002674.html).

29 Majidyar, op. cit.

30 Vanda Felbab-Brown, "No Easy Exit: Drugs and Counternarcotics Policies in Afghanistan," The Brookings Institution, April 29, 2015 (www.brook ings.edu/~/media/Research/Files/Papers/2015/04/global-drug-policy/Felbab Brown--Afghanistan-final.pdf?la=en).

31 Majidyar.

32 Alberto Mucci, "Hezbollah Profits from Hash as Syria Goes to Pot," July 9, 2014 (www.thedailybeast.com/hezbollah-profits-from-hash-as-syria-goes -to-pot?ref=scroll).

33 U.S. Drug Enforcement Administration, Drug Enforcement Administration (DEA), "DEA and European Authorities Uncover Massive Hizballah Drug and Money Laundering Scheme," press release, February 1, 2016 (www.dea.gov/press-releases/2016/02/01/dea-and-european-authorities-uncover-massive-hizballah-drug-and-money).

34 U.S. Department of Treasury, "Treasury Targets Hizballah Fundraising Network in the Triple Frontier of Argentina, Brazil, and Paraguay," press release, December 6, 2006 (www.treasury.gov/press-center/press-releases/Pages/hp190.aspx).

35 Vanda Felbab-Brown's interviews with Iraqi journalists, security experts and Western diplomats, and members of *hashd* groups in Baghdad, Erbil, and Mosul, December 2018.

36 Najia Houssary, "Saudi Arabia 'Will Stand Resolute' against Hezbollah," *Arab News*, November 1, 2017 (www.arabnews.com/node/1186436/middle-east).

6

Girls of Revolution Street
Iranian Women since 1979

SUZANNE MALONEY *and* ELIORA KATZ

In the forty years since Iran's 1979 revolution, no aspect of U.S. policy toward Tehran has produced more heat—and less light—than the question of external efforts to advance political change in Iran. Secretary of State Mike Pompeo stepped squarely into that contested terrain with his 2018 speech to an audience of Iranian Americans at the Reagan Library, coming down forcefully in favor of strenuous American and international advocacy but offering little in the way of specific fresh ideas. "While it is ultimately up to the Iranian people to determine the direction of their country," Pompeo said, "the United States, in the spirit of our own freedoms, will support the long-ignored voice of the Iranian people. Our hope is that ultimately the regime will make meaningful changes in its behavior both inside of Iran and globally."[1]

Pompeo's speech met with equal parts praise and scorn. Critics emphasized the checkered history of U.S.-backed efforts toward Iran, from the Central Intelligence Agency's (CIA's) role in the 1953 coup that ousted Iran's nationalist hero, Prime Minister Mohammad Mossadegh, to the Reagan-era Iran-Contra scandal, to the Obama administration's calculated neutrality toward 2009 pro-democracy protests.[2] Many observers express equal skepticism about any role for the Iranian diaspora, whose passions traditionally have concentrated around the long-exiled son of the late shah or an even more unsuitable alternative, the cult-like Mujahideen-e Khalq, a group whose partisans fought alongside Saddam Hussein.[3]

These concerns are not unfounded, but they may be a bit outdated. A variety of factors, including time and technology, has begun to create new opportunities for expatriate Iranians and others to contribute to charting a better course for the future of Iran. No one demonstrates those possibilities better than Masih Alinejad, a journalist who fled Iran after the 2009 upheaval and later launched an innovative human rights campaign that she chronicles in her 2018 book, *The Wind in My Hair*.[4] With the same audacity that propelled her out of the tiny, impoverished village where she was raised and fueled her crusading work during the heyday of Iran's reformist press, Alinejad in exile has shattered long-standing assumptions about the salience of external activism.

Hijab and History

Alinejad's campaign focuses on one of the central symbols of theocratic rule: obligatory hijab, or modest dress, which was enshrined in Iran's post-revolutionary legal framework on the basis of Quranic injunctions. Her project was borne of an expression of joy: a photo that Alinejad posted of herself running through a London street with her hair aloft, which she noted would be a crime in Iran. The photo and message went viral,[5] and that unexpected outpouring of support launched a movement. First, a Facebook page branded as "My Stealthy Freedom" invited Iranians to post images of themselves without hijab; within a month, the page had nearly 500,000 "likes." That was followed in 2017 by a hashtag campaign encouraging women to wear white scarves on Wednesdays to protest laws requiring hijab. Alinejad has hosted a weekly show on Voice of America (VOA) television, and her campaign engages on multiple social media apps, where some of the photos and videos draw millions of views and thousands of comments.

Veiling in Muslim societies has always been heavily contingent on geographic, socioeconomic, and historical context, and in contemporary Iran, the issue has long been politicized. In 1936, the first Pahlavi shah issued a decree that prohibited veiling in a bid to modernize his country and inculcate a sense of national identity; he also mandated European-style hats for men. The edict lapsed a few years later, when the shah was forced into exile and his young son took the helm. Mohammad Reza Pahlavi doubled down on his father's secular, pro-Western orientation, and in the 1970s, as anti-government activism gained momentum, many women consciously adopted headscarves or all-enveloping chadors as tangible rejections of the monarchy.

Still, even from the start of the post-revolutionary era, the efforts by the state to impose and enforce hijab provoked intense resistance. In the weeks after the monarchy was toppled, hints of a crackdown on women's dress prompted some of the first protests of the post-revolutionary era, drawing thousands of women to the streets in March 1979 to warn that the imposition of headscarves by the new leadership threatened their rights.[6] "In the dawn of freedom," their slogan went, "there is an absence of freedom."

Despite this and other shows of public opposition, compulsory hijab became one of the essential features of the post-revolutionary system, first by force and eventually by law. Today, any violation is punishable by modest fines and a two-month prison sentence.[7] Compulsory hijab was the sartorial manifestation of a broader imposition of legal and cultural misogyny by Iran's post-revolutionary leaders. They quickly nullified the monarchy's nascent efforts to advance the status and rights of women, and instead erected a legal framework that enshrines gender discrimination.

Nothing in Iran goes uncontested, and the restrictions on women's rights have drawn intense pushback over the past forty years. Advocacy by Iranian human rights activists has reopened additional professional opportunities for women, mitigated some of the most egregious discrimination in family laws, and inspired creative workarounds to official constraints. And yet, as evidenced by Iran's near-last ranking on the 2015 World Economic Forum report on the global gender gap, a dense "web of restrictions" on women remains intact,[8] as does the regime's enforcement of compulsory hijab.

Girls of Revolution Street

Alinejad's activism was controversial from the start. Iran's state broadcasters sought to smear her with horrific falsehoods, regime hackers tried to cut off her social media accounts, and she has received death threats from government paramilitary groups.[9] Her family in Iran has suffered harassment and imprisonment. Surprisingly, she has also faced backlash from some Iranians in the diaspora. Some questioned her focus on hijab, dismissing the fascination with women's dress as a Western fixation and arguing that Iranian women face more important issues than the piece of cloth on their heads. "Most activists in Iran are more concerned with matters from women's unemployment to domestic violence," Iranian-American author Azadeh Moaveni insisted in 2016. "While mandatory hijab certainly matters, it is for Iranian women to determine what level of priority to accord it."[10]

Then, in December 2017, on the eve of a spasm of protests over economic issues that briefly convulsed Iran, a 31-year-old mother named Vida Movahed stood atop a utility box on a busy street named for the country's 1979 revolution, silently waving her white hijab like a flag. She was arrested an hour later, but before she was incarcerated, Iranians captured her quiet rebellion on camera and shared it over social media, where it became one of the iconic images of the brief uprising. A few weeks later, Narges Hosseini climbed upon the same utility box and repeated Movahed's protest, and over the course of the following months, dozens of Iranian women followed their lead, their images shared under the hashtag #girlsofrevolutionstreet.[11]

In the months that followed, authorities arrested more than thirty-five women on charges such as "a sinful act" and "inciting corruption and prostitution"; some have reportedly been tortured and beaten while in custody.[12] Shaparak Shajarizadeh, a 42-year-old who peacefully waved her white hijab from a stick in December 2017, was sentenced to two years in prison in addition to an eighteen-year suspended prison term before fleeing the country. The renowned human rights lawyer who has defended several of the women, Nasrin Sotoudeh, was rearrested in June 2018 after her conviction in absentia on unknown charges. She is serving a five-year sentence, and her husband, Reza Khandan, was later detained in a new round of repression that jailed several leading women's rights activists.[13] Still, Iran's hijab protests persist: six women were arrested in Khuzestan in July 2018 for removing their scarves;[14] in October 2018, a still-unidentified woman climbed atop a turquoise dome in Revolution Square, where a statue of the shah once stood, and waved her headscarf along with a bouquet of balloons. Meanwhile, the commander of Iran's domestic security forces announced stepped-up efforts to enforce hijab compliance, threatening to impound the cars of female drivers who fail to cover their hair. And a controversy briefly erupted in June 2019, after a ride-share driver refused to transport a Tehran woman on the basis of "bad hijab." Thousands of social media messages called for a boycott of the ride-share app, but the company commended the driver for following the law.[15] The message is clear: Iranian women have no sanctuary from the long arm of the laws on modest dress.

Outside Influences

Did the Stealthy Freedom campaign help instigate this wave of activism? Neither Vida Movahed, who waved her white scarf on a Wednesday, nor those who followed in her footsteps have publicly attributed their actions to Alinejad. Several, including Hosseini, have sought to dissociate themselves from any outside involvement in the press and via social media. For their part, Iranian authorities clearly saw a connection. On International Women's Day, the country's Supreme Leader, Ayatollah Ali Khamenei, gave a blistering speech about hijab, blaming Iran's "enemies" for trying to "deceive a handful of girls to remove their hijabs on the street."[16] Since the protests, official efforts to smear Alinejad have intensified, with her family paraded on state television to engage in a Stalinist ritual of denunciation and her brother and other relatives detained.

Of course, even as Khamenei insisted that the protests had fizzled, he inveighed against the "journalists, semi-intellectuals, clerics. . .pursuing the same direction that the enemy is" by expressing doubts about compulsory hijab.[17] Indeed, a number of prominent voices within Iran came to the defense of the Girls of Revolution Street, including a female member of Iran's parliament who noted that the protestors were "the same girls who for years have been left behind the gates of gender discrimination."[18] President Hassan Rouhani seemed to hint sympathetically, and in February 2018 his office released a four-year-old public opinion survey showing that at least half the country believes that the government should not require or regulate hijab.[19] A study released in early 2019 by the parliament's research center suggests a steady decline in public support for mandatory hijab.[20]

And in the months that followed, new photos and videos and stories of women removing their hijab or resisting the morality police flooded social media, many via Alinejad, who has become the conduit and the champion of a social movement that is directly challenging the theocratic system.

Why Hijab Matters

In a country where women require a man's approval for travel and marriage, where laws surrounding divorce and custody and inheritance favor men, and where female labor force participation is among the lowest in the world despite high educational attainments, it is understandable that some downplay the significance of hijab "as secondary to other matters such as political or gender equality rights."[21] Compared with all this, a headscarf may seem trivial. After all, the Islamic Republic's cultural norms have evolved over time, with steady shrinkage of hems and emboldened colors, and ever-creative Iranians have contrived mechanisms for evading enforcement, including a smartphone app that warns users of nearby morality police.[22]

But even with updated styles, the impact of these rules is anything but trivial. By focusing on the legal requirement, rather than relitigating the theological debate around veiling, Alinejad has helped illuminate how deeply many Iranian women resent compulsory hijab as both the symbol and the instrument of official repression—and the extent to which that repression is meted out disproportionately on Iranian women. In other words, it is not about the clothes, it is about the coercion. And that looms large in the day-to-day lives of ordinary women: in the recurrent anxiety about an encounter with the morality police,[23] the discomfort and humiliation of having no agency over something as simple as your wardrobe, the hypocrisy of a system whose public figures extol the chador in public and conveniently discard it while on European vacations.[24] Alinejad's campaign channeled these frustrations into action, with the invitation to "create your own stealthy freedom so you are not ruined by the weight of coercion and compulsion."[25]

For something that is only a secondary concern, the Islamic Republic goes to great effort to ensure that its injunctions for modest dress are enforced. Newspapers penciled in a scarf for an obituary feature on Maryam Mirzakhani, a brilliant young mathematician who died in exile[26]; a clerical oversight body retroactively disqualified a successful candidate in the 2016 parliamentary election over leaked photos of foreign travel sans headscarf.[27] Simply organizing a discussion around compulsory hijab can result in detention, and films that mock the morality police have been banned.

In 2013, nearly 3 million women received official warnings for loose or "bad hijab" in a single year, with 18,000 cases referred for prosecution.[28] Meanwhile, Iran's judiciary recently closed the 2014 case of ten women in Isfahan who were attacked with acid shortly after a law was enacted empowering private citizens to verbally confront those who fail to comply with morality laws.[29] No one was ever charged with those crimes.

For young Iranian women, compulsory hijab is just one manifestation of a ruling system that seems to have criminalized every opportunity for self-expression: dancing,[30] modeling,[31] singing[32] or playing music[33] or shaking hands with men,[34] riding a bicycle,[35] doing Zumba,[36] posting dance videos to Instagram,[37] going to a pool party,[38] celebrating the winter solstice,[39] or cheering at a volleyball[40] or soccer[41] match in a public stadium. It is almost as though the Islamic Republic has outlawed happiness. In fact, seven young Iranian men and women were arrested in 2014 for a viral video they recorded of themselves dancing to the song "Happy."[42]

The Failure of Gradualism

Many Iranian activists and intellectuals sought to effect change by focusing on a broader effort to liberalize Iran's legal framework, through initiatives like the One Million Signatures for the Repeal of Discriminatory Laws. This agenda meshed neatly with the overall approach of the Iranian reform movement, which emerged as a force to be reckoned with in the late 1990s and sought to use Iran's routinely disregarded constitutional guarantees as an avenue for strengthening representative rule. That formula promised to temper the system's excesses from within, and combined with the inexorable force of sociocultural evolution, some anticipated that this would gradually but inevitably resolve the hijab question.

Unfortunately, that approach has failed—not simply on the question of hijab, but across the board. At every turn, incremental reform has been blunted and subverted by the post-revolutionary structure of power. Reformist victories at the ballot box cannot overcome the levers wielded by unelected authorities who remain committed to preserving the authoritarian control. After decades of public debate, even relatively innocuous improvements, such as permitting women to attend sports matches at public stadiums, are blocked or undermined by clerical opposition, despite evidence of support from across Iran's factional divide for change.[43] Elections and gradualism simply cannot overcome the roadblocks of a system where unelected clerics and security officials denounce those who oppose mandatory hijab as "prostitutes."[44]

Even worse, Iranian leaders became adept at using the debate itself to their advantage, in a seemingly endless game of raising hopes to sustain a modicum of support for the ruling system. The surprise 1997 election of reformist cleric Mohammad Khatami benefited from rumors that his opponent intended to mandate the most conservative interpretation of hijab, the all-enveloping chador. And in the lead-up to his 2017 reelection bid, President Rouhani posted a photo of himself on Instagram hiking near Tehran, posed alongside several young women wearing the most modern and minimalist interpretation of the hijab requirement. It was a savvy campaign move; as renowned human rights lawyer Mehrangiz Kar noted at the time, the Supreme Leader might have done the same if he had to face a popular vote.

Despite his campaign tactics, Rouhani's two terms as president have generated no change in Iran's policies on women's dress or, more broadly, on their legal rights and status. In fact, only months after his risqué photo op and two full decades after resentment of the chador helped sink a prior presidential candidacy, Rouhani required his vice president for legal affairs to supplement her headscarf with a chador, explaining that it remains government protocol.[45] As time passes, gradualism looks more like a hamster wheel, endlessly raising expectations for forward motion before careening right back down to where things began.

Hashtag Activism

Alinejad's campaign, and the hijab protests that have emerged in her wake, reflect a different model of advancing change, one that eschews incrementalism for confrontation and relies on individual acts of civil disobedience rather than collective appeals or coordinated mobilization. This approach has practical value in a country where organized activism exacerbates vulnerability. As one of the Girls of Revolution Street remarked to an interviewer: "This is a kind of movement that does not need to organize and gather people and groups. It is one of the few protests that you can do on your own."[46]

These solitary acts are amplified by a set of crucial tools—smart phones and social media. Smart phone penetration has increased at rapid rates over the past decade. Whereas in 2009, when massive protests shook the capital and several other cities, approximately 15 percent of Iranians had access to the internet, by March 2018 the country of 80 million people boasted at least 53 million mobile internet devices, according to Iran's ministry of telecommunications. And this number continues to multiply, by approximately 1 million new devices per month over the course of the past year.[47] According to state media, nearly 160 million

SIM cards were in use in 2018.[48] High-speed connectivity is available in all major cities, and while the government has sought to restrict access to popular messaging apps such as Telegram, along with Twitter, Facebook, YouTube, and now likely Instagram—all while the country's Supreme Leader and president actively use these platforms— Iranians have become adept at evading official filters.

As a result, the images of the Girls of Revolution Street quickly went viral, inspiring others to follow Vida Movahed's lead and provoking an intense debate about compulsory hijab that reached all the way up to Iran's senior leadership. Whatever her role in galvanizing the hijab protestors themselves, Alinejad's Stealthy Freedom advocacy offered proof of concept around the efficacy of "hashtag activism" in generating new fault lines by interrogating the symbols of state power.[49] A photo circulated widely is not simply a "selfie" when it calls into question the ideological claims of authoritarian control, and videos of Iranian women shouting down the harassment they receive from mullahs and morality police have gone viral.

And that is precisely what unnerves Alinejad's critics: her campaign strikes at the heart of the ideology that validates arbitrary and unaccountable power in Iran. To question hijab is to question the essence of the Islamic Republic, and to express those questions in a way that demonstrates impatience with the perennial assurances of "peaceful reform" confounds the deeply held political narratives of many, both inside and outside Iran.

Whether Alinejad or the Girls of Revolution Street can generate durable policy change is hardly certain. Tehran has massive repressive capacity at its disposal that extends well into the online space. While Alinejad has received thousands of videos and photos of women challenging the hijab mandate, those actively protesting remain a miniscule proportion of Iran's population. But their actions represent an implicit recognition that a new set of tools is needed to advance change in the Islamic Republic—that instead of working within the beleaguered rules of the game, it is time to contest the levers of power and the symbols that underpin the Islamic Republic's claims to legitimacy. Instead of gradualism, it is time for at least a hint of confrontation.

And sometimes, even in Iran, it seems possible that more assertive tactics can pay dividends. Iranian women have scored a few modest victories as of late. After years of fierce opposition, in June 2018 women were permitted to enter Tehran's famed Azadi Stadium for the first time to view a crucial World Cup game from Russia on a jumbotron. Just hours before the game was to commence, officials tried to shut down the event on the grounds of "infrastructure difficulties."[50] Thousands of women and men, already gathered outside the stadium to watch the match, refused to leave. After a tense pause, the doors were opened. Without explanation, one small barrier to Iranian women was broken, at least for one day. In 2019, Iran came under renewed international pressure over these issues after the death by self-immolation of Sahar Khodayari, a young woman facing a prison sentence for sneaking into a stadium to watch her favorite soccer club.

What Comes Next?

Alinejad has lived in exile outside Iran for nearly a decade, a factor that has typically undercut the efficacy and relevance of political activism. Post-revolutionary Iran has a disproportionately young population, and its politics entail an intense and often personalistic struggle for influence; both of these factors tend to relegate those who operate from a distance to little more than incisive commentary. In Alinejad's case, distance offered crucial insulation for internet-based advocacy; given the official backlash within Iran, it seems inconceivable that My Stealthy Freedom would have survived long if its servers or spokesperson had remained inside the country.

In that sense, she is not alone; a new generation of Iranian activists and dissidents are finding mechanisms for engaging with debates and shaping political outcomes inside the country via journalism sites like IranWire, Shirzanan, and Small Media, and human rights groups such as the Center for Human Rights in Iran, Justice for Iran, and many others.

The Trump administration has episodically invoked the cause of Iran's hijab protestors, as part of a broader social media campaign that seeks to highlight human right abuses in Iran. While Alinejad's message has been amplified by her VOA appearances, the new generation of Iranian expatriate activists do not require heavy-handed intervention by Washington or other outside governments.

Still, their efforts should prompt a debate about the role of governments and other interlocutors with Iran around the issues they are raising, including compulsory hijab. Without any credible religious rationale, the Islamic Republic has effectively extended the legal mandate for modest dress beyond its own citizenry, to include all women who visit Iran. As Tehran sought to raise its profile for, and revenues from, tourism and entertainment, this has occasionally provoked backlash, with Air France flight attendants forcing the company to change its policy and a number of athletes and chess players refusing to participate in tournaments in Iran rather than submit to Tehran's wardrobe dictates.[51]

For the most part, however, foreign officials and diplomats have submitted to Tehran's clothing dictates to avoid alienating or embarrassing their hosts. Even a delegation representing Sweden's avowedly feminist government deferred to local protocol and donned headscarves in 2017 trade talks.[52] The rare exceptions have generated a firestorm in Iran's official media or simply a cheery reprimand from the country's foreign minister.[53]

The Girls of Revolution Street movement should prompt a belated reconsideration of that approach. After all, a similar transformation occurred in the hijab requirements for foreign officials visiting Saudi Arabia. For a number of years, female U.S. service members stationed in Saudi Arabia were ordered to wear the all-enveloping abaya even as they were helping to defend the country. That policy only changed in 2002, after a female American fighter pilot, Martha McSally—who would go on to represent Arizona in the House of Representatives and the Senate—took the U.S. Department of Defense to court. Since then, senior U.S. and European officials visiting Saudi Arabia have quietly followed her lead; the abaya has been noticeably absent during visits by first ladies Laura Bush, Michelle Obama, and Melania Trump, as well as secretaries of state Condoleezza Rice and Hillary Clinton, German chancellor Angela Merkel, and British prime minister Theresa May.

Officials from Europe and elsewhere should borrow that script on their visits to Tehran. At a time when Iran's leadership is especially eager for diplomatic and economic engagement with the West, officials such as European Union foreign policy chief Federica Mogherini could make a simple, powerful statement in support of the fundamental rights that Iranians want and deserve by simply forgoing any deference to forced modesty on their next trip to Tehran. Forty years after Iranian women first went to the streets to denounce mandatory veiling, international advocacy for the rights and dignity of all people should not be stealthy.

NOTES

1 Remarks by Secretary of State Michael R. Pompeo, Ronald Reagan Presidential Foundation and Library, Simi Valley, CA, July 22, 2018 (www.state. gov/supporting-iranian-voices/).

2 Doug Bandow, "Trump's Iran Regime Change Fantasies," *The American Conservative*, July 26, 2018 (www.theamericanconservative.com/articles/trumps-iran-regime-change-fantasies/).

3 Nahal Toosi, "Trump Has Tough Sell Recruiting Iranian Americans in Campaign against Tehran," *Politico*, July 18, 2018 (www.politico.com/story/2018/07/18/trump-iran-iranian-americans-pompeo-731736).

4 Masih Alinejad, *The Wind in My Hair: My Fight for Freedom in Modern Iran* (New York: Little, Brown and Company, 2018.)

5 Beth Greenfield, "'My Hair Was a Hostage,' Says Iranian Hijab Activist," *Yahoo*, April 8, 2016 (www.yahoo.com/lifestyle/freeing-iranian-women-one-head-1403236247207990.html).

6 Gregory Jaynes, "Bazargan Goes to See Khomeini as Iran Rift Grows," *New York Times*, March 9, 1979, p.1 (www.nytimes.com/1979/03/09/archives/bazargan-goes-to-see-khomeini-as-iran-rift-grows-ayatollah-to-meet.html).

7 "Iran's Prosecutor Dismisses Hijab Protesters as Childish and Ignorant," IranWire, January 31, 2018 (iranwire.com/en/features/5136).

8 David Blair, "Iran's Big Woman Problem: All of the Things Iranian Women Aren't Allowed to Do," *The Telegraph*, September 21, 2015 (www.telegraph. co.uk/women/womens-life/11875128/Irans-women-problem-All-of-the-things-Iranian-women-arent-allowed.html).

9 "Iranian TV Slanders the Woman Who 'Unveiled' Iran," France 24 (June 3, 2014) (observers.france24.com/en/20140603-iranian-television-slanders-woman-who-unveiled-iran); "My Stealthy Freedom: The Hijab in Iran and in the West," Aero magazine (July 12, 2017) (https://areomagazine.com/2017/07/12/my-stealthy-freedom-the-hijab-in-iran-and-in-the-west/); Alinejad, "Iran's Basij Promised to Butcher Me for Fighting Compulsory Hijab," *Washington Post*, March 28, 2018 (www.washingtonpost.com/news/global-opinions/wp/2018/03/28/irans-religious-police-promised-to-butcher-me-for-fighting-against-the-hijab/?utm_term=.43e0cadaea6a).

10 Azadeh Moaveni, "Your Boycott Won't Help Iranian Women," *New York Times*, October 7, 2016, p.A26 (www.nytimes.com/2016/10/08/opinion/your-boycott-wont-help-iranian-women.html).

11 Saeed Kamali Dehgan, "Second Woman Arrested in Tehran for Hijab Protest," *The Guardian*, January 29, 2018 (www.theguardian.com/world/2018/jan/29/second-woman-arrested-tehran-hijab-protest-iran).

12 Amnesty International statement, "Dozens of Women Ill-treated and at Risk of long Jail Terms for Peacefully Protesting Compulsory Veiling," February 26, 2018 (www.amnesty.org/en/latest/news/2018/02/iran-dozens-of-women-ill-treated-and-at-risk-of-long-jail-terms-for-peacefully-protesting-compulsory-veiling/).

13 Robin Wright, "Iran's Orwellian Arrest of Its Leading Female Human-Rights Lawyer," *The New Yorker*, June 14, 2018 (www.newyorker.com/news/news-desk/irans-orwellian-arrest-of-a-leading-human-rights-lawyer).

14 Human Rights Activists News Agency (HRANA), "Five Girls Were Arrested in Dezful for Unveiling," July 23, 2018 (www.hra-news.org/2018/hranews/a-16262/).

15 Golnaz Esfandiari, "Snapp Judgment: Iran Ride-Sharing Company at Center of 'Bad Hijab' Dispute," RFE/RL, June 15, 2019 (www.rferl.org/a/snapp-judgment-iran-ride-sharing-company-at-center-of-bad-hijab-dispute/30000859.html).

16 The text of the speech can be found on Khamenei's website, in English (http://english.khamenei.ir/news/5535/Islam-dignifies-women-Liberalism-wants-them-humiliated-exposed).

17 Ibid.

18 "Iranian Female MP Voices Support for Women Arrested on Charges of Violating Hijab Code," *Rudaw News*, March 2, 2018 (www.rudaw.net/english/middleeast/iran/03022018).

19 Thomas Erdbrink, "Iran Can't Keep Dictating Lifestyle, Its President Warns," *New York Times,* January 8, 2018 (www.nytimes.com/2018/01/08/world/middleeast/iran-rouhani-protests.html); Erdbrink, "Compulsory Veils? Half of Iranians Say 'No' to Pillar of Revolution," *New York Times*, February 4, 2018 (www.nytimes.com/2018/02/04/world/middleeast/iran-hijab-veils.html). The text of the report itself, "Hijab: The Pathology of Past Policies, Looking to the

Future," can be found on the website of the Center for Strategic Studies, in Persian (www.css.ir/Media/PDF/1396/11/14/636532375414083535.pdf).

20 "Factors Affecting Implementation of Hijab Policies and Leading Solutions," in Persian (www.mizanonline.com/files/fa/news/1397/5/6/1727106_316.pdf).

21 Nahid Siamdoust, "Why Iranian Women Are Taking Off Their Head Scarves," New York Times, February 6, 2018, p. A21 (www.nytimes.com/2018/02/03/opinion/sunday/iran-hijab-women-scarves.html).

22 Peter Kenyon, "Springtime in Iran Means the 'Morality Police' Are Out in Force," NPR, All Things Considered, May 3, 2016 (www.npr.org/sections/parallels/2016/05/03/476511439/springtime-in-iran-means-the-morality-police-are-out-in-force).

23 Denise Hassanzade Ajiri, "Why So Many Iranians Have Come to Hate the Hijab," The Guardian, Tehran Bureau, April 28, 2016 (www.theguardian.com/world/2016/apr/28/iranian-women-hate-hijab-tehranbureau).

24 Patrick Evans, "Azadeh Namdari: Backlash over Conservative Iranian Television Host," BBC, July 25, 2017 (www.bbc.com/news/blogs-trending-40715595).

25 "Exiled Journalist Continues to Fight For Women's Rights In Iran," NPR, Fresh Air, May 30, 2018 (www.npr.org/2018/05/30/615457127/exiled-journalist-continues-to-fight-for-womens-rights-in-iran).

26 "They've Got Her Covered: Iran Photoshops a Veil on Its Deceased Math Genius Maryam Mirzakhani," IranWire/The Daily Beast, July 18, 2017 (www.thedailybeast.com/iran-photoshops-a-veil-on-its-deceased-math-genius-maryam-mirzakhani).

27 Thomas Erdbrink, "She Won a Seat in Iran's Parliament, but Hard-liners Had Other Plans," New York Times, May 11, 2016 (www.nytimes.com/2016/05/12/world/middleeast/iran-parliament-minoo-khaleghi.html).

28 "Naja: Approximately 3 Million Morality Patrol Warnings Last Year," Alef, in Persian, May 29, 2014 (http://old.alef.ir/vdcfced0cw6d0ya.igiw.html?227188).

29 Thomas Erdbrink, "Arrests Follow Acid Attacks on Iranian Women," New York Times, October 20, 2014 (www.nytimes.com/2014/10/21/world/middleeast/arrests-follow-acid-attacks-on-iranian-women-.html?_r=0).

30 "Iran Arrests Culture Ministry Official over Public Dance," France 24, April 19, 2018 (www.france24.com/en/20180419-iran-arrests-culture-ministry-official-over-public-dance).

31 "Iran Arrests 46 in Fresh Crackdowns on Instagram Models," Associated Press, July 16, 2018 (www.usnews.com/news/entertainment/articles/2018-07-16/iran-arrests-46-in-fresh-crackdowns-on-instagram-models).

32 Elliot Hannon, "Iran Makes Arrests for 'Vulgar' Celebratory Music Video Supporting Its World Cup Team," Slate, June 23, 2014 (slate.com/news-and-

politics/2014/06/iran-makes-arrests-for-world-cup-celebration-video.html).

33 "Iranian Singer Cancels Concert After Female Players Banned from Stage," *Kayhan Life*, February 4, 2018 (kayhanlife.com/culture/stage/iranian-singer-cancels-concert-female-players-banned-stage/).

34 Golnaz Esfandiari, "Iran Sentences Poets, Filmmaker to Prison, Lashings," RFE/RL, October 14, 2015 (www.rferl.org/a/iran-jails-lashes-poets-filmmaker/27306541.html).

35 Lizzie Dearden, "Women 'Arrested for Riding Bicycles' in Iran and Made to Sign Pledge Never to Cycle in Public again," *The Independent,* July 28, 2016 (www.independent.co.uk/news/world/middle-east/women-arrested-for-riding-bicycles-in-iran-and-made-to-sign-pledge-never-to-cycle-in-public-again-a7159761.html).

36 "Iran Arrests Six for Zumba," BBC, August 9, 2017 (www.bbc.com/news/world-middle-east-40880420).

37 Thomas Erdbrink, "Iran's Shaming of Young Dancer Draws Backlash, *New York Times*, July 9, 2018 (www.nytimes.com/2018/07/09/world/middleeast/irans-instagram-dancer-teen.html).

38 "Iranian Police Arrest Dozens of 'Half-Naked' Youths at Pool Party," RFE/RL, August 9, 2017 (www.rferl.org/a/iran-pool-party-arrests-young-half-naked/28667649.html).

39 "Iran's Morality Police Storm Solstice Parties to Arrest 230 People," BBC, December 22, 2017 (www.bbc.com/news/world-middle-east-42459544).

40 Josh Halliday and Saeed Kamali Dehghan, "Ghoncheh Ghavami's Brother Pleads with Iranian President to Free Sister," *The Guardian*, September 23, 2014 (www.theguardian.com/world/2014/sep/23/ghoncheh-ghavami-brother-pleads-iranian-president-free-sister).

41 "Iran Detains 35 Women for Going to Football Match," BBC, March 1, 2018 (www.bbc.com/news/world-middle-east-43243414).

42 Doug Stanglin, "Iranians Escape Lashing for Dancing in 'Happy' Video," *USA Today*, September 19, 2014 (www.usatoday.com/story/news/world/2014/09/19/iran-happy-pharrell-williams-sentenced-suspended/15879809/).

43 For example, during his early days as president, hard-liner Mahmoud Ahmadinejad sought to lift the ban on women's attendance at public sports matches, only to see his order reversed by clerical opposition. See Brian Whitaker, "President Lifts Ban on Women Watching Football in Iran," *The Guardian*, April 24, 2006 (www.theguardian.com/world/2006/apr/25/iran.gender); Frances Harrison, "Iran clergy Angry Over Women Fans," BBC, April 26, 2006 (http://news.bbc.co.uk/2/hi/middle_east/4947508.stm).

44 "Commander Naqdi: Today America Knows It Can Do Nothing," Iranian Students News Agency (ISNA), in Persian, August 10, 2018 (www.isna.ir/news/97051909894/).

45 Golnaz Esfandiari, "In Controversial Move, Iran's New Female Vice President Ordered to Wear Chador," RFE/RL, August 23, 2017 (www.rferl. org/a/iran-rohani-cabinet-joneydi-chador-chadori-/28692682.html).

46 "Interview with an Enghelab Street Woman Protesting Compulsory Hijab," Zamaneh Media, February 16, 2018 (en.radiozamaneh.com/28836/).

47 Hamed Jafari, "53 Million Mobile Internet Users in Iran Until March 2018," TechRasa, May 29, 2018;

"47 Million Mobile Internet Users in Iran Until September 2017," TechRasa, November 11, 2017 (http://techrasa.com/2017/11/11/47-million-mobile-internet-users-iran-sep-2017/).

48 "Iran Shining in ICT Development," Islamic Republic News Agency, March 14, 2018 (en.irna.ir/news/82862603/Iran-shining-in-ICT-development-index).

49 Lauren Katz, "Say It with a Selfie: Protesting in the Age of Social Media," NPR, *All Tech Considered*, May 10, 2014 (www.npr.org/sections/alltech considered/2014/05/10/311143584/say-it-with-a-selfie-protesting-in-the-age-of-social-media).

50 Rebecca Tan, "For the First Time Since 1980, Iranian Women Allowed to Watch World Cup in Same Stadium as Men," *Washington Post*, June 20, 2018 (www.washingtonpost.com/news/worldviews/wp/2018/06/20/for-the-first-time-since-1980-iranian-women-allowed-to-watch-world-cup-in-same-stadium-as-men/?utm_term=.fcc398e579af).

51 Liam Stack, "Air France Faces Backlash over Veil Policy on Route to Iran," *New York Times*, April 5, 2016 (www.nytimes.com/2016/04/06/world/europe/air-france-veil-policy-iran.html); "Compulsory Hijab Rule Makes Heena Sidhu Pull Out of Asian Airgun Championship in Iran," *India Today*, April 29, 2016 (www.indiatoday.in/sports/other-sports/story/heena-sidhu-asian-airgun-championship-iran-shooting-349165-2016-10-29); Cleve R. Wootson Jr., "'I Will NOT Wear a Hijab': U.S. Chess Star Refuses to Attend World Championships in Iran," *Washington Post*, October 6, 2016 (www.washingtonpost.com/news/worldviews/wp/2016/10/06/i-will-not-wear-a-hijab-u-s-chess-star-refuses-to-attend-world-championships-in-iran/?utm_term=.50aec88172f0).

52 Adam Taylor, "Sweden's 'Feminist' Government Criticized for Wearing Headscarves in Iran," *Washington Post*, February 13, 2017 (www.washingtonpost.com/news/worldviews/wp/2017/02/13/swedens-feminist-government-criticized-for-wearing-headscarves-in-iran/?utm_term=.ad70830f3479).

53 Bethan McKernan, "Iranian Media in Tailspin over Female British Diplomat's Lack of Headscarf," *The Independent*, December 12, 2017 (www.independent.co.uk/news/world/middle-east/iran-british-diplomat-karen-pierce-no-headscarf-hijab-uk-media-anger-muslim-clothing-rules-a8105966.html).

PART II

The Revolution and Washington

7

"We Used to Run This Country"
How the Revolution Upended an
American-Iranian Alliance

SUZANNE MALONEY

Four decades have now passed since a mass political movement espousing the triumph of sacral authority over secular toppled Iran's absolute monarch, Mohammad Reza Pahlavi, and his seemingly impregnable state. Just as definitively, the revolution that abrogated the Pahlavi dynasty in 1979 scuttled a set of assumptions about religion, modernity, and political development that were previously considered axiomatic. Widely considered unthinkable even as it was unfolding, the ouster of the shah and the assumption of authority by an inchoate coalition of leftists, liberals, and Muslim clerics captivated the world. The subsequent establishment of the Islamic Republic of Iran dramatically transformed the nation's internal politics, economy, and society, and its impact echoed well beyond its borders to reconfigure the regional landscape, the geostrategic balance in the Middle East.

For Washington, the revolution represented a devastating strategic loss. Since the British withdrawal from the Persian Gulf in 1971, Iran had become the cornerstone of America's security architecture for protecting Western interests across the region.[1] As both the "pivot in the price hike" and the sole regional leader willing to buck the Arab oil embargo, the shah had made himself equally consequential for energy markets and the global economy. Iran's revolution reshaped the country, the region, and its interaction with the rest of the world, especially the United States. Forty years later, the legacy of the revolution lives on in both Washington and Tehran in the mutual antagonisms it brought to the fore.

An Auspicious Beginning

The United States and Iran were not old allies, but Americans had played a crucial—and until 1953, constructive—role in each of the formative experiences in the birth of modern Iran. An American teacher died in the fight to advance rule of law during Iran's 1905 Constitutional Revolution. American missionaries established dozens of hospitals and schools around the country, training a generation of future leaders and helping expand female education. In the final years of the Qajar dynasty and the early years of the Pahlavi reign, U.S. officials were seconded to help strengthen the state's fiscal management, advance administrative reforms, and reorganize its gendarmerie. Washington advocated on behalf of Iran, then occupied by the Allied powers, during the Paris Peace Conference after World War I and again after World War II, when Russian troops helped instigate secessionist movements in northern Iran and refused to withdraw as agreed.

This propitious start to the relationship, which positioned Washington more favorably than the imperial machinations of Great Britain and Russia, is all but forgotten today, thanks to the U.S. role in ousting Iran's nationalist prime minister in 1953 and the subsequent embrace of Shah Mohammad Reza by successive American administrations. The coup was a momentous turning point for Iran; coinciding with a broader imperative around American engagement in the Middle East, the actions of the Central Intelligence Agency (CIA) in preserving the monarchy meant that for the first time, Washington assumed a real stake in Iran's fate. The generous American program of technical and financial assistance that followed the shah's reinstatement enabled him to impose greater central control and reassemble the instruments of the state under his personal authority. Over time, it would become painfully clear that the costs of the coup in stoking paranoia, enabling repression, and undermining the Pahlavis' legitimacy vastly outweighed its short-term benefits, but at the time the preoccupation with the Cold War obscured Iranian resentment fueled by the American intervention.

Instead, Americans and the world marveled as Iran made epic progress over the next quarter-century. Under the auspices of the shah's "White Revolution," a multifaceted set of political and economic reforms, together with the oil boom, helped generate rapid growth and a dynamic, cosmopolitan society. Average annual growth rates between 1959 and 1972 were 9.8 percent—on par with the more recent experience of China. The number of primary school students increased from 286,000 to 5.2 million, and adult literacy rates shot from 16 percent to 36 percent in the monarchy's final fifteen years.[2] Women secured the right to vote and run in parliamentary elections, and their political participation helped advance a progressive new family law. Iran's middle class approached one-fourth of the labor force, composed of an estimated 700,000 salaried professionals and an additional 1 million families associated with the *bazaar* and small manufacturers.[3] For millions of Iranians, the shah's development program generated tangible improvements in their quality of life and expectations of upward mobility for their children.

And yet, Iran's aggressive modernization triggered deep fissures that, over time, escalated to corrode the foundations of the monarchy. The launch of the shah's reform agenda met with fierce opposition among influential constituencies in the clergy, the merchant class, and major landholders. They saw land reform as an encroachment on their income, the extension of women's suffrage as an assault on their values, and the legal protections afforded to Americans in Iran as an intolerable capitulation of Iran's sovereignty. In 1963, Ayatollah Ruhollah Khomeini emerged as the most powerful voice of opposition, denouncing the shah as a "miserable wretch" and a puppet of American and Israeli masters.[4] Khomeini's arrest and deportation to Iraq a year later seemed to neutralize the threat;

as would eventually become clear, his arms-length distance from the shah's steady attenuation of Iran's political opposition only magnified the cleric's influence.

Iran's Thirst for "Modernity"

Through the 1960s and 1970s, the embrace between the shah and Washington grew ever closer. With commercial ties expanding steadily, Iran's great leap forward had direct beneficiaries in the United States. The floodgates opened—especially for military hardware—after the price of oil quadrupled in 1973. The shah launched a big-budget defense buildup, purchasing more than $16 billion in arms from the United States between 1972 and 1977, on top of approximately $3 billion per year in bilateral civilian trade.

The bilateral relationship transcended the obvious energy and military trade. Between 1973 and 1978, telephone calls between the United States and Iran skyrocketed by 1,600 percent. At least 60,000 Iranians lived or studied in the United States, while 50,000 Americans were working in Iran. More than fifty American universities had campuses in Iran or partnerships with Iranian counterparts. Tehran, Isfahan, and Shiraz became chic destinations for tourists: Andy Warhol went there to paint the empress's portrait; Elizabeth Taylor visited, drinking vodka with her caviar.[5] And the shah invited his son's favorite actor, Lee Majors, the star of the 1970s television hit *The Six Million Dollar Man*, who brought his starlet wife, Farrah Fawcett.[6] "This is an enchanted land in which modernity, thanks to an enlightened young ruler and the presence of an enormous supply of petroleum, harmonizes with one of the earliest civilizations known to recorded history," gushed the *New York Times* in 1965.[7] The Pahlavis' Iran was distant but familiar for Americans—and firmly on the path to "modernity."

The shah thought so as well. He abhorred traditionalism; as he declared in his memoirs, "I could not stop building supermarkets. I wanted a modern country."[8] Giddy with success and eager to expedite Iran's transformation, he boasted that Iran's economy would outpace that of Germany and France by the turn of the century, overriding his advisors' objections and doubling government spending in 1973. But even with record oil revenues, the scope and pace of his ambitions outstripped the country's absorptive capacity. Iran suffered all the predictable consequences of hyper-growth: rising inflation, corruption, and income inequality; rapid urbanization and inadequate public services; structural bottlenecks, vast inefficiencies, and an influx of foreign workers and associated cultural frictions. As Tehran sought to manage the disruptive impact of volatile energy markets, its remedies often exacerbated the problems, especially given the shah's increasingly autocratic political impulses. Since 1953, he had taken care to eliminate any potential threats to his reign, through the much-feared secret police and restrictions on political activity. Soon enough, the monarchy found itself facing a steadily escalating barrage of protests, as an improbable cooperation among Iran's traditional nationalists, radical Marxists, and a highly politicized faction of the clerical establishment came together to confront the shah.

Shock Wave

The revolution took Washington by surprise, though it should not have. The rumblings of trouble in Iran had been evident for years, in the attacks on Americans in Iran by radical groups; the burst of intellectual activism in moments of openness; the protestors who besieged the Pahlavis (and the White House on one occasion) on multiple U.S. visits[9]; and a hundred other indicators of political alienation and economic dislocation. Still, the rapidity of the monarchy's collapse was breathtaking. Only a year before the shah prepared for his final, ignominious flight from Tehran, he was lauded by President Jimmy Carter in a New Year's Eve toast that described Iran as "an island of stability in a turbulent corner of the world."[10]

The phrase remains a kind of shorthand for American failure to anticipate developments in Iran and the broader Middle East. However, it was not only Americans who misread the monarchy's vulnerabilities. The "island of stability" catchphrase was borrowed from remarks made by then-prime minister Amir Abbas Hoveyda on a 1968 visit to Washington.[11] Detained by the shah in November 1978 in a bid to assuage rising public fury, Hoveyda was executed in the post-revolutionary purges, the highest-ranking of the shah's officials to lose his life in the transition. The tsunami of political change that overtook Iran in 1978 took Iranians by surprise as well, including some of the leading voices in the opposition.

For many in the United States, where scenes of the mass demonstrations played on the nightly news, the upheaval in Iran compounded a sense of disarray and futility surrounding America's role in the world that remained potent in the aftermath of the Vietnam War. "America cannot do a damned thing," Khomeini liked to say, and the monarchy's demise and its early aftermath offered ample evidence. Days after Khomeini returned to Iran and the last vestiges of the shah's government fell, Iranian demonstrators briefly attacked the U.S. embassy in Tehran. "We used to run this country," an American diplomat commented bitterly in February 1979 as he prepared to leave Iran. "Now we don't even run our own embassy."[12]

These words would prove horribly prescient. Iran's provisional foreign minister defused the February siege on the U.S. embassy, but over the next nine months, the balance of power within Iran's still-evolving new order shifted in favor of the radical Islamists. Washington's clumsy efforts to maintain normal diplomatic and economic relations with the new authorities posed no match for the chaos and conspiracy theories still sweeping Iran. In November 1979, the U.S. embassy was overrun by student protestors yet again, and this time they secured Khomeini's blessing. Their seizure of the embassy staff launched a hostage crisis that became a 444-day national ordeal, dooming Carter's reelection prospects and forever altering the way that Americans engage with the Middle East. Khomeini described the embassy takeover as "Iran's second revolution," since it handily sidelined more moderate forces in the government and expedited the consolidation of clerical rule. It also precipitated a full-blown breach with Washington, which had sought to build relations with the post-revolutionary leadership.

"Who Lost Iran?"

Iran's abrupt transformation from a reliable U.S. security partner and hub for American investment to a seethingly anti-American regime led by an ascetic cleric confounded Washington. "How could Iran, with its oil and its strategic situation between the Soviet Union and the Persian Gulf, between Europe and the Middle East, fall under the sway of a holy man out of the mists of the thirteenth century?" a *New York Times* columnist beseeched in March 1979. "How could the shah, a monarch who commanded more tanks than the British Army, more helicopters than the United States First Cavalry in Vietnam, be pressured so neatly out of power?"[13]

The highly charged battle cry of "who lost Iran?" echoed through the American establishment in the aftermath of 1979. Some blamed the State Department, which had few Persian speakers stationed in Tehran before the revolution and discouraged U.S. diplomats from engaging with opponents of the shah. Others blamed the intelligence community, which infamously reported to Carter in August 1978 that "Iran is not in a revolutionary or even a 'pre-revolutionary' situation."[14] Some blamed Carter, who repeatedly gave public reassurances that the monarchy would stand but failed to provide clear and effective guidance to the shah as he obviously lost the capability to manage the situation. Within Iran, conspiracy theories abounded, continuing to this day, with many suspecting it was all somehow a British plot. For his part, the shah died convinced that his success in wresting control of Iran's oil sector away from the international oil companies had precipitated a scheme to unseat him.

None of these narratives are entirely accurate. American intelligence, diplomacy, and leadership each exhibited shortcomings, but as a study published in the CIA's in-house journal acknowledged, insufficient information did not cause the fiasco of U.S. policy toward Tehran in 1978–1979. In fact, the study notes, "the US compiled a substantial amount of accurate information and analysis about major events, particularly the demonstrations and riots."[15] And recently declassified information has documented the Carter administration's efforts to broker a peaceful transition directly with Khomeini after the shah had left.[16]

Washington's failure to anticipate the revolution in Iran arose from a failure of political imagination, to borrow a phrase from my colleague Bruce Riedel. The presumption of the shah's durability was so deeply engrained that alternative trajectories seemed inconceivable, especially the unprecedented prospect of a religious caste taking control. No one in Washington was prepared to indulge in "thinking the unthinkable," as the last U.S. ambassador to Tehran described the prospect of the shah's overthrow, until it was essentially too late to alter the course of history.[17] And ultimately, as Carter himself acknowledged repeatedly in the aftermath, "Iran was not ours to lose in the first place. We don't own Iran, and we have never had any intention nor ability to control the internal affairs of Iran."[18]

Two Countries, Intertwined

The Iranian Revolution left a broad and complex legacy within Washington. It remains one of the seminal examples of a black swan national security crisis with a catastrophic impact on American domestic politics as well as on foreign policy. Today, the consequences of the revolution continue to shape the bilateral dynamic between Washington and Tehran, even as memories of the moment itself begin to fade in both countries. The events of 1978–1979 and the political system that it wrought placed Iran squarely at the heart of U.S. security challenges for the past forty years and will continue to do so well into the foreseeable future.

That revolution enshrined the world's first and only modern Muslim theocracy, and the violence that erupted in its wake situated Iran as the epicenter of a wave of religiously inspired activism and virulent anti-Americanism that would eventually radiate through the region and elsewhere. As Christopher Hitchens remarked with only minor exaggeration, Iran's transformation in 1979 "moved us from the age of the Red Menace to epoch of Holy War."[19]

By transforming the nature and locus of the threats to regional stability, Iran's revolution also drew Washington into the Middle East in increasingly thorny ways. Instead of merely seeking to deter Soviet influence, the United States was now forced to contend with an implacably hostile power in a strategically vital region that was ready and able to wreak havoc on American interests and allies. No longer was offshore balancing via regional partners a sufficient posture for U.S. presidents from either party; increasingly, Washington found itself drawn into much more substantial direct military engagement in the Middle East. Our track record in this endeavor has proven incredibly costly in both human and financial terms.

For their part, Iran's revolutionaries remain mired in the mess they created in 1979: a state whose ideological impulses cannot be fully overcome, even when they subvert its obvious interests. The founders of the Islamic Republic were determined to extricate their government from what they perceived as Washington's control. However, by grounding its identity and legitimacy in anti-Americanism, Tehran remains just as firmly contingent upon the United States as the shah ever was. The regime's pointless, destructive rivalry with Washington distorts any objective pursuit of Iran's real interests in a stable, prosperous region, and leaves its people vulnerable to the long reach of U.S. economic and military might. "Obviously this can't go on forever," an Iranian political scientist commented to a Western reporter in March 1979. And yet, forty years later, the revolutionary state remains firmly in place and the bilateral estrangement appears as intractable as ever.[20]

NOTES

1 Gholam Reza Afkhami, *The Life and Times of the Shah* (University of California Press, 2009), p. 278.

2 Hadi Salehi Esfahani and M. Hashem Pesaran, "Iranian Economy in the Twentieth Century: A Global Perspective," *Cambridge Working Papers in Economics*, no. 0815, March 2008, p. 7.

3 Ervand Abrahamian, *A History of Modern Iran* (Cambridge University Press, 2008), p. 138.

4 Speech by Ayatollah Ruhollah Khomeini, delivered at Feyziya Madrasa, Qom, on June 3, 1963, in Hamid Algar, tr., *Islam and Revolution: Writings and Declarations of Imam Khomeini* (Berkeley, CA: Mizan Press, 1981), p. 177.

5 "Here's How Andy Warhol Ended up in Iran during the Shah's Regime," *PRI's The World*, November 4, 2013 (www.pri.org/stories/2013-11-04/heres-how-andy-warhol-ended-iran-during-shahs-regime).

6 Clare Crawford and Parviz Raein, "The Charming Zahedi Ponders: Can Liz Taylor Be a Diplomatic Incident?" *People*, vol. 5, no. 23, June 14, 1976 (https://people.com/archive/the-charming-zahedi-ponders-can-liz-taylor-be-a-diplomatic-incident-vol-5-no-23/).

7 A.E. Woolley, "Festival in Iran: Celebration, Just Begun, to End with Coronation of the Shah in 1967," *New York Times*, December 26, 1965, p. 35 (https://timesmachine.nytimes.com/timesmachine/1965/12/26/issue.html?action=click&contentCollection=Archives&module=ArticleEndCTA&region=ArchiveBody&pgtype=article).

8 Mohammad Reza Shah Pahlavi, *Answer to History* (New York: Stein & Day, 1980), p. 156.

9 Linda Charlton, "Clashes and Tear Gas Mar Shah's Welcome in Capital," *New York Times,* November 16, 1977, p. 1 (www.nytimes.com/1977/11/16/archives/clashes-and-tear-gas-mar-shahs-welcome-in-capital-clashes-and-tear.html); Judith Cummings, "Lunch with the Empress Interrupted by Shout of 'Down with Shah,' " *New York Times,* July 8, 1977, p. 19 (www.nytimes.com/1977/07/08/archives/lunch-for-empress-interrupted-by-shout-of-down-with-shah.html).

10 Andrew Glass, "This Day in Politics: Carter Lauds Shah of Iran, Dec. 31, 1977," *Politico,* December 30, 2018 (www.politico.com/story/2018/12/30/this-day-in-politics-december-31-1077103).

11 U.S. Department of State Bulletin, vol. 59, no. 1359, December 13, 1968, pp. 659–62.

12 Youssef M. Ibrahim, "Iran Wants a New Era, But Only on Its Terms," *New York Times,* February 25, 1979, p. 2 (www.nytimes.com/1979/02/25/archives/iran-wants-a-new-era-but-only-on-its-terms.html).

13 R.W. Apple Jr., "Iran: Heart of the Matter," *New York Times,* March 11, 1979, p. 5 (www.nytimes.com/1979/03/11/archives/iran-heart-of-the-matter-iran.html).

14 Jimmy Carter, *Keeping Faith* (New York: Bantam Books, 1982), p. 438.

15 Allen H. Kitchens, "Crisis and Intelligence: Two Case Studies [Tet and Iran]," *Studies in Intelligence*, vol. 28, no. 3, 1984, p. 75 (www.cia.gov/library/center-for-the-study-of-intelligence/csi-publications/books-and-monographs/Anthology-CIA-and-the-Wars-in-Southeast-Asia/pdfs/kitchens-crisis-and-intel-two-case-studies.pdf).

16 Kambiz Fattahi, "Two Weeks in January: America's Secret Engagement with Khomeini," *BBC News*, June 3, 2016 (www.bbc.com/news/world-us-canada-36431160).

17 William Sullivan, "Thinking the Unthinkable," Cable from U.S. Embassy Tehran to U.S. State Department, November 9, 1978, text available at the

National Security Archive, "Iran's 1979 Revolution Revisited: Failures (and a Few Successes) of U.S. Intelligence and Diplomatic Reporting," Malcolm Byrne, ed., February 11, 2019 (https://nsarchive2.gwu.edu//dc.html?doc=5734181-National-Security-Archive-Doc-07-U-S-Embassy).

18 President Jimmy Carter, news conference, February 27, 1979, text available at the University of California at Santa Barbara American President Project (www.presidency.ucsb.edu/documents/the-presidents-news-conference -984).

19 Christopher Hitchens, "Iran's Waiting Game," *Vanity Fair*, July 2005 (www.vanityfair.com/news/2005/07/hitchens-200507).

20 Youssef M. Ibrahim, "Many Factions Begin the Real Struggle for Power," *New York Times*, February 18, 1979, p. 1 (www.nytimes.com/1979/02/18/arch ives/khomeini-leads-but-not-everyone-follows.html).

8

After 1979, America's Torch Song for Tehran

KENNETH POLLACK

An Arab foreign minister once asked me, "Why are you Americans so infatuated with Iran? She is like your insane ex-girlfriend whom you endlessly pine for even though she only wants to hurt you and your life is so much better without her. Meanwhile, we Arabs are like your long-suffering wife, who only wants a better relationship with you, only to have you abandon us whenever that Persian hussy bats an eye at you."

Sometimes others see us more clearly than we see ourselves.

For a great many Americans, the legacy of the Iranian Revolution is the enduring enmity of the Islamic Republic toward the United States. Iranians are increasingly at pains to rationalize their regular, if ritualized, chants of "Death to America," but for Americans, the words still bite. It is hard for Americans to reflect on the forty years since the revolution and understand why Tehran's antagonism has persisted for so long. So many Americans see it as irrational, wasteful, foolish, even childish. It is. But what we must realize, hard as it may be, is that it is not accidental. It is not the product of misunderstandings or missed opportunities. It is purposeful. It is deliberate.

While American leaders have run hot and cold on Iran, most of the presidents who have served during that forty-year span have sought genuine reconciliation with Iran. That they have failed time and again has little to do with their own mistakes and everything to do with the fact that Iran's leadership has never wanted the same.

The Long, Unrequited Courtship

Right from the start, the United States sought good relations with the Islamic Republic. After the shah's flight from Iran, the Carter administration tried to open a diplomatic channel to Tehran. For Carter, the fall of the shah was no great loss. He had railed against the shah's human rights abuses and was willing to embrace a new Iranian regime that seemed to be far more popular with the Iranian people.

Iran's response was swift and clear. No. Tehran did not want a relationship with Washington. The United States was Iran's eternal enemy, and the Islamic Revolution wanted only death to America. The seizure of the American embassy and the holding of fifty-two U.S. diplomats as hostages for 444 days became the defining statement of Tehran's policy toward Washington.

It is worth noting that the American overture followed a clandestine effort to encourage a counterrevolution by the shah's generals. However, there are three critical facts bearing on this issue. First, the American effort lasted little more than a week because Washington quickly recognized that such a gambit was impossible. Second, neither President Carter nor Secretary of State Cyrus Vance was ever enthusiastic about the idea, and both saw it as a last-resort contingency plan if all else failed and were relieved when it was mooted. They had always preferred to offer the new revolutionary Iranian regime the olive branch rather than the stick. Last, the Iranians were unaware of this effort until many years later, and so it cannot serve as an excuse for Tehran's snub.

For all his bluster, President Ronald Reagan tried, too. It began with his sincere desire to free American hostages being held by Iranian allies and proxies in Lebanon in the mid-1980s. (These captives were seized after Iran finally freed the original hostages from the embassy.) It was this desire that spawned the Iran-Contra imbroglio, in which the United States sold missiles to Iran—for its war with Iraq—and then channeled the money from those sales to the Contras, guerrillas fighting the Sandinista regime in Nicaragua. Sordid as the affair was, Reagan's hope was that the weapons sales would prompt Tehran to release the hostages, convince them not to take any more, and make possible a reduction of tensions between the two countries. Indeed, some of Reagan's key subordinates hoped that it could be the start of a wider rapprochement, and Reagan may have as well.

There were Iranians eager to reciprocate. The evidence suggests that they, too, hoped the arms sales might lead to a wider warming of relations. But their hopes withered under the hostility to America from the more powerful hard-line figures in the regime. The secret relationship was exposed, and its Iranian proponents were forced to disavow their intentions.

President George H. W. Bush was always more prudent, never rushing in where wise men feared to tread. Yet he, too, famously blew a kiss Tehran's way in his inaugural address, pointedly suggesting to Iran that "goodwill begets goodwill." From Iran there was no answer. But actions speak louder than words, and throughout the 1990s, Iran's actions spoke volumes about its true feelings toward America. Iran instigated repeated terrorist attacks against American allies from Israel to Bahrain, killed its own dissidents abroad, harassed American military forces in the Persian Gulf, and even attacked a U.S. military housing complex in Saudi Arabia, killing 19 Americans and wounding over 400 others.

Yet, through it all, even furious at Iran's seemingly gratuitous calumnies, America nursed its yearning for a better relationship.

In 1997, Iranians chose Mohammad Khatami as their new president. Khatami won in a landslide and in typically cryptic Persian fashion, he let it be known that he believed Iran should normalize relations with the United States. President Bill Clinton leapt at the chance. Against the advice of more cautious advisors, Clinton made a determined effort to demonstrate that the United States wanted the same.

Iran's bureaucracy remained fettered by the hard-line, anti-American leadership. So, Khatami had to pursue his outreach to Washington indirectly, employing academics, journalists, and other unofficial emissaries. Clinton's team eagerly met with Khatami's messengers and explicitly asked what steps the United States might take to signal its interest in rapprochement and enable Khatami to make it possible from the Iranian side. During Clinton's final two years in office, the United States made eleven separate, unilateral gestures to Iran, from allowing visits by Iranian wrestlers and clergy, to removing Iran from the U.S. list of major narcotics smuggling states, all the way to apologizing for America's role in the Mohammad Mossadegh coup and exempting Iranian pistachios and carpets from American sanctions.

It all came to naught. Iran's hard-liners struck back at Khatami and crushed him. Khatami's proposed reforms threatened their domestic policies and position as much as their cherished enmity with the United States. In 1999 and 2000, they forced him to crush student riots in support of his own reforms, much like Stalin had forced Vyacheslav Molotov to denounce his own beloved wife. Khatami was allowed to serve out his term—he was even reelected in 2001—but he was toothless, reduced to an impotent symbol of what might have been, left to taunt Iranians and Americans who had dreamed of a different relationship with the Tehran regime.

The failure of the Clinton-Khatami bid for rapprochement was not lost on President George W. Bush's foreign policy team. They never had any love for Iran, and whether this sentiment confirmed their belief that improved relations were a pipe dream or merely justified the course of action they always meant to take is impossible to know. But it was no accident that they included Iran as part of an "Axis of Evil" with Iraq and North Korea in Bush's infamous 2002 State of the Union address.

Of course, having declared Iran evil, they were immediately forced to ignore it. Their invasions of Afghanistan and Iraq proved something of an unexpected boon to Iran and something of an epic catastrophe for America. The invasions removed Iran's two worst antagonists: the Taliban and Saddam Hussein. Of course, the chaos that the United States left in their place to Iran's east and west created new problems for Tehran, but also new opportunities—opportunities that the Iranian regime would exploit to magnify its sway and further harm the United States.

Iran would repay the Bush administration many times over for the "Axis of Evil" speech. In Iraq in particular, Tehran supported a vast range of murderous anti-American groups. Iranian personnel and their Hezbollah allies not only encouraged and equipped these groups to kill Americans, but at times also planned and participated in the attacks themselves. Hundreds of Americans died as a result. The Bush administration did nothing in response, albeit largely because it was miserably bogged down in Iraq and Afghanistan, and wisely (for a change) recognized that picking still another fight with Iran was unlikely to improve its fortunes.

Their Last, Best Hope

Barack Obama came to the presidency with an eye toward making peace with Iran. From the very first, his administration broadcast on all frequencies, public and private, that it wanted to consummate the elusive rapprochement. In 2009, in the wake of Iran's stolen presidential elections, the Obama administration tried as hard as it could for as long as it could to say nothing, believing that any statement of American support for the millions of Iranians demanding the end of the Islamic regime might kill the bid for reconciliation. When the howls of American domestic and international outrage at Washington's silence became too much, the administration gave in, but even then, its criticisms were still bland and perfunctory to the point of being counterproductive. Nevertheless, Tehran seized on them to blame the would-be second Iranian Revolution on American machinations.

Yet, Obama would not be put off. In his second term he redoubled his efforts, this time aided by an equally ardent secretary of state, John Kerry. Then the Iranians seemed to signal some reciprocation by electing Hassan Rouhani as their new president. Rouhani explicitly ran on a platform of saving Iran's economy by cutting a deal on the country's nuclear program with the United States and the international community. Thus began the negotiations that would ultimately culminate in the Joint Comprehensive Plan of Action (JCPOA), colloquially known as the Iranian nuclear deal.

Both Obama and Kerry hoped that the nuclear deal would pave the way toward a wider reconciliation between the two countries. Indeed, it is hard to understand their willingness to agree to the terms of the JCPOA—which only maintained the tightest constraints on the Iranian nuclear program for ten to fifteen years—except in light of their expectation that the agreement would lead to a comprehensive settlement of the Iranian-American conflict that would eventually render the agreement unnecessary. Rouhani wanted that rapprochement, too. And so did his foreign minister, Mohammad Javad Zarif, who forged a close relationship with Kerry and also hoped to use the JCPOA as a wedge to open the door to normalized ties.

They were all disappointed. In the words of Karim Sadjadpour, senior fellow at the Carnegie Endowment for International Peace, while Obama and Kerry—and Rouhani and Zarif—all hoped the JCPOA would prove to be transformative, Ayatollah Ali Khamenei and Iran's hard-liners were determined that it remain merely transactional.[1] A simple deal, curbs on the Iranian nuclear program in return for a lifting of American and international sanctions. No more. Long before Donald Trump came to office and killed the deal, Khamenei had made clear that it would never be anything more than it was. He would never allow it to be the end to Iranian–American conflict.

The United States has never had a president more desirous of turning Iran from foe to friend, and we may never have another one. Obama openly disdained America's Middle East allies and even took Iran's side against them in regional disputes, going so far as to declare that the Saudis needed to learn to "share" the Middle East with Iran.[2] He agreed to the JCPOA in the face of tremendous political criticism. Both he and many of his key advisors hoped that a nuclear deal with Iran could be the gateway toward a wider rapprochement, and Secretary Kerry tried every door before, during, and after the nuclear negotiations to try to make that happen.

The Iranians never had an American president more willing to accommodate their needs and fears, and once again they spurned him. Yet, Ayatollah Khamenei and the rest of Iran's leadership were not interested in the better relationship that Obama and Kerry craved. If Iran could not accept what Obama and Kerry proffered, it is hard to conclude anything other than that those who matter in Tehran, those who actually make Iran's foreign policy, are determined to treat the United States as their enemy, regardless of what we do or why.

Coping with Hate

The history of Iranian-American relations in the forty years since the 1979 revolution is replete with mistakes, missed opportunities, and misunderstandings. Both sides have done terrible things to each other. Both can claim justification for their every savage act against the other. For every U.S. policy meant to hurt Iran, Americans can cite a prior Iranian action meant to hurt the United States. And for every Iranian action deliberately intended to hurt America, Iranians can cite a prior U.S. policy meant to hurt Iran.

Yet, the one vital difference is this: Of the seven American presidents to serve since the Iranian Revolution, at least four and arguably five wanted an end to the hostilities with Iran and made real efforts to bring that about. In most cases, they paid a considerable political price to do so. And while there certainly have been many Iranians, many Iranian officials, and at least three Iranian presidents who seemed to want the same, the Iranian regime as a whole and its two supreme leaders—Iran's equivalent to the American president—have never shown the least interest. Instead, they have systematically shut down every effort toward meaningful peace between the two countries.

Both Khomeini and Khamenei cherished their anti-Americanism. For them, it was never a tool toward a wider goal but a core element of their rule and their philosophies. It certainly has served certain specific aims, but even when American administrations have offered what could have been compelling incentives to embrace warmer ties and reduced tensions, Khomeini and Khamenei never would.

Perhaps someday America's cherished desire for better ties will be reciprocated by the leaders of Iran. But the history of the past forty years seems to suggest that will never be more than a tantalizing dream until new leaders take the helm in Tehran. Until then, the only intelligent course for the United States is to steer clear of the Iranians as best we can and treat them like enemies when we must, not because we want them to be, but because their leaders insist on it, no matter what we may do.

NOTES

1 Thomas L. Friedman, "Look Before Leaping," *New York Times*, March 25, 2015 (www.nytimes.com/2015/03/25/opinion/thomas-friedman-look-before-leaping.html).

2 Jeffrey Goldberg, "The Obama Doctrine," *The Atlantic*, April 2016 (www.theatlantic.com/magazine/archive/2016/04/the-obama-doctrine/471525/).

9

The Iranian Hostage Crisis and Its Effect on American Politics

ELAINE KAMARCK

Unlike many other countries, America has been blessed by two oceans and two friendly countries on its borders. Because of this, foreign affairs do not typically figure prominently in American electoral politics except when Americans are in danger for one reason or another. In the late 1970s, the American public had little knowledge of Iran, the shah, Islam, or terrorism. That would all change on November 4, 1979, when radical Iranian students took over the U.S. embassy in Tehran and held fifty-two Americans hostage for 444 days. The Iranian Revolution and the hostage crisis would take down President Jimmy Carter and make Americans aware of a part of the world and the roiling tensions within it that are still part of our politics today.

When the shah fell, I was working at the Democratic National Committee, getting ready for the 1980 presidential election. The turmoil in Iran and the fall of the shah had, frankly, very little impact on American politics. In fact, what I remember from that period of time is the

Jules Feiffer cartoon with a series of men in Middle Eastern dress lined up. And the gist of the cartoon was, Who knows the difference? Shiites, Sunnis, the differences between them, what their enmity meant to the region: most Americans remained unaware of the religious and political nuances of the region.

Most of that changed when the hostages were taken. Suddenly, this heretofore unknown country burst into the public's consciousness. There was the initial, predictable burst of patriotism. A 1973 hit by Tony Orlando and Dawn about a prisoner coming home, called "Tie a Yellow Ribbon 'Round the Ole Oak Tree," was appropriated to the hostage situation, and all over the land people began tying yellow ribbons on their trees.

At the center of this was President Carter, whose bid for reelection in 1980 was already being complicated by a primary challenge from Senator Ted Kennedy (D-Mass). Carter immediately suspended foreign travel and political campaigning to focus on the crisis. But there was no diplomatic solution to be had. And what came to be known as "the Rose Garden strategy" (referring to the White House Rose Garden) turned into a trap for the president. Stu Eizenstat, one of Carter's top aides and the author of *President Carter: The White House Years*, writes that the Rose Garden strategy "had another unintended and deeply pervasive effect. It totally personalized the crisis in the American media by focusing the responsibility on the Oval Office and showing the terrorists they could put the American presidency itself into dysfunction."[1]

Carter initially tried negotiating with Iran's government that had been thrown into new disarray by the hostage seizure. But given that it was Carter who had invited the shah into the United States, the students who were in control were not inclined to let him off the hook. Furthermore, Ayatollah Ruhollah Khomeini was calling the shots, and he opposed any early settlement. So month after month, as Carter was trapped in the White House, negotiations went nowhere. This is why, in the spring, he decided to mount a military rescue of the hostages.

Operation Eagle Claw was a disaster that ended with American deaths, ruined military planes, and the hostages no closer to freedom. The phone at my house rang early in the morning on April 25, 1980. It was Rick Hernandez, one of the president's senior political aides, who had heard about the aborted mission and subsequent disaster. He opened the conversation with, "We just lost the election." I was confused. It was the middle of the night, and, moreover, Carter had just beaten Kennedy in a string of southern primaries and had tied him in the Pennsylvania primary. Rick proceeded to describe, in fairly accurate terms, the debacle in the desert.

All of this happened at a very crucial time in the election cycle. The Carter-Kennedy fight was big news, and voters were just tuning in. To put these events in context, it is also important to remember that Americans had been enchanted with the story of the Israeli raid on Entebbe in 1976. This is one of the first special operations missions that burst into the public consciousness. The dramatic and stunning Israeli rescue of hostages who had been taken by Palestinians in Uganda captured the public imagination. Four years later, the United States tried its own daring rescue and fell flat on its face. That was devastating to Carter. And I believe to this day that my friend Rick Hernandez was right. Carter lost the election that night.

The failed mission was the last straw. Going into 1980, Jimmy Carter was seen as a weak and feckless president. The economy was going extraordinarily badly. His approval ratings were in the toilet. And the challenge from Kennedy, a lion of the Democratic Party, was the toughest nomination challenge any incumbent Democrat had had in many years. Although Carter won the Democratic nomination, he lost all but six states plus the District of Columbia to Ronald Reagan in November. By then, the Iranian students had played out their hand. They had held the hostages for longer than anyone (including themselves) had expected. The hostages were released on January 20, 1981—the day Ronald Reagan was inaugurated.

On a brighter note, the disastrous rescue mission had tremendous consequences for reform in the U.S. military. It should be noted that at the time of the attempted hostage rescue mission in 1980, there was no unified Special Operations Command in the U.S. military to coordinate the various commands and agencies involved in special operations warfare. In fact, these elements of U.S. military power were, after the wind-down of the Vietnam War, generally underfunded and mistrusted within the military establishment.

The failure of Operation Eagle Claw changed that. It was the straw that broke the camel's back when it came to military reform. Remember, this happened in 1980. Carter lost the election resoundingly to Ronald Reagan. And in 1985, the Senate began to look at a major military reform bill. Reformers faced intense opposition within the military, particularly from the Navy, and they also faced opposition from Reagan's secretary of defense. But it was clear that the failure of Operation Eagle Claw, in addition to Vietnam and several other smaller failures, contributed to a point in history where people said, it is time to do something with the United States military when the greatest power in the world cannot manage to rescue its own people.

So remarkably, after forty years of trying, in 1986 Congress passed the Goldwater-Nichols Department of Defense Reorganization Act, and Reagan signed it. That reorganization and the revival of special operations eventually transformed the American military from Operation Eagle Claw to Operation Neptune Spear (the successful operation that found and killed Osama bin Laden in 2011).

But the effects of the Iranian hostage crisis linger. Americans still harbor deep wells of suspicion about the Islamic world. Starting with the Iranian Revolution and the hostage crisis and continuing through the 9/11 attacks, a generation of Americans came to view the Islamic world with great distrust. (And they are still not clear about the differences between Sunni and Shia Muslims.) Some U.S. presidents have tried to soothe this fear; for instance, President George W. Bush visited a mosque right after 9/11. President Donald Trump, on the other hand, has gone in the opposite direction, engaging in incendiary rhetoric about radical Islam. The hostage crisis and subsequent acts of terrorism in the name of Islam created a powerful strain of public opinion that continues to play a role in American life and politics.

NOTES

1 Stu Eizenstat, *President Carter: The White House Years* (New York: St. Martin's Press, 2018), p. 784.

10

Washington, the Shah, and the Problem of Autocratic Allies

TAMARA COFMAN WITTES

The Islamic Revolution of February 1979 kicked off a polarized debate within the United States over President Jimmy Carter's human rights policy and, more broadly, over how concerned American foreign policy should be with human rights and democracy promotion. In many ways, we have been having this debate ever since.

Carter was the first modern president to elevate human rights within U.S. foreign policy, establishing a new Bureau of Human Rights and Humanitarian Affairs in the State Department and appointing his deputy campaign chair, Patricia Derian, as the first assistant secretary of state dedicated to human rights.[1] The emphasis on moral principles in U.S. foreign policy grew from Carter's own political ideology, and also the desire for a stark contrast to the Nixon administration's corruption, scandals, and amoral realism.

But the Iranian Revolution was a devastating blow to this approach. In November 1979, a political science professor and anti-communist activist named Jeane Kirkpatrick published an article in a conservative monthly that began thus: "The failure of the Carter administration's foreign policy is now clear to everyone except its architects."[2] The article blasted President Carter for his handling of the Iranian Revolution earlier that year, saying that both there and in Nicaragua he "actively collaborated in the replacement of moderate autocrats friendly to American interests with less friendly autocrats of extremist persuasion."[3] To Kirkpatrick, Carter's pressure on the shah to reform had encouraged the revolution, and his failure to support a friendly monarch facing a violent, communist-linked opposition had worsened the situation in Iran both for human rights and for American national interests.

Published just as the Iranian revolutionaries seized the U.S. embassy and took American diplomats hostage for what turned into 444 days of captivity, the article's critique of Carter's Iran policy seemed prescient. Jeane Kirkpatrick's "Dictatorships and Double Standards" probably did more than any other piece of writing to structure the way foreign policy elites came to view the Iranian Revolution and how they debate, even today, the proper place of democracy and human rights in American foreign policy—especially in relations with autocratic allies.

For the conservatives who embraced Kirkpatrick's argument (and embraced Kirkpatrick herself, who won a cabinet post in the Reagan administration as U.S. ambassador to the United Nations), President Carter's criticism of friendly autocrats and readiness to condition ties to them based on human rights grounds was both naive and counterproductive. Conservatives argued that pressuring friends weakened their ability to serve as bulwarks against the spread of communist influence and also sent a message of American unreliability to other allies around the world. The priority in U.S. foreign policy must be the fight against communism (and later, radical Islamism), the argument went—and thus, rights abuses by friends should be overlooked for the sake of the larger cause.

The most enduring, and perhaps the most powerful, component of Kirkpatrick's argument has been the notion that pressuring autocratic allies on human rights does not advance democracy, but only enables the rise of anti-American and often radical successor regimes. The loss of the shah as a U.S. partner in the Persian Gulf was widely understood as a major strategic defeat, at a key moment in the Cold War—and the humiliation of the hostage crisis only underscored this judgment.

This scenario, in which U.S. rights advocacy leads to the overthrow of friendly dictators by anti-American successors, has become the nightmare that rights advocates, both inside and outside government, have had to contend ever since the fall of the shah. And the wide embrace of this view within foreign policy circles has led autocratic allies to treat American support like a game of blackmail—whereby the fear of what might come next often deters American presidents from embracing change in friendly dictatorships, even when that change is peaceful. This view, for example, heavily colored the George H.W. Bush administration's response to the Algerian elections in 1991. When Islamists won the first round of elections and the military shut down the process to avoid their outright victory, it kicked off a civil war that lasted 10 years and cost as many as 150,000 lives. Yet Bush, along with most other Western leaders, supported the military's short-circuiting of the democratic process. I discuss the lingering effects of this choice on U.S. democracy promotion in my 2008 book, *Freedom's Unsteady March: America's Role in Building Arab Democracy.*[4]

Ironically, it was the very administration that first and most power-fully embraced Kirkpatrick's ideas that proved this nightmare scenario was not inevitable, and that it was possible to advance American ideals without sacrificing American interests. As pro-American dictators in Chile, the Philippines, and South Korea began to face growing internal dissent, key officials within the Reagan administration argued for a dif-ferent approach than uncritical support for autocratic allies. Through quiet dialogue with local opposition movements, these administration officials came to see the possibility of successor regimes that were demo-cratic and also open to working with the United States. They ultimately persuaded the secretary of state and the president to send strong mes-sages to these friendly dictators, warning against violent suppression of the opposition movements—and at a crucial moment in Manila, Presi-dent Reagan directly facilitated Ferdinand Marcos's exit from power. In all three cases, the United States proved able to stand up for human rights and democracy, and ultimately to embrace regime change in a friendly country while maintaining a working partnership throughout.

The cases of Chile, South Korea, and the Philippines, along with a few others, are often cited today by foreign policy elites arguing that American human rights advocacy need not come at the expense of American interests.[5] And yet, as we could see in the harsh Monday-morning quarterbacking of Obama's policy toward the Egyptian uprising against former president Hosni Mubarak, for example, this argument still faces a steep uphill climb.

It is notable that, forty years later, the trauma felt in Washington over the fall of the shah still weighs more heavily on foreign policy debates than the triumph of our lasting partnership with a democratic South Korea. Perhaps this anniversary is an opportunity to reexamine the record of U.S. relations with autocratic allies and begin to rewrite the narrative.

NOTES

1 Paul Vitello, "Patricia Derian, Diplomat Who Made Human Rights a Priority, Dies at 86," *New York Times*, May 20, 2016 (www.nytimes.com/2016 /05/21/us/patricia-derian-diplomat-who-made-human-rights-a-priority-dies-at-86.html).

2 Jeane J. Kirkpatrick, "Dictatorships and Double Standards," *Commentary*, November 1979 (www.commentarymagazine.com/articles/dictatorships-double -standards/).

3 Ibid.

4 Tamara Cofman Wittes, *Freedom's Unsteady March: America's Role in Building Arab Democracy* (Brookings Institution Press, 2008).

5 Ariel David Adesnik and Michael McFaul, "Engaging Autocratic Allies to Promote Democracy," *Washington Quarterly*, Spring 2006.

11

The Revolution and Washington's Reliance on Economic Pressure

KATE HEWITT *and* RICHARD NEPHEW

On November 14, 1979—ten days after Iranian students seized the U.S. embassy in Tehran and took American diplomats as hostages—President Jimmy Carter signed Executive Order 12170, freezing Iranian government assets held in the United States.[1] This was the first time a U.S. president used the expansive authorities offered by the 1977 International Emergency Economic Powers Act (IEEPA), but it was hardly the last example of American economic pressure applied against Iran. By mid-2019, nine executive orders were active against Iran, each of which begins with a declaration of a "national emergency" and involves applying sanctions against the country and many of its entities and individuals.[2] These measures, along with sanctions legislation enacted by Congress, are designed to address the full range of U.S. policy issues with Iran, from human rights to missile proliferation to terrorism.

More important, the decision to target Iranian government assets for sanctions in November 1979 set the context for U.S.-Iran relations since.

Washington has increasingly relied on economic pressure against Iran, despite persistent challenges in generating broad multilateral support.

Sanctions Options and Implementation

When the hostage crisis began, the United States had no formal sanctions in place against Iran. However, immediately following the onset of the crisis, President Carter sought options to pressure Tehran. The administration chose sanctions because it saw them as severe but incremental, intended to serve as both a source of pain for the Iranians—to motivate them to release the hostages swiftly—and a warning that the United States could escalate to other options, including military force, if needed. Carter began with the prohibition of military and oil trade with Iran and quickly progressed to the more aggressive option of the asset freeze of Executive Order 12170.

By late December 1979, the United States sought multilateral sanctions against Iran through the United Nations Security Council, but the Soviet Union vetoed the resolution.[3] Washington continued its unilateral sanctions and requested allied and partner support.

Several countries—including Mexico, Austria, Poland, and Sweden—joined the Soviet Union and China in countering U.S. sanctions by instead normalizing trade relations with Tehran, even expanding economic and commercial relations with Iran to offset U.S. effects in some cases.[4] In this, the dissenting countries acted much as the Soviet Union did with Cuba after the U.S. embargo was imposed in the early 1960s: aiding a country dependent on trade and business with the Western world to compensate for its sudden curtailment.

While few governments were willing to cut off oil imports from Iran, some countries belatedly or half-heartedly joined American efforts to pressure Tehran throughout 1980. Portugal was the first major U.S. ally to ban all trade with Iran in April 1980.[5] Japan, the largest purchaser of Iranian crude at the time, ceased all oil imports from Iran halfway through the fifteen-month hostage crisis.[6] Eventually, foreign ministers from the European Community and other Western European countries agreed to reduce financial and diplomatic relations with Iran. Australia also slowly imposed a trade ban without condition on all goods except foodstuffs, their primary interest with Iran, and medicine. However, unlike the Europeans who applied sanctions only to new contracts or ones entered into force post-November 1979, Australia made it clear that its sanctions would be on every non-food contract with Iran until the hostages were released. Australia, Denmark, Norway, and the United Kingdom all recalled their ambassadors from Iran. The governments of Denmark and the United Kingdom passed their own economic sanctions, followed shortly by West Germany, France, and Italy. And the U.S. neighbor to the north, Canada, banned all exports to Iran.

Impact on Iran

The cumulative effect of the sanctions had a substantial impact on Iran's economy. Definitive costs are difficult to assess, in no small part because the revolution and resulting chaos had already imposed a heavy toll on the Iranian economy. For example, in 1980, U.S.-Iranian trade plummeted when U.S. exports to Iran dropped from $3.7 billion to $23 million, while imports from Iran dropped from $2.9 billion to $458 million—mostly in oil.[7] One case study estimated that the total economic cost to Iran from 1980 to 1981 was roughly $3.3 billion.

But while these numbers are significant, the U.S. failure to motivate its partners to respond more aggressively to the hostage crisis underscored the degree to which it was still seen as a U.S.-Iran affair. Moreover, as our Brookings colleague Suzanne Maloney points out in her book *Iran's Political Economy since the Revolution*, "The European reluctance to sanction Tehran over the hostage seizure preserved its traditionally preferential place in the Iranian market and trade remained steady during the early war years, nearly doubling in 1983 with more than $6 billion in European exports to Iran."[8]

The most effective U.S. measure was the asset freeze, which "effectively immobilized $12 billion in Iran's assets, including most of its available foreign exchange reserves," according to Robert Carswell and Richard J. Davis.[9] Washington took advantage of the fact that, after the turmoil of the revolution, the Iranians were still sorting out how to manage their international financial relations and still maintained substantial reserves banked in the United States. Consequently, Washington was in a position to deliver acute, targeted, and highly disruptive pressure on a key vulnerability at the time.

The exposure to such direct pressure from the United States was a mistake that the revolutionary government tried to correct after sanctions were eventually lifted, with Tehran seeking to hold its reserves much closer to home. But in the meantime, the cumulative impact of the specific costs imposed by the United States—coupled with the growing financial and diplomatic international pressure to release the hostages—was effective in persuading the Iranians to negotiate.

Lessons Learned

The hostages were released on January 20, 1981, via the Algiers Accords.[10] The Accords also created an arbitration process, based in The Hague, in which the United States and Iran have negotiated solutions to various commercial disputes arising from the revolution, such as expropriations and canceled contracts. Most recently, this process awarded a settlement for a pre-revolutionary military equipment contract that, with interest, resulted in a $1.7 billion transfer to Iran in January 2016.

Three broader results, though, emerged from the crisis that still affect U.S.-Iranian relations and strategy to date.

First, the United States learned that Iranian leaders—even in post-revolutionary Iran—remain guided by rational cost-benefit calculations. The revolutionary fervor that Iran's leaders exploited to consolidate their power over internal rivals in November 1979 helped animate the decision to prolong the crisis. However, after a year that featured the shah's death and the invasion of Iran by neighboring Iraq, Iran's leaders understood that continuing the crisis posed far more significant risks than benefits. Iran's leaders did not release the hostages because they changed their view of the United States or lost interest in using the crisis domestically. Rather, Iran's leaders backed down and sought a negotiated outcome because they decided it was in their national interest, a fact that encouraged future U.S. policymakers to seek negotiations with Tehran.

In turn, each U.S. president who has subsequently sought to use sanctions against Iran has done so with the expectation that Iran's calculus can be shifted toward more constructive policies. For this reason, U.S. policymakers have viewed sanctions as a useful source of leverage to dissuade Iran's support for terrorism, violations of human rights, or nuclear weapons development. Arguably, this continues to be the case under the Trump administration, which has sought to use sanctions pressure to secure a "better deal" with Iran than the Joint Comprehensive Plan of Action (JCPOA) negotiated by President Barack Obama. Notably, this consensus is challenged by a substantial group of dissenting officials— including, prominently, former National Security Advisor John Bolton— who instead see Iran as irretrievably hostile to the United States and, consequently, less motivated by national interest.

Second, the experience of the hostage crisis demonstrated the advantages and limitations of applying multilateral pressure on Iran. The United States benefited from the cooperation of partners, even if that follow-on pressure was incomplete, sometimes slow, and in some cases more symbolic than substantive. Although the main economic pressure came from the United States, the broader sense of growing isolation likely incentivized Iran to cooperate. With important players like the Soviet Union and China defecting, the United States also had to find creative solutions to intensify its own sanctions—a task made harder by the fact that Iran and the United States were already less intertwined economically and politically. This creative application of U.S. sanctions pressure would find full maturity in the secondary sanctions programs of the mid-2000s, in which the United States had little to no economic contact with Iran, yet still was able to exert considerable leverage by threatening access to the U.S. economy for those countries still doing business with Iran.

Third, the hostage crisis set the emotional and psychological context among Americans for nearly everything that was to come between the United States and Iran. This context made restoring trade and business ties difficult, even if legal, due to the reputational risks (as the oil company Conoco discovered in 1995). It also, at times problematically, created a potential analogy for future attempts at transactional diplomacy, as President Obama experienced after the aforementioned $1.7 billion debt settlement was conflated with the release of U.S. citizens held in Iran in January 2016. This may be one of the most significant ramifications of the hostage crisis. In 1981, the incoming Reagan administration criticized the Algiers Accords as an enormous concession to an act of terrorism. All future U.S. negotiations with Iran would be met with the same accusation, especially wherever sanctions relief was to be applied; this was a critical element of the JCPOA's reception in Washington.

Such criticism did not stop U.S. administrations of both political parties from contemplating and concluding agreements with Iran involving sanctions relief and debt repayment. In this way, just as the Iran sanctions experience in 1979–1981 would teach the United States much about Iranian rationality in foreign affairs, Iran, too, would come to recognize that it can create and exert leverage with the United States. Tehran has characterized its nuclear expansion from 2006 to 2013, for example, as a means of generating leverage and creating a sense of urgency for negotiations as well as developing Iran's nuclear capacity. Iran may likewise see value in regional misbehavior as a way of not only advancing its security interests, but also creating asymmetric sources of leverage against its adversaries, the United States foremost among them.

Conclusion

In the decades following the 1979 hostage crisis, the United States and Iran have sought to demonstrate a readiness to engage but also the limits of engagement. The use of sanctions—based on the premise that Tehran remains guided by rational cost-benefit analysis and that even tough unilateral pressure can benefit from multilateral cooperation—has been a reliable mechanism for the United States, beginning in 1979 and refined in the years that followed. The question now is whether the limits of sanctions policy have also been incorporated into U.S. strategic thought in order to ensure that sanctions can still be used to guide negotiations.

NOTES

1 U.S. Treasury Department, *Executive Order 12170 44 F.R. 65729*, "Blocking Iranian Government Property," November 14, 1979 (www.treasury.gov/resource -center/sanctions/Programs/Documents/Executive%20Order%2012170.pdf).

2 U.S. Treasury Department, Iran Sanctions Resource Center (www.treasury.gov/resource-center/sanctions/Programs/Pages/iran.aspx).

3 Gary Clyde Hufbauer and others, "Case Studies in Economic Sanctions and Terrorism 79-1: US v. Iran," Peterson Institute for International Economics, May 1, 2008 (https://piie.com/publications/papers/sanctions-iran-79-1.pdf).

4 Ibid.

5 United States Congress, House of Representatives, the Committee on Foreign Affairs, *The Iran Hostage Crisis: A Chronology of Daily Developments*, Report Prepared by the Foreign Affairs and National Defense Division, Congressional Research Service, Library of Congress (https://archive.org/stream/IranHostageCrisisChronologyOfDailyEvents/Iran-Hostage%20Crisis%20Chronology%20of%20Daily%20Events_djvu.txt).

6 Ibid.

7 Kenneth N. Gilpin, "Iran-U.S. Trade Up from 1980 Plunge," *New York Times*, December 26, 1983 (www.nytimes.com/1983/12/26/business/iran-us-trade-up-from-1980-plunge.html).

8 Suzanne Maloney, *Iran's Political Economy since the Revolution* (Cambridge University Press, 2015), p. 436.

9 Warren Christopher and others (eds.), *American Hostages in Iran: The Conduct of a Crisis* (Yale University Press, 1985).

10 "Text of Agreement Between Iran and the U.S. to Resolve Hostage Situation," *New York Times*, January 20, 1981 (www.nytimes.com/1981/01/20/world/text-of-agreement-between-iran-and-the-us-to-resolve-the-hostage-situation.html).

12

The Rules of the Game

International Law and Iranian-American Relations

SCOTT R. ANDERSON

When student demonstrators overran the U.S. embassy in Tehran on November 4, 1979, the world did not know how Iran's new revolutionary government would respond. Just nine months earlier, Iran's own deputy prime minister had led a contingent of Revolutionary Guards to end a similar siege and put the embassy facility back under American control.[1] In November, however, the Iranian government's official response was limited to a statement of sympathy for the students—an approach directed by the Ayatollah Ruhollah Khomeini, whose supporters had spent the prior year gradually consolidating control throughout the country.[2] "The action taken today by a group of our countrymen," the statement said, "reflect[s] the feeling of the Iranian nation toward the U.S. government's disregard," specifically in relation to its recent decision to admit the deposed shah of Iran into the United States for medical treatment.

These words were more than just a rhetorical jab. By refusing to intervene as the embassy facility and dozens of Americans located there were taken hostage, the Iranian government was violating a widely respected set of international legal rules that plays a foundational role in international relations. Within days, what was arguably Iran's last secular government resigned in protest over this response, formally ceding control to Khomeini's Revolutionary Council. This not only ended any hopes for a quick resolution to the crisis, but also set the stage for a sudden and severe rupture in what had been one of the region's defining bilateral relationships— and a growing divide between Iran and the international community.

The international legal dispute that resulted from the Iran hostage crisis continues to have ramifications to this day in how Iran and the United States interact. Yet, in recent years, the parties' positions have taken an ironic twist. Whereas the United States used international law to help set revolutionary Iran on the path to becoming a pariah state, it has since severed its own ties to many of the international legal institutions that it once relied upon for this purpose. And while revolutionary Iran fervently rejected any external intervention, contemporary Iran has increasingly sought the international community's help in securing relief from various U.S. policies it claims are unlawful.

Bringing the Hostage Crisis to Court

The initial U.S. response to the fall of the embassy—followed a day later by the seizure of abandoned U.S. consular facilities in Shiraz and Tabriz— was surprisingly muted. U.S. officials hoped Iranian authorities would once again step in to resolve the situation, and quietly set about trying to open diplomatic channels for negotiations. As these hopes dimmed, the United States began to freeze U.S.-based Iranian assets and install other economic measures to secure some leverage over the Iranian government. And the United States initiated a more aggressive diplomatic strategy aimed at mobilizing the international community in opposition to Iran's actions.[3]

Pursuant to this strategy, the United States submitted a claim to the International Court of Justice (ICJ) on November 29, 1979, alleging that Iran's failure to oppose the student demonstrators' actions violated certain key international legal obligations regarding the treatment of foreign embassies and diplomatic personnel.[4] Officials initially hoped to pair this claim with United Nations (UN) Security Council resolutions multilateralizing the economic sanctions it had already imposed on Iran, but their efforts to secure anything more than rhetorical opposition to Iran's actions were stymied by the Soviet Union's veto. This left the ICJ as the main channel of recourse within the UN system.

The U.S. claims were rooted in the Vienna Convention on Diplomatic Relations (VCDR)[5] and Vienna Convention on Consular Relations (VCCR),[6] two multilateral treaties that codify long-standing rules regarding diplomatic and consular relations between states, including obligations to respect the inviolability of foreign embassies and diplomatic personnel. The United States also cited certain standards of treatment in the 1955 Treaty of Amity, Economic Relations, and Consular Rights, which Iran and the United States had signed shortly after a controversial U.S.-backed coup d'état restored the shah to power following a prior period of political unrest.[7] All three treaties subjected relevant disputes to the compulsory jurisdiction of the ICJ—the Treaty of Amity directly, and the VCDR and VCCR through separate optional protocols. This provided the United States with the hook it needed to bring its claim before the ICJ, whose jurisdiction is limited to circumstances consented to by the parties.

Despite these prior commitments, Iran refused to participate in the ensuing proceedings. Instead, in a short written response, it argued that the ICJ "should not take cognisance of the case" on the grounds that the hostage crisis was simply "a marginal and secondary aspect of an overall problem," namely the "more than 25 years of continual interference by the United States in the internal affairs of Iran." As such interference "is essentially and directly a matter within the national sovereignty of Iran," Iran contended, the ICJ should decline to exercise jurisdiction.[8]

The court was not persuaded. Just two weeks later, it unanimously granted a U.S. request for provisional measures that directed Iran to return the hostages and embassy facility to American control in order to avoid any more irreparable damage to U.S. interests while the court weighed its claim.[9] It followed up with a full judgment in May 1980, which also found that the United States was entitled to reparations in a form and amount to be determined.[10] Only two judges dissented from this latter holding, on the grounds that the United States had also violated its own international legal obligations, both by imposing increasingly stringent economic sanctions and by pursuing the failed April 1980 rescue attempt, which the dissenters viewed as tantamount to an unlawful military attack on Iran.

The ICJ's ruling was a legal landmark, as it not only reaffirmed the fundamental importance of the legal protections provided by the VCDR and VCCR, but also rejected the prospect that American malfeasance, even if proven, could justify Iran's actions. And while the decision did little to bring about an immediate end to the crisis, it contributed to revolutionary Iran's growing international isolation by highlighting the extent to which it had departed from widely accepted international norms. Further, if the United States were awarded reparations, the ICJ's decision could well threaten Iran's frozen overseas assets, which the United States could attempt to claim in its effort to collect. Both consequences were notable—and as Iran's relations with its neighbor Iraq rapidly deteriorated over the course of 1980, they became sources of serious concern.

Reaching Settlement

As war with Iraq grew more inevitable, the Iranian government became more intent on retrieving its frozen assets and stabilizing its global position. By the time of the Iraqi invasion in September 1980, Iran had finally begun to engage the United States in negotiations over the hostages.[11] On January 19, 1981, these efforts—with help from the Algerian government—yielded an agreement on a set of commitments to end the hostage crisis, dubbed the Algiers Accords.[12] In exchange for the release of the hostages, the United States agreed to return a portion of Iran's frozen assets, settle any remaining legal claims—including those by the hostages themselves—arising from the hostage crisis, and avoid future interference in Iran's internal affairs. The hostages were released a few days later. And per the terms of the agreement, the United States withdrew its ICJ claims within the year.[13]

Nor were these the only claims that the Algiers Accords addressed. The sudden disruption in economic ties brought about by the Iranian Revolution had left private citizens on both sides with an array of property claims against each other's governments, ranging from contract violations to alleged expropriations. And Iran's revolutionary government had leveled similar allegations against the United States itself in relation to the once robust arms sales program that had existed between the two countries. Yet, neither government was willing to submit itself to the domestic courts of the other, and the claims themselves were too complex to resolve through negotiations in any timely fashion. For this reason, the parties decided to pursue a more novel disposition: They channeled these claims into a new independent adjudicatory body created specifically for the purpose, called the Iran-United States Claims Tribunal (IUSCT).

Established later that year in The Hague, the nine-member IUSCT—which consists of three members appointed by each party and an additional three selected by those appointees—was given jurisdiction over all relevant bilateral property claims that were outstanding when the agreement was signed, as well as disputes regarding the interpretation and implementation of the Algiers Accords themselves. To ensure this jurisdiction was exclusive, the parties also agreed to bar any related domestic litigation by private parties—a controversial step whose constitutionality was challenged in U.S. courts but ultimately upheld.[14] As a result, the IUSCT became the only venue through which Americans and Iranians whose property rights were damaged as a result of the revolution could pursue recompense. And to ensure funds were available to pay the resulting claims, the parties agreed to channel half of Iran's restored assets into an account specifically designated for that purpose.

Over the ensuing four decades, the IUSCT has quietly pursued its mandate under the Algiers Accords, providing an early model for the growing field of international arbitration. By May 2016, it had resolved around 4,000 claims, resulting in the transfer of about $2 billion to U.S. parties and $1 billion to Iranian parties, leaving only large state-to-state claims unresolved.[15] In January of that year, Iran and the United States settled one such claim relating to funds that pre-revolutionary Iran had deposited into a trust fund for potential arms sales,[16] restoring $400 million to Iran along with $1.3 billion in interest.[17] The remaining claims are large and complex, leading one departing tribunal member to posit that they could still take decades to resolve.[18]

Trading Places

As the IUSCT has gone about its work, the broader legal relationship between Iran and the United States has shifted. Since the 1980s, the United States has increasingly used its central position in the global economy to put economic pressure on Iran to stop its support for terrorism and nascent nuclear program. The primary mechanism for this effort has been economic sanctions that impose domestic legal penalties on entities that do business in the United States—or are in some cases even further removed from the U.S. economy—but try to maintain various prohibited ties with Iran.[19] Congress has also enacted exceptions to U.S. sovereign immunity laws that make Iran and other state sponsors of terrorism subject to terrorism-related lawsuits in U.S. courts, resulting in awards of more than $50 billion in damages against Iran.[20] Tehran has refused to dignify many of these claims by opposing them in court, a stance that has produced judgments for claims as dubious as Iranian involvement in the September 11 attacks.[21] Congress has occasionally made Iranian assets, sanctions-related proceeds, or other funds available to satisfy these outstanding judgments,[22] but the sheer scale of the damages has left most judgment-holders with no clear way of securing compensation.[23]

Iran has not taken these measures lying down. To the contrary, unlike during the hostage crisis, it has repeatedly turned to the international community in pursuit of relief. In the 1990s, Iran argued before the IUSCT that economic sanctions and other U.S. policies violated the obligation not to interfere with Iran's internal affairs, set forth in the Algiers Accords.[24] And it has relied on the Treaty of Amity to bring a number of claims before the ICJ. Most notably, in 2015, Iran argued that an American law making certain frozen Iranian assets available to U.S. judgment-holders violated the Treaty of Amity and other international legal obligations[25]—a case the court has ruled that it has the jurisdiction to consider on the merits in part.[26] And when the Trump administration reimposed economic sanctions following its highly controversial 2018 withdrawal from the Joint Comprehensive Plan of Action (JCPOA) regarding Iran's nuclear program, Iran filed a Treaty of Amity-based claim similarly seeking to prohibit those actions. The ICJ rejected Iran's request for provisional measures ordering an end to these sanctions in October 2018[27] but did require exceptions for certain humanitarian goods and civil aviation-related equipment—all of which the United States maintains are already eligible for exemptions.[28] Both cases remain ongoing as of late 2019.

Until recently, the United States appeared content to dutifully respond to these claims and defend the legality of its policies. But in October 2018, the Trump administration responded to the ICJ ruling on provisional measures in the JCPOA case by announcing that the United States was withdrawing from the Treaty of Amity, effective in one year pursuant to the treaty's terms.[29] That same day, it also withdrew from the optional protocol for the VCDR,[30] following the same path of action that the George W. Bush administration had pursued to withdraw from the VCCR's optional protocol in 2005.[31] Together, these acts officially severed the last of the legal ties that the United States had relied on to pursue its hostage claims before the ICJ. Both of Iran's existing ICJ claims will proceed, as will any other claims it files under the Treaty of Amity before the U.S. withdrawal goes into effect. But future disputes related to these treaties will not fall within the ICJ's jurisdiction. Whether this will result in a new set of claims before the IUSCT remains to be seen.

The Trump administration has been careful to make clear that it still views the substantive obligations of the VCDR and VCCR as legally binding.[32] In February 2019, it even recorded a video message to the Iranian people[33] showing that it was still maintaining the abandoned Iranian embassy building in Washington, D.C., pursuant to its VCDR obligations—a sharp contrast with how Iran has treated the former U.S. embassy building in Tehran, which is now an anti-American museum displaying official documents and other items looted from the site in flagrant violation of the VCDR.[34] But Trump administration officials have been equally explicit that they have no interest in subjecting U.S. policies to the scrutiny of "politicized and ineffective" international institutions like the ICJ.[35]

History Lessons

From the perspective of history, there is some irony in this shift. Iran's refusal to defend the legality of its actions during the hostage crisis reinforced the extent to which it was willing to spite the international community, and set it on the road to becoming a global pariah. Now that Iran is seeking to repair its international status, it has turned to the ICJ to try and paint the United States as an "outlaw regime" whose unilateral campaign against Iran similarly spits in the face of international law—a narrative that the Trump administration's resistance to ICJ scrutiny only serves to reinforce. The parallels should not be overstated: Iran's current claims stand on far weaker legal grounds than the U.S. hostage claims, and U.S. efforts to limit the ICJ's jurisdiction are entirely consistent with international law. Nonetheless, there may be lessons to be drawn from the two states' prior experiences.

True pariah status is a long way off for the United States. But since its controversial 2018 withdrawal from the JCPOA, the United States has stood largely alone when it comes to Iran. The UN Security Council removed multilateral sanctions on Iran when it endorsed the JCPOA in 2015[36] and has declined to reinstate them, in large part because Iran is widely believed to have remained in compliance with the JCPOA's terms through the summer of 2019.[37] European allies who wish to preserve the JCPOA have gone so far as to establish a special-purpose vehicle to allow European companies to trade with Iran without triggering reimposed U.S. economic sanctions.[38] Yet, this has not stopped the Trump administration from pursuing its unilateral "pressure campaign"—one officially aimed at ending the various objectionable activities Iran engages in that were not covered by the JCPOA, but that the Trump administration often discusses in terms that sound like regime change.[39]

Whether this effort succeeds will ultimately depend on the extent to which the United States can either coerce or persuade the international community into cooperating. Thus far the Trump administration has focused on the former, but there may be limits on how far even the United States can leverage its global economic and political power. Pursuing the latter, however, almost certainly would require demonstrating how U.S.

policies are consistent with the international legal regime that helps protect the interests of various members of the international community—and adjusting those policies accordingly where they do not. This does not necessarily require submitting to ICJ jurisdiction, but it does require serious consideration of the international community's concerns. Revolutionary Iran's failure to take this into account has cost it more than four decades of international isolation. And while the United States is unlikely to face as severe a consequence, the Trump administration's unwillingness to learn from Iran's example may prove no less self-defeating.

NOTES

1 Nicholas Gage, "Armed Iranians Rush U.S. Embassy," *New York Times*, February 15, 1979, p. 1 (www.nytimes.com/1979/02/15/archives/armed-iranians-rush-us-embassy-khomeinis-forces-free-staff-of-100-a.html).

2 Nicholas Cumming-Bruce, "Iranians Seize U.S. Mission, Ask Shah's Return for Trial," *Washington Post*, November 5, 1979, p. A1 (www.washingtonpost.com/world/iranians-seize-us-mission-ask-shahs-return-for-trial/2011/11/29/gIQAWxhs8N_story.html?utm_term=.14d796fa8884).

3 Gary Sick, *All Fall Down: America's Tragic Encounter with Iran* (New York: Random House, 1985), pp. 241-93.

4 Application Instituting Proceedings Submitted by the Government of the United States of America, November 29, 1979 (www.icj-cij.org/files/case-related/64/9545.pdf#page=19).

5 Vienna Convention on Diplomatic Relations, 1961 (legal.un.org/ilc/texts/instruments/english/conventions/9_1_1961.pdf).

6 Vienna Convention on Consular Relations, 1963 (legal.un.org/ilc/texts/instruments/english/conventions/9_2_1963.pdf).

7 Treaty of Amity, Economic Relations, and Consular Rights between the United States of America and Iran, August 15, 1955 (www.state.gov/treaty-of-amity-economic-relations-and-consular-rights-between-the-united-states-of-america-and-iran-aug-15-1955/).

8 See Iran-United States Claims Tribunal, Order re: Request for the Indication of Provisional Measures in Case Concerning United States Diplomatic and Consular Staff in Tehran (United States of American v. Iran), December 15, 1979, p. 7 (www.icj-cij.org/files/case-related/64/064-19791215-ORD-01-00-EN.pdf).

9 Ibid.

112   SCOTT R. ANDERSON

10 See Iran-United States Claims Tribunal, Judgment in Case Concerning United States Diplomatic and Consular Staff in Tehran (United States of American v. Iran), May 24, 1980 (www.icj-cij.org/files/case-related/64/064-19800524-JUD-01-00-EN.pdf).

11 Sick (1985), op. cit., pp. 360–75.

12 Declaration of the Government of the Democratic and Popular Republic of Algeria, General Declaration and Claims Settlement Declaration, January 19, 1981 (www.iusct.net/Pages/Public/A-Documents.aspx).

13 See Iran-United States Claims Tribunal, Order in Case Concerning United States Diplomatic and Consular Staff in Tehran (United States of American v. Iran), May 12, 1981 (www.icj-cij.org/files/case-related/64/064-1981 0512-ORD-01-00-EN.pdf).

14 See U.S. Supreme Court, Opinion in Dames & Moore v. Regan (No. 80-2078), July 2, 1981 (scholar.google.com/scholar_case?case=15483881597751001372&q=dames+%26+moore+v.+regan&hl=en&as_sdt=20006).

15 See Office of the Secretary-General, Iran-United States Claims Tribunal, Communiqué no. 16/1, May 9, 2016 (www.iusct.net/General%20Documents/Communique%2016.1%20(9%20May%202016).pdf).

16 See U.S. Secretary of State John F. Kerry, Press Statement on Hague Tribunal Claims Settlement, January 17, 2016 (2009-2017.state.gov/secretary/remarks/2016/01/251338.htm).

17 Emma Borden, "The United States, Iran, and $1.7 Billion: Sorting Out the Details," *Brookings Markaz*, October 3, 2016 (www.brookings.edu/blog/markaz/2016/10/03/the-united-states-iran-and-1-7-billion-sorting-out-the-details/).

18 Statement of Judge Charles N. Brower, Iran-United States Claims Tribunal, December 2015, (http://res.cloudinary.com/lbresearch/image/upload/v1449481124/statementcnb_711115_938.pdf).

19 See Chapter 11 of this volume, "The Revolution and Washington's Reliance on Economic Pressure," by Kate Hewitt and Richard Nephew.

20 See 28 U.S.C. § 1605A.

21 Aaron Katersky, "Iran Ordered to Pay Billions to Relatives of 9/11 Victim," *ABC News*, May 1, 2018 (abcnews.go.com/International/iran-ordered-pay-billions-relatives-911-victims/story?id=54862664).

22 See, e.g., 22 U.S.C. § 8772.

23 Frances Stead Sellers, "Americans Held in Iran Waited Decades for Relief. Now They Face a New Challenge," *Washington Post*, February 23, 2019 (www.washingtonpost.com/national/americans-held-in-iran-waited-decades-for-relief-now-they-face-a-new-challenge/2019/02/22/c8b03de4-308f-11e9-8ad3-9a5b113ecd3c_story.html?utm_term=.6091dd9e8cff).

24 See Digest of United States Practice in International Law 1991–1999 (2005), pp. 1094–95 (2009-2017.state.gov/documents/organization/139394.pdf).

25 International Court of Justice, Application Instituting Proceedings in Certain Iranian Assets (Islamic Republic of Iran v. United States of America), June 14, 2016 (www.icj-cij.org/files/case-related/164/164-20160614-APP-01-00 -EN.pdf).

26 International Court of Justice, Judgment on Preliminary Objections in Certain Iranian Assets (Islamic Republic of Iran v. United States of America), February 13, 2019 (www.icj-cij.org/files/case-related/164/164-20190213-JUD-01-00-EN.pdf).

27 International Court of Justice, Order on Request for the Indication of Provisional Measures in Alleged Violations of the 1955 Treaty of Amity, Economic Relations, and Consular Rights (Islamic Republic of Iran v. United States of America), October 3, 2018 (www.icj-cij.org/files/case-related/175/175-20181003-ORD-01-00-EN.pdf).

28 U.S. Secretary of State Michael Pompeo, remarks to the press, October 3, 2018 (www.state.gov/remarks-to-the-media-3/).

29 Ibid.

30 Roberta Rampton, Lesley Wroughton, and Stephanie van den Berg, "U.S. Withdraws from International Accords, Says UN World Court 'Politicized,'" Reuters, October 3, 2018 (www.reuters.com/article/us-usa-diplomacy-treaty /u-s-reviewing-agreements-that-expose-it-to-world-court-bolton-idUSKCN 1MD2CP).

31 Adam Liptak, "U.S. Says It Has Withdrawn from World Judicial Body," *New York Times*, March 10, 2005, p. A16 (www.nytimes.com/2005/03/10/politics /us-says-it-has-withdrawn-from-world-judicial-body.html).

32 See Rampton and others (2018), quoting National Security Advisor John Bolton as saying, "I'd like to stress . . . the United States remains a party to the underlying Vienna Convention on Diplomatic Relations and we expect all other parties to abide by their international obligations under the convention."

33 U.S. Department of State, "Brian Hook Addresses the Iranian People from Iran's Former Embassy," February 19, 2019 (www.youtube.com/watch?v =Lsa2le8_j44).

34 William Brangham, "Photos: Eerie Remnants of the Former U.S. Embassy, 35 Years after Iran Hostage Crisis," *PBS News Hour,* March 2, 2015 (www.pbs. org/newshour/world/what-became-of-the-former-u-s-embassy-in-tehran).

35 Rampton and others, op. cit., quoting National Security Advisor John Bolton.

36 See UN Security Council Resolution 2231, UN doc. S/RES/2231, 2015 (undocs.org/S/RES/2231).

37 Iran publicly announced its intent to cease compliance with the JCPOA in May 2019. See Michael Birnbaum, Tamer El-Ghobashy, and Carol Morello, "Iran Announces It Will Stop Complying with Parts of Landmark Nuclear

Deal," *Washington Post*, May 8, 2019 (www.washingtonpost.com/world/iran-to-take-steps-to-reduce-its-commitment-to-landmark-nuclear-deal/2019/05/07/90cc3b1c-70fe-11e9-9331-30bc5836f48e_story.html).

38 Stephanie Zable, "Instex: A Blow to U.S. Sanctions?" *Lawfare*, March 6, 2019 (www.lawfareblog.com/instex-blow-us-sanctions).

39 See U.S. Department of State, "Outlaw Regime: A Chronicle of Iran's Destructive Activities," September 25, 2018 (www.state.gov/outlaw-regime-a-chronicle-of-irans-destructive-activities/).

13

1979 and the World's Second Oil Shock

SAMANTHA GROSS

The Iranian Revolution sparked the world's second oil shock in five years. Strikes began in Iran's oil fields in the autumn of 1978 and by January 1979, crude oil production declined by 4.8 million barrels per day, or about 7 percent of world production at the time. Other producers were able to make up some of the volume, resulting in a net loss of supply of about 4 to 5 percent. Nevertheless, oil prices climbed rapidly, rising from $13 per barrel in mid-1979 to $34 per barrel in mid-1980.[1]

The loss of production was important, but panic among crude oil buyers was an important driver of price. Buyers were concerned that the crisis would only get worse, that the combination of religious fundamentalism and nationalism would spread to other oil-producing countries in the region, and that ever-growing oil demand would continually drive up the price. As a result, crude oil buyers not only bought to cover current demand, but also increased their crude oil inventories, deepening the shortage and further driving up prices. Panic buying more than doubled the actual shortage. Oil on the spot market sold for as much as $50 per barrel.

The Iranian Revolution and the oil price shocks that followed catalyzed a number of important changes in petroleum markets that remain in place today.

Deregulation of American Fuel Market

Endless lines at gasoline stations are the overwhelming image in the minds of Americans who lived through the oil shocks. There was a genuine shortage of gasoline in the United States for a while, as refineries geared to running Iranian crude oil could not produce as much gasoline from other types. However, government policies that regulated the petroleum industry made the situation much worse.

Price controls on gasoline exacerbated shortages by not allowing rising prices to curb demand. The controls allowed refiners to raise gasoline prices each month based on the previous month's crude oil price. In an environment of rising prices, the price controls incentivized refiners to withhold gasoline and sell it later at higher prices rather than sell it today.[2] Further aggravating the shortages, the federal government had an allocation system that did not allow gasoline distribution to adjust to demand conditions around the country. Some states also established a policy that only allowed drivers to buy $5 of gasoline at a time, meaning that they had to buy more frequently, virtually assuring longer lines.

Crude oil markets were regulated as well. Different prices for "old" and "new" oil were a relic of the earlier oil shock in 1973–1974 that established perverse incentives, reducing domestic production and increasing imports. Additionally, in April 1979, the Department of Energy ordered large refiners to sell crude oil to smaller refineries that could not obtain affordable supply on the market. However, these smaller refineries were generally less complex and able to produce less gasoline from a given crude oil than their larger counterparts, deepening the supply shortage.[3]

The situation drove a groundswell of anger against U.S. oil companies and public support for President Jimmy Carter dropped substantially. The crisis highlighted the inefficiencies inherent in government control of fuel markets, although the public wanted the government to do something about high prices and long lines. President Carter began to repeal price controls on crude oil in 1979, but the energy crisis, along with the Iran hostage situation, were significant factors in Carter's 1980 election loss. Soon after his inauguration, President Ronald Reagan removed the remaining federal controls on domestic production and distribution of crude oil and gasoline.

Rise of Non-OPEC Oil Production

Some of the most important lingering effects of the Iranian Revolution occurred afterward, as the market recovered from the price and supply shock. Oil producers around the world responded to the two crises of the 1970s by investing in exploration and production. Additionally, several large fields that had been discovered in the previous decade began substantial production.

The North Sea, Alaska, and Mexico were very large new sources of oil at this time. Oil was first discovered in the British North Sea in 1965 and in Norway in 1967. Norway began production in the giant Ekofisk field in 1971, and the British Forties field began production in 1975. In the United States, the Prudhoe Bay field in Alaska was discovered in 1968 and oil began flowing through the Trans-Alaska Pipeline in 1977. Approval and construction of the pipeline was rushed after the first oil crisis in 1973. In 1976, Mexico discovered the super-giant Cantarell field, named after the fisherman who noticed an oil seep in the Gulf of Mexico. At the same time, Mexico was pouring money into its oil industry, and production increased from 1.3 million barrels per day in 1978 to 2.8 million barrels per day in 1984.[4]

In total, non-OPEC producers added 5.6 million barrels per day of crude oil production from 1979 to 1985.[5] In response, OPEC drastically cut production, setting a limit of 18 million barrels per day in March 1982, compared with the 31 million barrels per day it had been producing at the time of the Iranian Revolution.

At the same time, the high oil prices of the previous years and a global recession in the early 1980s brought about declining oil demand. World oil demand fell by about 10 percent from 1979 to 1983. Because of growing supply and shrinking demand, oil prices crashed in the 1980s, declining 40 percent between 1981 and 1985 before collapsing another 50 percent in 1986, down to $12 per barrel.[6]

Development of Crude Oil Spot Market

Long-term contracts were the primary means of buying and selling oil at the time of the Iranian Revolution. Therefore, the loss of Iranian oil unevenly affected buyers during the immediate crisis. Buyers with Iranian contracts scrambled to replace the missing oil, while buyers who held contracts with other producers dealt with higher prices but not actual scarcity.

Before the shock, spot markets for crude oil and refined products had made up no more than 8 percent of the market, as most oil was sold under long-term contracts at set prices. Spot markets at the time were a place to buy unguaranteed oil at a discount. However, as buyers scrambled to find additional supply, they bid up prices in the spot market. In late February 1979, spot market prices reached double the official price level.[7] The role of the spot market grew, and some producers canceled contracts burdened with official prices to sell oil on the more lucrative spot market.

The crude oil shortage after the Iranian Revolution increased the role of the spot market, but the oversupply that followed cemented the demise of long-term contracts at set prices. The surge of supply that came online in response to the second oil shock made spot prices lower than contract prices. Right after the revolution, buyers turned to the spot market willing to pay almost anything for scarce oil. However, in the early 1980s, they turned to the spot market to shop around and find the cheapest source of supply.

A *New York Times* article in April 1983 described the immature and chaotic spot market at the time. "The spot market mostly consists of an amorphous network of traders . . . working over telephone lines without the benefit of a trading floor or public disclosure of what prices are being paid elsewhere for the kind of oil they are negotiating at any given time."[8]

Two additional events cemented the centrality of the spot market for crude oil during the early 1980s. First, in 1983 the New York Mercantile Exchange (NYMEX) introduced a futures contract on crude oil. NYMEX had already introduced futures contracts for home heating oil and gasoline, but the crude oil contract was focused on a global commodity rather than local ones. Futures contracts can play an important role in markets, allowing both buyers and sellers to lock in prices and reduce their exposure to volatile prices. Futures contracts also allow price discovery, with supply and demand conditions on display for all to see, through trades taking place on the exchange. The NYMEX contract ended the Wild West atmosphere and brought legitimacy to the oil spot market.

Second, under the production cuts that OPEC established in 1982 in response to falling prices, Saudi Arabia did not have an official quota. Instead, Saudi Arabia intended to act as the swing producer, raising and lowering its output to balance the market and maintain a reasonable price level. However, the other OPEC members rampantly cheated on their production quotas and discounted their oil to maintain sales and revenues in the oversupplied market. Saudi oil production reached as low as 2.2 million barrels per day in 1985—a mere 20 percent of the level it had been producing five years earlier.[9] By 1985, the Saudis lost their patience with this situation and changed their pricing structure, intending to recover their market share. Instead of selling at an established contract price, they created a pricing structure known as "netback." The price for Saudi crude was set based on the price a refiner received for the resulting products plus a set profit for the refiner. With its profits locked in, the refiner did not need to shop around for the lowest-price crude oil. Instead, the more crude oil it processed, the more profits it made. The result of the new Saudi pricing scheme was a war for market share among oil producers, total price collapse, and a turbulent end to the era of contract oil prices.

NOTES

1 Daniel Yergin, *The Prize: The Epic Quest for Oil, Money & Power* (New York: Simon & Schuster: 1990), pp. 677–714.

2 Philip K. Verleger Jr., "The U.S. Petroleum Crisis of 1979," *Brookings Papers on Economic Activity* (1979), 10:2, p. 475.

3 Ibid.

4 Michael Gavin, "The Mexican Oil Boom, 1977–85," in *Trade Shocks in Developing Countries, Volume 2: Asia and Latin America*, Paul Collier and Jan Willem Gunning, eds. (Oxford University Press, 2000).

5 I.A.H. Ismail, "Shifting Production Trends Point to More Oil from OPEC," *Oil & Gas Journal*, vol. 92, no. 52, 1994, pp. 36–40.

6 Dermot Gately, Lessons from the 1986 Oil Price Collapse," *Brookings Papers on Economic Activity* (1986), 17:2, p. 238.

7 Yergin, op. cit., p. 688.

8 Thomas J. Lueck, "The Rise of Oil's Spot Market," *New York Times*, April 8, 1983, p. D1.

9 Yergin, op. cit., p. 748.

PART III

The Ripple Effect of Iran's Revolution across the Middle East

14

How 1979 Transformed the Regional Balance of Power

ITAMAR RABINOVICH

L ike other major revolutions—such as the French and the Russian—
the 1979 Islamic Revolution in Iran did not remain a domestic affair.
Its authors and Iran's new ruling elite were determined to export their
revolution, but the impact of that determination was not readily apparent. The regime needed time to consolidate, to go through internecine
conflicts, and to see through the protracted Iran-Iraq war that Iraq
started.

But as early as 1982, the effort to mobilize and recruit Shia communities in the Middle East was manifested in Lebanon. That effort, furthermore, was conducted in partnership with the Islamic Republic's first
regional ally, Hafez al-Assad's Syria, a country whose leadership has been
dominated by members of a Shia sect. By the early 2000s, Iran's quest for
regional hegemony and the resources it brought to bear in the service of
that end came to rattle the Middle East. In recent years, these ambitions
have been particularly evident in the Syrian civil war.

Iraq and Turkey

Iran's regional drive was facilitated by the 2003 American invasion of Iraq. Washington's action destroyed Iran's arch enemy, Saddam Hussein, removing an obstacle to the westward projection of Iranian influence and transferring power in Iraq to the Shia majority. Instead of a hostile neighbor, Iran now faced a fertile field for building its influence.

During the same years, another development took place that had a profound impact on the regional politics of the Middle East: the emergence and consolidation of Recep Tayyip Erdoğan's Islamist regime in Turkey. Iran and Turkey are neither enemies nor allies, but the parallel unfolding of Iran's quest for regional hegemony and Turkey's return to a central position in the Middle East transformed the region's politics.

During most of the twentieth century, the two successor states of the Ottoman and Persian Empires played only a limited role in Middle Eastern politics. The shah of Iran did have foreign policy ambitions, and his impact on the Middle East was felt mostly in the region's east and in its petro-politics. Iran's ability to project power and influence in its immediate environment and beyond was constrained by Soviet pressure and domestic problems. Turkey, for its part, was ruled by a secular elite oriented toward Europe. As such, during most of the latter half of the twentieth century, the regional politics of the Middle East were shaped mostly by the dynamics of inter-Arab relations and by the Arab-Israeli conflict.

Iran's quest for regional hegemony after 1979 and Turkey's shift away from Europe to its neighborhood (sometimes called neo-Ottomanism) transformed the region. The Middle East was now joined by two large, powerful Muslim states. The impact of their new roles was magnified by the atrophy of the Arab system and the diminished influence of major Arab states such as Egypt and Iraq. One important illustration of the new regional reality is the Astana Forum—composed of Russia, Iran, and Turkey—that since 2017 has been the major arena of the efforts to resolve the Syrian crisis. Not a single Arab state is a participant in that forum.

Of the two new actors, Iran is the more ambitious and more active. It is driven by religious zeal; the geopolitical ambitions of a successor state to a great imperial past; and the anxieties of a regime worried by the enmity of the United States and such regional enemies as Israel, Saudi Arabia, and, until 2003, Iraq. The Iranian leadership may well see some of its actions as defensive, but they serve in fact to exacerbate the anxieties of its rivals, thus creating a vicious cycle of defensive-offensive action and reaction.

Egypt, Lebanon, and Israel

Iran's progression as a Middle Eastern power was punctuated by opportunity and challenge.

One such opportunity was provided by the toppling of President Hosni Mubarak's regime in Egypt and the rise to power of Mohammed Morsi's government. In response—and for the first time—Iran sent warships through the Suez Canal to the Mediterranean Sea. Although only a single act, it provided a clear indication of Iran's interests in expanding beyond its position in the region's east and reaching the Mediterranean.

By that point, Iran had already established itself firmly in Lebanon (through Hezbollah) and in the Gaza Strip (through its support of Hamas). Iran's efforts to mobilize and harness the Shia community in Lebanon go back to 1982 (though in fact, the investment in Lebanon's Shia community began in the days of the shah). Of revolutionary Iran's early investments in foreign policy, the investment in Lebanon proved to be the most effective. Hezbollah gradually became the most powerful actor in Lebanon, more powerful than the state and the Lebanese Army.

Championing Hezbollah enabled the Islamic Republic to claim the mantle of leading the conflict against Israel at the time when Arab regimes, including Iran's Syrian allies, entered into a peace process with Israel. By providing Hezbollah with a huge arsenal of rockets and missiles, Iran was building a deterrent against a prospective Israeli or American attack on its nuclear program. The course and outcome of Israel's second Lebanon war in 2006 demonstrate Tehran's effectiveness in its trilateral partnership with President Bashar al-Assad's Syria and Hezbollah.

For the Iranian leadership, Israel was not merely a competitor for regional influence or an extension of the American archenemy (the "Little

Satan"). According to Karim Sadjadpour of the Carnegie Endowment for International Peace:

> Distilled to its essence, Tehran's steadfast support for Assad is not driven by the geopolitical or financial interests of the Iranian nation, nor the religious convictions of the Islamic Republic, but by a visceral and seemingly inextinguishable hatred of the state of Israel. Senior Iranian officials like Ali Akbar Velayati . . . have commonly said 'The chain of resistance against Israel by Iran, Syria, Hezbollah, the new Iraqi government and Hamas passes through the Syrian highway. . . . Syria is the golden ring of the chain of resistance against Israel. . . . Though Israel has virtually no direct impact on the daily lives of Iranians, opposition to the Jewish state has been the most enduring pillar of Iranian revolutionary ideology. Whether Khamenei is giving a speech about agriculture or education, he invariably returns to the evils of Zionism.[1]

The Arab Spring, which resonated across the Arab world beginning in 2010 and 2011, provided Iran with additional opportunities: the revolt against the Bahraini government (a Sunni regime dominating Shia majority) was suppressed by Saudi Arabia, but the civil war in Yemen created an arena where Iran has been stoking the fires and Saudi Arabia has not yet been able defeat its rivals.

Syria

But it was Syria where the repercussions of the Arab Spring confronted Iran first with a major challenge and then with a major opportunity.

As the demonstrations against Bashar al-Assad developed into the Syrian civil war, Iran detected a severe challenge to its regional policy. If the Syrian regime—Iran's oldest regional alliance—fell, it would be a major blow to Tehran, and Hezbollah's position in Lebanon could become untenable. Iran therefore rallied to support the regime, first by providing military aid, then by dispatching Hezbollah and other Shia militias (from Iraq, Afghanistan, and Pakistan), and in 2014 sending its own troops. (Like the United States and Russia, Iran was and is sensitive to casualties and preferred to delegate fighting.) In 2015, when the Assad regime faced a prospect of collapse, the Iranians helped persuade Russia to send its air force to Syria, promising to provide the "boots on the ground" itself.

At the height of the Syrian civil war, Assad's regime—supported by Russia, Iran, and the latter's auxiliary forces—fought against a motley group of opposition forces armed and financed by regional Sunni states (Turkey, Saudi Arabia, Qatar, and Jordan) as well as by the United States, France, and the United Kingdom. The joint Iranian-Russian effort met with success and led, in December 2016, to the capture of Aleppo from anti-government forces, the turning point that marked the regime's victory in the Syrian civil war.

This conflict was compounded and, for some time, overshadowed by the rise of ISIS in both Iraq and Syria. ISIS and other jihadi groups were, among other things, a manifestation of Sunni opposition to the Shia takeover in Iraq and Alawite domination of Syria, and had a sharp anti-Iranian edge. The Obama administration, reluctant to join the war against the Assad regime, had no ambivalence about organizing and leading a large international coalition against ISIS, thus sharing an interest with Iran.

In addition, Iran's ambitions in Syria led to a direct military conflict with Israel in 2018, with Israel determined to prevent a repetition of Iran's success in building military infrastructure in Syria directed against Israel (as it had done in Lebanon). Until then, Iran and Israel fought indirectly in Lebanon and conducted a shadow war over Iran's nuclear program.

Iran's success in its Syrian venture inflated its self-confidence, and Tehran has now sought to take advantage of its success in Syria and expand its regional influence. Whereas before 2011, Tehran saw Syria as an ally and as a partner providing access to Lebanon and Hezbollah, as of 2016 Iran began to see Syria as an asset in its own right, as a second front against Israel in addition to Lebanon. Related to its interest in having a presence near the Mediterranean, Iran sought Syrian agreement to build a naval base on the Syrian coast and to embed itself in Syria with strategic infrastructure (including long-range missiles and missile production facilities). Iran has sought to build what has become known as "a land bridge" through Iraq and Syria to Lebanon; Iranian supplies to Lebanon had previously been provided by air, by sea, and only occasionally over land. The air and sea routes had challenges, so secure access by land would be a significant improvement for Iran's access to the Mediterranean. In November 2016, the chief of staff of the Iranian Army, General Mohammed Hussain Baqri, declared in front of Iranian naval commanders that in the future, Iran might construct long-range naval bases on coasts, on islands, or as floating bases, and that it could possibly build bases on the coast of Yemen or Syria.

The Ongoing Question of Iran in Its Neighborhood

And so, as it marks the fortieth anniversary of the Islamic Revolution, Iran finds itself a major actor in a transformed Middle Eastern system shaped to a considerable extent by its own actions. It is deeply invested in two crises, in Syria and in Yemen, that are still unfolding, and is confronted by a hostile American administration whose willingness to match its anti-Iranian rhetoric with action is uncertain.

Forty years after its birth, the Islamic Republic is still fueled by a blend of religious zeal, geopolitical ambitions, and vested interest. The question remains open as to when—as has been the case with other great revolutions—a phase of consolidation and moderation will set in.

NOTES

1 Karim Sadjadpour, "Iran's Real Enemy in Syria," *The Atlantic*, April 16, 2018 (www.theatlantic.com/international/archive/2018/04/iran-syria-israel/558 080/).

15

The Iranian Revolution's Legacy of Terrorism

DANIEL BYMAN

The 1979 Islamic Revolution in Iran proved one of the most consequential events in the history of modern terrorism. The revolution
led to a surge in Iranian-backed terrorism that continues, albeit in quite
different forms, to this day. Less noticed, but equally consequential, the
revolution also generated a response by Saudi Arabia and various Sunni
militant groups that set the stage for the rise in Sunni jihadism. Finally,
the revolution sparked fundamental changes in American counterterrorism institutions and attitudes.

The new clerical regime in Iran initially viewed the world in revolutionary terms.[1] Tehran's leaders saw foreign policy through the lens of
ideology, downplaying the strategic and economic interests of the country in pursuit of an Islamic revolution. In addition, like many revolutionary states, the new regime overestimated the fragility of neighboring
regimes, believing that their people, too, would rise up and that they were
ripe for revolution. The charisma of Iran's new leader, Ayatollah Ruhollah Khomeini, the compelling model of religious activism he offered, and
the numerous ties between Shia community and religious leaders in Iran

to Shia leaders in other countries led to a surge in militant groups in Iraq, Kuwait, Saudi Arabia, and other states that cited Iran as a model.

In addition, Iran declared its revolution to be an Islamic revolution, not a Shia one, and it hoped to inspire Sunni Muslims as well. Although many Sunni militants saw Iran's Shia theology as anathema, the idea of a religious revolution was compelling and gave new energy and hope to existing organizations. The Iranian Revolution helped inspire the assassins of Egyptian president Anwar Sadat in 1981 and the Hama uprising in Syria in 1982.

The new regime's ideology and misperceptions had several consequences. First, the new leaders often instinctively aided like-minded revolutionary groups, even when they had relatively little chance of success. So, they supported the Islamic Liberation Front of Bahrain, backed the assassination of the Kuwait emir, and otherwise sowed mayhem even when the chances of reaping revolution were low.[2] Second, the new regime tried to delegitimize its rivals. For example, it accused the Saudi regime of practicing "American Islam"[3] and otherwise criticized its religious credentials. Third, the regime managed to alienate both the United States and the Soviet Union at a time of intense superpower rivalry. The 1979–1981 hostage crisis and the Iranian-backed attacks by Hezbollah on the U.S. embassy and Marine barracks in Lebanon in 1983 that killed over 300 Americans were, until 9/11, the deadliest terrorist attacks on Americans. Tehran, however, was also avowedly anti-communist and believed the Soviet Union was supporting Marxist rebels in Iran.

This aggressive approach quickly led to a strategic backlash. In Iraq, Saddam Hussein saw the new regime as militarily weak yet feared its ideological sway over his country's Shia majority, contributing to his decision to invade Iran.[4] Saudi Arabia, Kuwait, and other states all rallied to Iraq's side, despite bearing no love for the bellicose Iraqi dictator, because they feared Iran's ideological power and revolutionary meddling. The United States, too, shifted firmly into the anti-Iran camp, imposing sanctions, aiding Iraq in its bitter war with Iran,[5] and stopping arms sales to Iran. (An exception to this was the Reagan administration's covert provision of weapons in an attempt to free U.S. hostages in Lebanon through the Iran-Contra program from 1985 to 1987.[6]) Terrorism began to take on a more strategic logic, with Iran and its allies, such as the Lebanese

Hezbollah, attacking backers of Iraq, like France, and otherwise using terrorism to undermine its enemies.[7]

The United States labeled Iran the world's leading supporter of terrorism, a deleterious status it enjoys to this day.[8] Tehran's support for a range of militant groups continues, with Iranian leaders seeing them as a form of power projection and a way to undermine enemies as well as help like-minded groups become stronger. Iran also uses these groups in conjunction with traditional insurgent warfare, above-ground political mobilization, and other means of increasing its influence. The Islamic Revolutionary Guard Corps and Iran's intelligence service[9] developed a range of connections to militant groups of many stripes and has recently used militants to great effect[10] in Syria and Yemen. Tehran's relationship with Hamas has also made Iran a player in the Israel-Palestine dispute.[11] Iran's zealotry may have diminished since the revolution, but its skill in using militants has steadily improved.

Even as Iran remains committed to working with militant groups, the broader nature of state sponsorship has evolved since the 1979 revolution. State sponsorship is still a danger beyond Iran, with countries like Pakistan arming, training, and funding an array of dangerous militant groups.[12] Yet, the ideological fervor that motivated Iran in 1979—and motivated Libya when Muammar Qaddafi took power[13] in 1969 and Sudan in the mid-1990s[14]—is now lacking among sponsors. Even states like Iran are more pragmatic and transactional rather than seeing the world in black and white. With the rise of Sunni jihadist groups like al Qaeda, which often had their own transnational funding and recruitment networks, "passive sponsorship"—when states knowingly turn a blind eye to terrorist activities on their soil—became more important and shifted the nature of the challenge.[15]

The Iranian Revolution and Tehran's subsequent support for militant groups also created new regional dynamics that shape the Middle East and the nature of terrorism today. One of the most significant effects was the religious mobilization of Saudi Arabia. Before the Islamic Revolution, Saudi Arabia's religious establishment primarily looked inward and even saw many other Sunni Muslims as undeserving of aid because they were deviant (that is, non-Salafi) Muslims whose faith was impure.[16] The Iranian Revolution, and the attacks on the regime's legitimacy, led the Al

Saud both to rely more on the religious establishment at home to shore up its credentials and to play up its support for Sunni Islam abroad. To undermine Iran's influence, Saudi Arabia poured hundreds of billions of dollars into support for Salafism in Europe, the United States, Asia, and much of the Muslim world.[17] In many countries, such funding supported radical mosques that become hubs for recruiting terrorists or led to much broader support for radical ideas that made it far easier for groups like the Islamic State to recruit.[18]

The competition with Iran fostered a sectarian dynamic in the Middle East.[19] After the fall of Saddam Hussein's regime in Iraq and the rise of an Iran-aligned Shia regime in Baghdad, clerics in Saudi Arabia began to play up the illegitimate nature of the regime there. This dynamic exploded when Syria slipped into civil war in 2011, with preachers in Saudi Arabia praising the resistance to the Bashar al-Assad regime because the resistance opposed a deviant, Iran-backed regime. The war heightened sectarian tension and increased Iran's regional influence with Riyadh, which increased efforts to counter Iranian influence in Lebanon and Yemen.[20]

The Iranian Revolution also led to profound changes in U.S. counterterrorism. The disastrous "Eagle Claw" hostage rescue operation in 1980, which resulted in eight American deaths when a helicopter and a transport aircraft collided, led to the creation of special operations forces focused on hostage rescue and counterterrorism.[21] The Joint Special Operations Command, which has emerged as a lethal terrorist-hunting machine in the post-9/11 era, arose from this wreckage.[22] In 1986, the Central Intelligence Agency (CIA) created its counterterrorist center, which after 9/11 became an intelligence behemoth.[23]

Finally, for many Americans, the terrorism associated with the Iranian regime seemed to mark a new era in the very nature of terrorism.[24] Religious inspiration, more than Marxism or nationalism, would define this period. Iranian-backed groups like Lebanese Hezbollah represented an early stage in this trend, but Hamas, al Qaeda, the Islamic State, and many like-minded movements would emerge as the most deadly type of terrorism violence facing the United States and its allies.

For the clerical regime in Iran, support for terrorism offered many tactical benefits, but it was often strategically self-defeating. Because Iran works with militant groups opposed to Sunni regimes and the United

States, it cements its image as a rogue power, angers potential allies, and increases U.S. pressure on the regime. This in turn increases Iran's dependence on militant groups and limits its foreign policy options.

NOTES

1 Stephen M. Walt, "Revolution and War," *World Politics*, vol. 44, no. 3, April 1992, pp. 321–68.

2 Hasan Tariq Alhasan, "The Role of Iran in the Failed Coup of 1981: The IFLB in Bahrain," *Middle East Journal*, vol. 65, no. 4, Autumn 2011, pp. 603–17; Kristian Coates Ulrichsen, "Iran-Saudi Crisis 'Most Dangerous for Decades'," BBC, January 4, 2016 (www.bbc.com/news/world-middle-east-35219693).

3 Behnam Ben Taleblu, "Iran's Greatest Fear: 'American Islam,'" *The National Interest*, January 1, 2015 (nationalinterest.org/feature/irans-greatest-fear-american-islam-11951).

4 Kenneth M. Pollack, *The Persian Puzzle: The Conflict Between Iran and America* (New York: Random House, 2005.)

5 Bruce Riedel, "Lessons from America's First War with Iran," Brookings Institution, May 22, 2013 (www.brookings.edu/articles/lessons-from-americas-first-war-with-iran/).

6 Tower Commission, President's Special Review Board, John G. Tower, Edmund S. Muskie, and Brent Scowcroft. *Report of the President's Special Review Board* (Washington: Government Printing Office, February 1987) (https://archive.org/details/TowerCommission).

7 Jeremy Shapiro and Bénédicte Suzan, "The French Experience of Counter-Terrorism," *Survival* 45, no. 1, Spring 2003, pp. 67–98.

8 Bureau of Counterterrorism, "Select Iran-Sponsored Operational Activity in Europe, 1979–2018," U.S. Department of State, July 5, 2018 (www.state.gov/j/ct/rls/other/283789.htm).

9 Ariane M. Tabatabai, "Other Side of the Iranian Coin: Iran's Counterterrorism Apparatus," *Journal of Strategic Studies*, vol. 41, no. 1–2, 2018, pp. 181–207.

10 Daniel Byman, "Why States Are Turning to Proxy War," *The National Interest*, August 26, 2018 (https://nationalinterest.org/feature/why-states-are-turning-proxy-war-29677).

11 Daniel Levin, "Iran, Hamas and the Palestinian Islamic Jihad," *The Iran Primer* (blog), United States Institute of Peace, July 9, 2018 (https://iranprimer.usip.org/blog/2018/jul/09/iran-hamas-and-palestinian-islamic-jihad).

12 Maria Abi-Habib and Salman Masood, "Pakistan's Shields Suddenly Step Aside, Placing It on Terrorism Listing," *New York Times*, March 1, 2018 (www.nytimes.com/2018/03/01/world/asia/pakistan-terrorism-china-saudi-arabia.html).

13 Sara Obeidat, "Muammar Qaddafi and Libya's Legacy of Terrorism," *Frontline*, October 13, 2015 (www.pbs.org/wgbh/frontline/article/muammar-qaddafi-and-libyas-legacy-of-terrorism/).

14 "Sudan—State Sponsor of Terrorism," Global Security (www.globalsecurity.org/military/world/sudan/terrorist.htm).

15 Daniel Byman, "Passive Sponsors of Terrorism," *Survival*, vol. 47, no. 4, 2005, pp. 117–44.

16 Thomas Hegghammer, "The Rise of Muslim Foreign Fighters: Islam and the Globalization of Jihad," *International Security*, vol. 35, no. 3, Winter 2010–2011), pp. 53–94.

17 Ben Hubbard and Mayy El Sheikh, "WikiLeaks Shows a Saudi Obsession with Iran," *New York Times*, July 16, 2015 (www.nytimes.com/2015/07/17/world/middleeast/wikileaks-saudi-arabia-iran.html).

18 Patrick Wintour, "Saudi Arabia Boosting Extremism in Europe, Says Former Ambassador," *The Guardian*, July 13, 2017 (www.theguardian.com/world/2017/jul/13/saudi-arabia-boosting-extremism-in-europe-says-former-ambassador); Carlotta Gall, "How Kosovo Was Turned into Fertile Ground for ISIS," *New York Times*, May 21, 2016 (www.nytimes.com/2016/05/22/world/europe/how-the-saudis-turned-kosovo-into-fertile-ground-for-isis.html?module=inline).

19 F. Gregory Gause III, "Beyond Sectarianism: The New Middle East Cold War," Brookings Doha Center Analysis Paper, no. 11, July 2014 (www.brookings.edu/wp-content/uploads/2016/06/English-PDF-1.pdf).

20 Priyanka Boghani, "The Rivalry Behind Three Wars: How Saudi Arabia and Iran Fueled Conflicts in Iraq, Syria and Yemen," *Frontline*, February 27, 2018 (http://apps.frontline.org/bitter-rivals-maps/).

21 Steve Balestrieri, "Operation Eagle Claw, Disaster at Desert One Brings Changes to Special Operations," *Special Operations*, April 24, 2017 (https://specialoperations.com/30764/operation-eagle-claw-disaster-desert-one-brings-changes-special-operations/).

22 Sean D. Naylor, "Inside the Pentagon's Manhunting Machine: A Brief History of Special Operations, from Panama to the War on Terror," *The Atlantic*, August 28, 2015 (www.theatlantic.com/international/archive/2015/08/jsoc-manhunt-special-operations-pentagon/402652/).

23 Sean D. Naylor, "Government Terrorist Trackers Before 9/11: Higher Ups Wouldn't Listen," *History*, August 30, 2017 (www.history.com/news/government-terrorist-trackers-before-911-higher-ups-wouldnt-listen).

24 David C. Rapoport, "The Fourth Wave: September 11 in the History of Terrorism," *Current History*, vol. 100, no. 650, December 2001, pp. 419–24.

16

Iraq and the "First Islamic Revolution"

RANJ ALAALDIN

The 1979 Iranian Revolution had a cataclysmic impact on the region, and forty years since the Islamic Republic's founding, the legacy of the revolution is still being debated. The emergence of the Islamic Republic represented what scholar Yitzhak Nakash described as the "surge of Shiism as a political force," creating a sense of unease and uncertainty among Arab, Sunni-led autocratic regimes and monarchs across the region.[1] For decades, they had worked on cultivating foundational, pluralistic values and a unified identity to manage and engage their (at times) restive Shia communities.

For some in those communities, including Shia Islamist movements and activists, the revolution in Iran created a sense of opportunity, a chance to trigger their own, indigenous revolutions. In Iraq, Ayatollah Ruhollah Khomeini, the revolution's chief architect, had spent thirteen years exiled in the holy city of Najaf. Khomeini taught seminars and cultivated ties with students and religious scholars from near and far, as well as leading members of the Shia clerical establishment in Najaf and Karbala.

135

It was while exiled in Iraq that Khomeini devised the intellectual and ideological framework that underpins Iran's system of governance today. Known as *velayat-e faqih*, or rule of the jurist, it advocates direct and executive rule by Shia clergy and constitutes the Iranian model of theocracy based on a jurisprudential interpretation of Islam. Its execution after the revolution represented a radical departure from Shia Islam's centuries-old tradition of separating religion from politics.

When the 1979 Iranian Revolution unfolded, Iraq's Shia movement was in no position to emulate its co-religionists across the border. The failed uprising resulted in brutal repression for the Shia community, but it also shaped the state's relationship with its Shia community for decades to come, arguably setting the tone and conditions for other Shia insurrections, including most notably during the 1990s.

The Rise and Fall of Dawa

Khomeini was not the first to advocate clerical involvement in politics. Iraq's Islamic Dawa Party—established in 1958—was the first modern Shia Islamist party and movement, resulting in the creation of separate branches in other Arab countries with significant Shia populations, such as Bahrain and Kuwait. Founding members of the party included the sons of the leading Shia clergymen Grand Ayatollah Muhsin al-Hakim, whose modern-day equivalent in terms of stature in the clerical community would be Grand Ayatollah Ali Sistani.

The party's ideological founder, Mohammad Baqir al-Sadr, sought to develop an Islamic framework that aimed to reconcile Western-dominated modernity with classical Shia thought but did not go as far as embracing what would become the Iranian model of theocracy. Bahraini and Saudi students were among the many foreign junior scholars following his teachings. Dawa founding members longed for a movement that was not defined along communal or sectarian lines, and established the party on the basis of an ecumenical, intellectual, and Islamic revivalist outlook, one that drew inspiration from Egypt's Muslim Brotherhood.

However, al-Sadr and the Dawa Party were targeted on two fronts. The Dawa Party was established from within Shia clerical networks as a response to the ascent of the Iraqi Communist Party after the fall of the monarchy in 1958. Communism drew support from large sections of the Shia population, including the relatives of leading Shia clerical figures. While the party was viewed with caution by the regime in Iraq, during its formative years it was actually from within the Shia religious establishment in Najaf that the party suffered its first major hit.

Just as the party started to gain traction and popularity, the clerical establishment pushed back against the formation of a Shia Islamist movement that looked to engage politics and power structures, warning that this violated the centuries-old quietist tradition of Shia Islam and could provoke a dangerous response from the state against the *hawza,* or religious seminaries. Critics of Dawa and al-Sadr launched a smear campaign against the cleric, and mobilized enough support to force al-Sadr's retreat from the party.

Indeed, tensions over the extent to which the Shia clergy should involve themselves in politics and governance were central to the thorny relations Khomeini developed with leading quietist clerics in Najaf while in exile, including Grand Ayatollah Abu al-Qasim al-Khoei. And these same frictions have loomed large in the rivalry between Najaf and Iran's holy city of Qom since the revolution in 1979. Through mid-2019, Grand Ayatollah Sistani, al-Khoei's student, has continued the quietist tradition and has assiduously protected Najaf from *velayat-e faqih,* despite Iran's best efforts.

Dawa took another major hit after the Baath Party came to power in 1968, which also targeted the mobilizing capacity of the Shia religious establishment, particularly after Grand Ayatollah Muhsin al-Hakim's death in 1970. By the time the Iranian Revolution unfolded, Dawa had already been forced underground and had lost many of its members and supporters, who were imprisoned, killed, or forced into exile.

A Failed Revolution

Still, although dilapidated and distressed, the broad-based, loosely organized Shia Islamist movement that had emerged in Iraq since 1958—composed as it was of Dawa Party supporters, members of Iraq's Shia clerical networks, and ordinary members of the Shia community— saw its own opportunity in 1979.

In the aftermath of Iran's revolution, Iraq's Shia community called on

Mohammad Baqir al-Sadr to be their "Iraqi Ayatollah Khomeini" and to lead a revolt against the regime. Community leaders, tribal heads, and hundreds of ordinary members of the public paid their allegiance to al-Sadr. Protests then erupted in Baghdad and the predominantly Shia provinces of the south in May 1979. Every Friday, Iraqis from across Baghdad and the southern Shia-dominated provinces visited al-Sadr in his home in Najaf to declare their allegiance and readiness to support the revolution.

For nine days, protests against the regime unfolded, but the regime suppressed them and arrested al-Sadr. The cleric's imprisonment led to another wave of protests in June, after a seminal, powerful appeal from al-Sadr's sister, Bint al-Huda, a preeminent activist in her own right and icon of Islamic feminism. Further clashes broke out between the security forces and protestors. Najaf was put under siege. The magnitude of the violence was such that the regime released al-Sadr, concurrently repressing his representatives and supporters to diminish the cleric's network and the mobilizing capacity of the protestors. Thousands were tortured and executed.

The Dawa Party and Iraq's Shia movement was in no position to emulate the revolution in Iran. For starters, the party was fragmented and lost much of its initial leadership to Baath repression when events in Iran unfolded, meaning it lacked strategic direction and organization. Dawa leaders either had fled the country or were imprisoned and killed by the regime. Indeed, in the years after the revolution, the Dawa Party in its literature conceded how costly and disastrous the uprisings were. A failed assassination attempt in 1980 on the then-deputy prime minister, Tariq al-Aziz, resulted in the regime's torture and execution of al-Sadr and his sister, Bint al-Huda. Baath repression after 1979 depleted the party's resources and capacity to mobilize against the regime, forcing the Dawa Party to rely on intermittent, usually unsuccessful insurgent attacks.

Unlike their Iranian co-religionists, Iraq's Shia community lacked the active participation of other sections of society, including groups such as the Kurds or Arab Sunnis. In other words, the protests failed to reach critical mass. There was sympathy toward the Shia cause from Kurdish revolutionaries in the north, given their historically close relationship and coordination, but the Kurds were confined to the mountains and engulfed in their own war against the regime. Others adopted the regime's anti-Shia polemics, dismissing Shia activism as sectarian or part of an

Iranian conspiracy. In this respect, the Iranian Revolution had a negative, polarizing impact on sectarian relations.

The Baath regime itself was aware of this shortcoming. In records captured by the United States after the 2003 invasion, the Baath senior leadership, including Saddam Hussein himself, pointed out that Khomeini was "riding the wave of the revolution" and "national, regional and international political events interacted to let Khomeini take hold of the revolution and access the power." Unlike in Iran, Iraq's Shia religious establishment was also severely weakened in the decades before 1979 and had nowhere near the numbers of clerics and seminary students that Iran's religious establishment enjoyed. By the time the revolution unfolded, Iraq's Shia were lacking the structural conditions for a successful revolution.

The collective victimhood and memory generated by the post-1979 events also resulted in a distinctly Iraqi form of Shia rebellion, which forms part of the Iraqi narrative of nationalism and patriotism today. Indeed, it would be wrong to attribute the 1979 protests in Iraq solely to events in Iran. As scholar Michelle Browers explains, discourses of reform and resistance characterized Iraq's Shia community long before the 1979 Iranian Revolution. What unfolded in 1979 was a national Iraqi affair years in the making, enabled by the activism of the Dawa Party and the Shia religious establishment. In fact, the little-known seminal protests in 1977 known as the *Safar* Intifada (named to mark the second month in the Islamic calendar) erupted after the regime attempted to ban Shia religious processions. That uprising aimed to topple the Baath regime and was met with a brutal crackdown. Shia activists refer to the protests of 1977 as "the first Islamic revolution, the one that came before the one in Iran."

NOTES

1 Yitzhak Nakash, *Reaching for Power: The Shi'a in the Modern Arab World* (Princeton University Press, 2011).

17

Saddam's Monumental Mistakes

BRUCE RIEDEL

The collapse of the shah's government in Iran in early 1979 had an impact on the entire world, but no country was more affected than Iraq. Saddam Hussein's regime was the shah's deadly enemy and had hosted the Ayatollah Ruhollah Khomeini in exile for years, but Saddam became the top foreign target of the revolutionaries in Tehran once they took power. Many countries were caught off balance by the Iranian Revolution, but none got it as wrong as Iraq. Its response—war—led to decades of conflict that have yet to end.

The shah sent Ayatollah Khomeini into exile in Turkey in 1964 for his role in leading protests against Iran's close relations with the United States. In October 1965, Khomeini moved to Iraq, to the Shia holy city of Najaf. The Iraqi government had a bitterly disputed border with Iran. The two governments were on the opposite sides of the Cold War, and Iraq was the beneficiary of large-scale Soviet military assistance.

The United States, on the other hand, had built its Middle East policy around Iran and the shah. He was the anchor of the American posture in the Persian Gulf. Billions of dollars in arms went to the shah's army. His downfall was a disaster in the minds of most Americans.

At the same time, the United States had no relations with Iraq. It was a challenging intelligence target. The Iranians under the shah were quick to tell the Americans what they thought was going on inside Iraq; their assessments were often way off the mark.

The Iraqi intelligence services helped Khomeini run a clandestine subversion operation from Najaf against the shah. The Iranian Shia pilgrimage to Najaf was a useful cover for communicating with operatives inside Iran. Cassette tapes of Khomeini's preaching were smuggled into Iran from Najaf.

In 1968, Saddam Hussein came to power in a coup. For the next decade, he ruled Iraq from behind the scenes. Saddam continued using Khomeini against the shah. For his part, the shah backed a Kurdish insurgency against Saddam with the support of the Central Intelligence Agency (CIA). Then in 1975, Saddam and the shah signed a peace agreement in Algiers, which awarded Iran disputed territory along the Shatt al-Arab in return for abandoning the Kurds. Saddam did not abandon Khomeini along with the Kurds, and he remained at the center of Islamic militancy against the shah right up to the start of the revolution.

I was assigned to the Iran desk in the CIA in November 1978 amidst widespread allegations that the intelligence community had failed to anticipate the revolution. Whatever the failing of America's intelligence, the Iraqis had clearly not anticipated the strength and magnitude of the revolution that they had helped create by supporting Khomeini for years in Najaf. On October 5, 1978, Saddam expelled Khomeini from Najaf. The ayatollah found new refuge in France, outside of Paris. From Neauphle-le-Chateau, Khomeini commanded the final months of the revolution and triumphantly returned to Tehran on February 1, 1979. Saddam alienated the man who had been laboring for years against the shah just before the moment of his triumph. It was a monumental mistake.

Within weeks of the creation of the Islamic Republic, Khomeini reverse engineered the smuggling routes he had used against the shah from Najaf to now try to subvert Saddam's Baathist regime in Baghdad. At the CIA, we forecast in the spring of 1979 that Iran-Iraq relations were heading toward conflict. The new revolutionary regime in Tehran began sponsoring a wave of terror attacks inside Iraq aimed at toppling Saddam and creating a second Islamic (and Shia) Republic in Baghdad. Border clashes became the norm.

Saddam was determined to fight back. He invited disgruntled generals from the shah's former army to Baghdad to arrange a coup to oust the ayatollah. Both sides engaged in conspiracies and plots to subvert the other. Both sides also targeted minority communities in the other for subversion: Iran worked on the Kurds, Iraq on the Arabs in Khuzestan and the Baluchis.

After the seizure of the American embassy in Tehran, the CIA Task Force on Iran redoubled efforts to monitor the Iran-Iraq border for signs of a coming war. Among the generals who were assisting the Iraqis was Gholam Ali Oveissi, who had been the shah's last army commander. He left Iran in January 1979 for exile in Paris. He continued to have close contacts with the American military that had developed during his years with the shah. Oveissi trained in the United States in Virginia and Kansas.

In September 1980, Oveissi came to New York and I debriefed him. He had just been in Baghdad and seen Saddam. War was imminent, according to what Oveissi had been told. The Iraqi Army was poised to invade. Oveissi promised Saddam that Iran was weak and its military was in disarray. Of course, that is what Saddam wanted to hear.

The intelligence community issued an immediate warning memo indicating that the Iraqis were going to invade and assessing the implications. The memo concluded that Iraq was not likely to win a quick and cheap war. National Security Advisor Zbigniew Brzezinski summed it up crisply: "Iraq has bitten off more than it can chew," he wrote to President Jimmy Carter.[1]

Oveissi was assassinated in Paris on February 7, 1984, by an Iranian hit team. The war lasted eight years and cost the lives of a half million people, another million injured, and over a trillion dollars in damage. It set in motion the march of folly that led to three more wars. It all began with Saddam's mistakes in 1978 and 1979.

NOTES

1 James G. Blight and others, *Becoming Enemies: U.S.-Iran Relations and the Iran-Iraq War, 1979–1988* (Lanham, MD: Rowman and Littlefield, 2012), p. 303.

18

Hezbollah: Revolutionary Iran's Most Successful Export

JEFFREY FELTMAN

Like others who had the privilege of serving as U.S. ambassador in Beirut, I often took the downhill walk from the official residence to a modest memorial nearby. There, like my predecessors and successors, I presided over anniversary remembrances to honor those who lost their lives serving the U.S. government in Lebanon: 63 people slaughtered in the April 1983 embassy bombing; 241 Marines and other U.S. service personnel murdered in the October 1983 Marine barracks bombing; 23 (including Lebanese visa applicants) killed in the October 1984 bombing of the temporary embassy in Awkar, East Beirut; individuals held hostage, tortured, and killed for their service to the United States; a Navy Seabee murdered and dumped on the tarmac during a 1985 plane hijacking.

The emotional reunions of the embassy's Lebanese employees, many retired, who survived the bombings, along with the relatives of their colleagues who did not, made these remembrances particularly poignant.

The story of an Armenian Lebanese woman always touched me: She still toiled for the embassy during my 2004 to 2008 tenure, more than 20 years after she had been left for dead in April 1983 and sent for medical care only when a morgue worker glimpsed a slight twitch. And what did the embassy's Lebanese commercial specialist tell his mother when he accepted a job at the very compound where his father had worked and then been killed in 1984? Even Americans who did not experience the bombings recognized the sacrifices of those who did. While we did not in those days have many Marines visiting Beirut, whenever we did, it was a special but somber honor for me to accompany the visitor to pay respects at the memorial.

The remembrance commemorations also prompted reflections on the history and power of Hezbollah, the presumed (and in some cases indicted) author of the murders of all of the hundreds of victims—American and Lebanese—whose names were inscribed on the embassy's memorial. Most were killed by the suicide bombings that Hezbollah did more than any other group to popularize in the modern era. Hezbollah's methods have evolved as its military and political powers and sophistication have expanded since the mid-1980s, with Lebanon itself rather than American citizens now held hostage. But then as now, Hezbollah serves as the most successful, and the most deadly, export of the 1979 Iranian Revolution.

Hezbollah's Origins: Iran Seizes the Opportunity

Hezbollah emerged during the chaos of Lebanon's civil war. As Lebanese factions, Palestinians, Israelis, Syrians, and various proxy powers destroyed the country, the ground was fertile for Iran's post-1979 revolutionary leaders to demonstrate that their example could be replicated in the Arab world, by exploiting long-standing grievances of Lebanon's Shia Muslim underclass.

In the complicated balance of the so-called confessional system adopted in 1943 upon Lebanon's independence, government positions are allocated according to religious sect. These are apportioned by the demographic weight of each group as reflected in a now wildly outdated

1932 census that, given the political implications for Lebanon's shrinking Christian population, has never been updated. Thus, the presidency of the republic is held by a Maronite Christian, the prime minister comes from the Sunni Muslims, the speaker of the parliament must be Shia Muslim, and so forth. Originally, government positions and parliamentary seats were divided in a six-to-five ratio favoring Christians over Muslims; the 1989 Taif Agreement ending Lebanon's civil war amended this to fifty-fifty. Further divisions allow for representation of Lebanon's eighteen recognized religious sects or confessions (for example, the Muslim 50-percent share is divided between Sunnis, Shia, Druze, and Alawites, and the Christian half, while dominated by the Maronites, has reserved slots for the other Christian denominations).

Confessional allocations aside, Lebanon's Maronite-Sunni elite (and even some traditional Shia feudal families) tended to treat the Shia with disdain and neglect. Enmeshed in poverty and high rates of illiteracy, Shia peasants concentrated in the south also suffered disproportionately from the Palestinian-Israeli conflict, as the Palestine Liberation Organization (PLO) attacked Israel from southern Lebanon, and the Israelis retaliated in kind. Given years of PLO abuses, Shia residents of the south briefly welcomed the 1982 Israeli invasion, although Israeli tactics quickly alienated them, driving thousands from ancestral villages to the slums of Beirut's impoverished southern suburbs.

Meanwhile, the Multinational Force in Lebanon (consisting of U.S., French, Italian, and U.K. military personnel and established in 1982 to oversee the evacuation of the PLO from Lebanon) was increasingly viewed as a partisan belligerent rather than a neutral player, especially after the September 1982 assassination of President-elect Bashir Gemayel.

The Iranian mullahs thus had a perfect stage on which to export their revolutionary drama: an increasingly disliked Western coalition on the ground; a brutal Israeli occupation and victimized Palestinians in squalid camps; the distracting chaos of an ongoing civil war; and, most importantly, an alienated and despised Shia population desperate for political and economic salvation and security. An earlier attempt at awakening Shia political activism by the charismatic Shia cleric Imam Musa Sadr lost its unique momentum with Sadr's disappearance during a 1978 visit to Libya. Albeit with more dangerous intent, Iran picked up what Sadr started and transformed Shia from underclass to what today is Lebanon's most powerful political force, one willing to impose its will on the country—including, if needed, by assassinations and militia force.

Conveniently for the newly minted Islamic Republic of Iran, fighting the "Imperialists" and "Zionists" could bolster the Shia fortunes in Lebanon simultaneously with enhancing the revolutionary reputation of Iran's government at a time when it was enmeshed in war with Saddam Hussein's Iraq. Initially hardly noticed in the "noise" of the Lebanese civil war, Iranian Revolutionary Guards (as many as 1,000) established training camps in the Bekaa Valley in the early 1980s. Iran committed tens of millions of dollars (some estimates exceed $200 million) annually to cover salaries and services for the Shia that the Lebanese state neglected to extend. As opposed to the corruption and cronyism of traditional Lebanese leaders, Hezbollah cultivated an image of crisp efficiency and honesty. But by 1985, when Hezbollah's initial manifesto (calling for, among other things, the establishment of an Iran-style Islamic republic in Lebanon) was issued, the group was already notorious internationally for its methods of simultaneous suicide attacks, later copied by other terrorist groups, and for its hostage-taking.

For Iran, Hezbollah was already a success story by this point. Hezbollah claimed credit for the departure of U.S and French military personnel in 1984 and the 1985 retreat of the Israelis from Beirut to a security zone in southern Lebanon. Hezbollah's seizure of hostages gave Iran leverage, with the Reagan administration's attempts to explain away the Iran-Contra scandal by claiming the arms sales to Iran were intended to secure the release of Americans from Hezbollah. While the group's leaders today downplay the bloody legacy of suicide bombing, hijacking, hostage-snatching, torture, and murder, this history foreshadows Hezbollah's subsequent success in using Israeli hostages and remains to secure the release of Palestinian and Lebanese prisoners from Israeli custody. As in 1985, Hezbollah also declared victory for "the resistance" in forcing the Israeli withdrawal from southern Lebanon in 2000 and for having survived the Israeli ground and air attacks in the devastating war that Hezbollah provoked in the summer of 2006.

Hezbollah as Iran's Multipurpose Tool

For Iran, Hezbollah is a strategic asset that extends Iranian influence to the Mediterranean. The group's rockets and missiles are tangible demonstration of the Islamic Republic's anti-Israel credentials. But Hezbollah's value to Tehran transcends the Lebanese theater. The group, like a "Beltway bandit" government subcontractor, has provided technical assistance and training to Iraqi militias supported by Iran and, more recently, Yemen. When tasked by Tehran or Damascus, Hezbollah provides assassination services, with operatives indicted by the Special Tribunal for Lebanon in the February 2005 murder of former Lebanese Prime Minister Rafiq Hariri and under suspicion for the elimination of many other anti-Syrian and anti-Hezbollah Lebanese politicians in the 2005 to 2008 period.

As the 1992 and 1994 suicide attacks against, respectively, the Israeli embassy and a Jewish center in Buenos Aires illustrate, Hezbollah's terrorism does not stop at the Mediterranean water's edge. More recently, the group stands accused of perpetrating the 2012 assault against a bus of Israeli tourists in Bulgaria and planning attacks, subsequently foiled, in Azerbaijan and Cyprus. Argentina announced the arrest of Hezbollah operatives in advance of the 2018 G20 summit. Hezbollah also developed the capability of helping Iran evade sanctions: Drawing on an extensive expatriate Lebanese Shia population in Latin America and Africa, Hezbollah has mastered the criminal links of smuggling, money laundering, and drug trafficking. Most importantly for Iran, Hezbollah fighters, backed by Russian air power, have been an essential part of Bashar al-Assad's survival in Syria. Put simply, for Iran, Hezbollah is a malevolent version of the Swiss Army knife, with special capabilities always at the ready for distinct tasks.

Hezbollah as a Lebanese Actor

When people would describe Hezbollah as a "state within a state," Fred Hof, a distinguished fellow at the Atlantic Council, would gently correct them, describing Hezbollah as "a state within a non-state." Unlike other

Lebanese militias that battled each other, Hezbollah evaded the disarmament requirements of the 1989 Taif Agreement by citing the Israeli occupation of southern Lebanon (and sometimes, the very existence of Israel). Especially since the 2006 war, Iran has facilitated an exponential increase in the size, sophistication, and lethality of Hezbollah's arsenal—a reality not lost upon other Lebanese political leaders and one-time warlords who willingly dismantled their militias in accordance with Taif.

Under Hassan Nasrallah, the secretary-general who replaced Abbas Musawi (assassinated by Israel) in 1992, Hezbollah decided to participate in that year's parliamentary elections for the first time and has shifted more recently from having loyal allies in the cabinet to insisting its own members also take ministerial portfolios. Hopeful speculation that Hezbollah's growing role in politics and governing would diminish the importance of its arms and transform Hezbollah into a "normal" party proved naive.

Today, Hezbollah uses the combination of its genuine popularity among the majority of Lebanon's Shia, its positions in Lebanon's parliament and cabinet, and its militia power to exercise effective veto over any Lebanese government policy it opposes—while at the same time constructing an impenetrable wall against any public or parliamentary accountability over Hezbollah's decisions. The Israeli discovery in late 2018 and early 2019 of Hezbollah tunnels from southern Lebanon into Israel is just the latest example of dangerous Hezbollah decisions, similar to its directive to kidnap Israeli soldiers from Israeli sovereign territory in July 2006, which could lead Lebanon into a devastating war—without any public debate, transparency, or governmental oversight.

Should any Lebanese question Hezbollah's autonomous decisions, the group will deploy fighters and supporters to physically stifle the scrutiny (and if needed, to eliminate the critic). When the Lebanese government in 2008 tried to dismantle an illegal Hezbollah telecommunications system, Hezbollah fighters physically seized control of West Beirut. Characteristic of its intolerance to others' views, Hezbollah's ability to mobilize intimidating mobs quickly has repeatedly thwarted any serious discussion of its arms or the special treatment it insists on assuming (but never bestowing).

Michel Aoun Provides Christian Cover to Hezbollah

What gives Hezbollah particular potency in the current Lebanese environment is Hassan Nasrallah's ability to assert that the group represents national Lebanese interests rather than narrow parochial Shia goals or the positions of Tehran and Damascus. With political venality astonishing even by Lebanese standards, President Michel Aoun, a Maronite Christian whose followers once idolized him as the symbol of courageous resistance against Damascus, has embraced his role as Hezbollah's enabler in this regard. His son-in-law, current foreign minister Gebran Bassil, midwifed a 2006 memorandum of understanding (MOU) between Aoun's Free Patriotic Movement (FPM) and Hezbollah, and the two groups have maintained a close Shia-Christian alliance ever since.

With their cult-like, personality-based followings, neither Aoun nor Nasrallah had to bother with the political acrobatics of trying to reconcile previous hostile positions with their 2006 bromance. Bassil in particular has been a notorious apologist for Hezbollah, insisting that Lebanon needs it as a defense against Israel (ignoring the reality that Hezbollah is primarily responsible for the threat from Israel that Bassil, like Nasrallah, cites as justification for Hezbollah's arms). Even today, with the discovery of the tunnels into Israel, it is apparently impossible for President Aoun, who was by all accounts taken by surprise, to acknowledge that Hezbollah's unaccountable behavior puts Lebanon at risk of war, undermines the very institutions of the state he was elected to lead, humiliates his own authority as president, and unveils the true nature of the supposedly equal partnership between the FPM and Hezbollah.

For Aoun, the MOU his son-in-law brokered with Hezbollah was a step on the route to achieving Aoun's long-standing ambition to be elected president, with his narcissism overriding his earlier opposition to Syria's dominance of Lebanon. For Nasrallah, the MOU with a major Christian bloc was Hezbollah's coming-out party as a leader of a national, rather than sectarian Shia, movement. With the FPM's Christian ministers and parliament members enthusiastically subservient to his objectives, Nasrallah has been able to exploit the peculiarities of Lebanon's democracy to assert his will constitutionally.

For both leaders, their enduring alliance is also intended to sideline once and for all any independent political competition and, especially, to send a message to (and about) Lebanon's Sunnis. In Lebanese-style race-baiting, Aoun's FPM multiplies and exploits Lebanese Christian insecurities about the Sunnis. Given the well-documented horrors of ISIS and a Lebanese Christian lifestyle as remote as imaginable from austere Saudi-style Wahhabi Muslim traditions, FPM leaders argue that an alliance with Hezbollah is the best protection for the Christians against a hyped-up Sunni demographic, cultural, and security threat. The FPM-Hezbollah alliance is rooted on a narrative appealing to some Christians that Sunnis (portrayed as agents of Saudi Arabia) are a bigger danger to Lebanon than a heavily armed, religious-based political movement contemptuous of public oversight and allied with mullahs in Tehran and a serial murderer in Damascus. Some particularly delusional FPM members even argue that, despite the relative demographic decline of Christians in Lebanon, Hezbollah will help them reverse the rebalancing of Christian-Muslim political power that was part of the 1989 Taif Agreement that Aoun despises.

Having succeeded with astonishing ease in co-opting Aoun and those Christians who follow him, Nasrallah spent weeks blocking Lebanon's cabinet formation in 2018 by insisting that individual Sunni proxies of Hezbollah, who won parliamentary seats in districts with significant Hezbollah voters, be awarded cabinet representation at the expense of caretaker prime minister Saad Hariri's larger and more representative Sunni bloc. With the ludicrous Druze politician Talal Arslan already parroting Hezbollah positions, Nasrallah now seeks to create an equally pliable Sunni version of Michel Aoun, to allow Hezbollah to claim Sunni credibility as well. Nasrallah may not yet have the power to name the prime minister in the same way that he appealed to Aoun's vanity to create the Aoun presidency, but Nasrallah is patiently expanding his alliances. Considering the uncanny similarity of the challenges provoked by Shia militias in the post-election Iraq government formation exercise, the question is whether this is all part of the unseemly business of local Lebanese politics or whether Nasrallah is also representing Iranian designs of wielding power through both militias and constitutional positions. After all, Nasrallah's attempts to use Aoun's ready acquiescence and Hezbollah's militia to monopolize internal Lebanese politics would not be contradictory to Iran's regional ambitions.

Hezbollah Today, and Lessons

Iranian leaders can look with satisfaction on what their nearly four-decade investment in Lebanon has yielded. With its fighters having experienced real-world battles over several years in Syria and due to its expanded and sophisticated military arsenal, Hezbollah, as a force multiplier for Iran and threat to Israel, is stronger than ever militarily. It is also clear now that the Iran-style Islamic Republic demanded in Hezbollah's 1985 manifesto (and now conveniently ignored by Nasrallah and Aoun alike) is not essential to the group's ability to protect its own, and Iran's, interests. The alliance with Michel Aoun gives Hezbollah constitutional levers to manipulate and paralyze the government at will, while Hezbollah has successfully demonstrated that it can use intimidation and threats to prevent public scrutiny and debate over its arms. Moreover, given demographic realities, momentum is building behind an idea for further revisions to Lebanon's confessional divide—shifting from fifty-fifty Christian-Muslim to equal thirds for Christians, Sunnis, and Shia. If ever enacted, such revisions would essentially assure Hezbollah, given its dominance over Shia politics, of a permanent, constitutional "blocking third" over important parliamentary and government decisions, without having to worry whether the alliance with the FPM will outlive Aoun.[1]

Finally, Iran can anticipate that an increasing number of self-serving Lebanese political figures, anticipating how the regional and international political winds are blowing, may decide that joining the Tehran-Damascus-Hezbollah alliance is the safe bet, especially given uncertainties about American leadership and reliability in light of the Trump administration's decision to withdraw U.S. forces from Syria.

Yet, perceptive Iranian analysts might detect some emerging, cautionary trends; all is not well in Hezbollah's earthly Lebanese paradise. Demobilized Hezbollah fighters from Syria return to Lebanon with no job prospects (and fewer abilities than other Lebanese to migrate or work abroad). Hezbollah is reportedly struggling to cope with former fighters with post-traumatic stress disorder (PTSD), drug addiction, or thuggish behavior incubated in Syria's lawless environment. Late salaries to Hezbollah's social service employees and delayed payments to suppliers are interpreted as signs that U.S. sanctions against Iran and Hezbollah are taking a toll. Hezbollah's insistence on getting the Health Ministry in the 2019 cabinet can be explained, in part, as an effort to burnish its credentials in terms of relatively honest service delivery, but it does not seem to be a coincidence that control of the Health Ministry gives Hezbollah authority over significant amounts of cash. (While larger in terms of amounts, the budgets of the Defense, Education, and Interior ministries are mostly mortgaged to salaries and pensions; the Health Ministry, by contrast, has discretionary funds.) The Lebanese Armed Forces (LAF), while devoid of the offensive rockets and missiles of Hezbollah, are an increasingly coherent and sophisticated military defense force, thanks in large measure to years of patient U.S. support. In light of the LAF's improved capacities, Nasrallah's arguments that Hezbollah is needed to defend Lebanon begin to sound increasingly hollow, especially when, as with the tunnels and in 2006, Hezbollah is the party most responsible for placing Lebanon in danger of a catastrophic war.

Given the Trump administration's stated policy of pressuring Iran, it seems an opportune time for increased focus on Hezbollah, revolutionary Iran's most successful export and one of its primary tools for deadly mischief, both regionally and internationally. As the Israeli experience has shown, a purely military approach to Hezbollah provides, at best, only temporary setbacks. Questions to consider include how to prevent a blurring between the LAF and Hezbollah—which, with careful diplomacy, should be possible, given the LAF's improved capacities and the resentment many proud LAF officers quietly voice about Hezbollah's arrogance. Related, it is time for the United States at last to seriously contemplate how to show FPM officials and supporters, many of whom have U.S. ties, that there are consequences for the FPM's alliance with a designated terrorist organization that has American blood on its hands. Bassil's slavish embrace of Hezbollah, for example, should not be cost-free in terms of his access to Washington officials. Scrutiny of World Bank commitments in light of what ministries fall under Hezbollah's control in the cabinet also seems wise. Decisive, rapid U.S. action along these lines can help mitigate the impression in Lebanon, after the Syria troop withdrawal decision, that the U.S. has lost interest and influence in the region and that Washington's Iran policy is rhetorical only.

More broadly, the United States might consider how to work with others to prevent the emergence of other Hezbollah-like entities elsewhere in the region. The benefit of hindsight shows clearly what those Islamic Revolutionary Guard Corps (IRGC) trainers in the Bekaa Valley, as well as the Iranian subsidies of jobs and services, did in terms of creating momentum behind Hezbollah's growth. However, for something even that heavily subsidized to take permanent root and flourish, fertile ground is required. The utter neglect, for decades, of Lebanon's Shia population by the Sunni-Maronite elite and the Shia feudal families, exacerbated by the contempt for and brutality toward the locals as demonstrated by the Palestinians and Israelis in southern Lebanon, prepared the land for the seeds Iran then planted and nurtured. Unlike Michel Aoun's calculated embrace of Hezbollah, the Lebanese Shia did not collectively decide one day to become tools of Iran (and many still resent having their political interests hijacked by Hezbollah and Iran). But devoid of prospects for respect and a better future, they gravitated to the opportunities Iran provided in nascent Hezbollah.

The leaders of Bahrain, Saudi Arabia, and the supporters of Yemen's recognized government need to consider whether they are creating the very conditions by which a portion of their own citizenry, whose political and professional aspirations seem constantly thwarted, will at some point give up on their own national leaders in frustration and see no alternative to the offers of help that Iran will be willing to extend (even in its own tightened financial condition). These countries risk making the same mistakes the Lebanese elite committed in creating the opportunity Iran was all too happy to exploit.

A Brief Aside: Hezbollah, My Mother, and Me

A friend in Beirut enjoys amusing me by sending links to speeches by Hezbollah Secretary-General Hassan Nasrallah in which he invokes my name—as he did at least twice in 2018, a decade after I concluded my tenure as U.S. ambassador to Lebanon and six years after my last trip to Beirut, in May 2012 as assistant secretary of state for Near Eastern Affairs. My wife, Mary, teases me that, for Nasrallah, I serve the same function as Hillary Clinton does for President Trump: a way to excite the base.

Like other U.S. ambassadors in Lebanon and elsewhere, I was seen to personify the "Great Satan." Until Nasrallah feared alienating the embassy's Christian neighbors he hoped his seduction of Michel Aoun would woo, Nasrallah deployed rent-a-mobs to weekly demonstrations outside the embassy gates. A fun by-product was the vivid confirmation of how diplomatic service alters perspectives. Alarmed by the news coverage, my mother in small-town Ohio sent an e-mail to announce that she was flying to Beirut to join the Hezbollah protests, because, yes, Feltman did need to go home. Mary, a U.S. Foreign Service Officer then at Stanford University, reacted to the same reports by asking where the protestors had found the image of me for the giant posters they were enthusiastically striking with their shoes—it is a really good photograph, she noted. Live footage of me waving farewell to a ship evacuating U.S. citizens during the summer 2006 war also caught my mother's attention: "Don't wave to the ship; get on it!" her message advised.

Nasrallah's use of me as a convenient stage prop peaked during the 2006–2008 Hezbollah sit-in that paralyzed the government and crippled Beirut's downtown over ministerial demands. Even inside the grand offices of the prime minister, the rhythmic Hezbollah chants attempting to discredit the cabinet of Prime Minister Fouad Siniora were audible: "Feltman government! Feltman government!" In one of my calls with him, Siniora reacted to a crescendo of chants by wearily joking, "Jeff, they say it's your government: So, take it!" A few years later, when as a UN official I joined UN Secretary-General Ban Ki-moon's meeting with Iranian Supreme Leader Ali Khamenei in Tehran, my Lebanese friends laughed: Was Nasrallah's favorite object of scorn now discussing possible "Feltman governments" for Iran?

NOTES

1 Constitutionally, to prevent domination by one religious group, important government decisions or parliamentary legislation in Lebanon need to pass by a two-thirds majority. So even if the Shia proportion of positions increases from its current 21 percent to one-third of the total under the idea being discussed, Hezbollah—which can be assured of all Shia votes—would need one additional supporter for the "blocking third." Given Hezbollah's various levers of power, finding a single Sunni, Druze, or Christian vote would be easy.

19

The Origins of the Saudi-Iranian Battle for the Broader Middle East

SUZANNE MALONEY *and* BRUCE RIEDEL

"Please, my brother, modernize," Iran's last king, Mohammad Reza Pahlavi, reportedly advised his Saudi counterpart in the late 1960s. "Open up your country. Make the schools mixed women and men. Let women wear miniskirts. Have discos. Be modern. Otherwise, I cannot guarantee you will stay on your throne."

The Saudi monarch, King Faisal, responded pointedly: "Your Majesty, I appreciate your advice. May I remind you, you are not the shah of France. You are not in the Élysée. You are in Iran. Your population is 90 percent Muslim. Please don't forget that."[1]

For all his self-assured counsel, Pahlavi's throne crumbled less than a decade later. Iran's revolutionary leaders especially reviled the shah's secularism and his pro-Western orientation. And the complicated relationship between the shah and his Gulf counterparts—prickly, competitive, but ultimately aligned by common interests—was supplanted by a destructive new rivalry that has wrought havoc across the broader

Middle East and fueled sectarianism. As the self-proclaimed leader of the Sunni world, which includes approximately 87 to 90 percent of Muslims, Saudi Arabia condemns the largest Shia state, Iran, as polytheist. Tehran is ecumenical in its outreach, but its regional influence correlates overwhelmingly with large Shia communities. Sectarianism is more vicious today than at any time in modern Islamic history.

Prior to the shah's ouster, Washington relied on both Tehran and Riyadh to help guarantee regional stability and vital energy transit corridors. By transforming Iran from a valued security partner to the region's paramount threat, the Iranian Revolution magnified the interdependence between Washington and Tehran and ultimately triggered the expanding U.S. military footprint in the Gulf.

Origins of the Rift

The roots of the Saudi-Iranian rivalry long predate the 1979 Revolution. They are grounded in the ideology of the Saudi state, Wahhabism. Muhammad ibn Abd al Wahhab, for whom Wahhabism is erroneously named, was a preacher in the Arabian desert who spent an informative part of his life in the Iraqi city of Basra, which then and now has a Shia majority. Wahhab was appalled by the Shia veneration of Ali, the nephew and son-in-law of the prophet Muhammad, believing that the practice violated Islam's core principle of monotheism. Wahhab's biographer, Michael Crawford, argues that his time in Basra was critical to the formulation of his doctrine of *tawhid,* or oneness.[2] Since God is the sole creator and orderer of the affairs of the universe, Wahhab emphasizes that God alone should be the addressee of prayers, supplications, and all forms of worship. At the center of the Wahhabi objection to Shia jurisprudence lies a fundamental divergence over authority, both temporal and spiritual.[3]

Wahhabi beliefs are core to Saudi policy at home and abroad. There are almost 100,000 mosques in the kingdom, and the royal family is intimately connected to the clerical establishment by intermarriage and professional collaboration. Since 1744, when the Saudi state was created in a marriage of the house of the al-Saud family and Wahhab's descendants, the al Shaykh family, its leaders have pursued an anti-Shia agenda in the Arabian Peninsula.

Iran has been a predominantly Shia state since the sixteenth century, when a mystical order aligned with Turkmen tribes consolidated control and eventually extended its dominion from Baghdad to Herat and northward into modern Azerbaijan. The Safavid Empire revived an independent Persian state for the first time in nine centuries, and the deployment of religious fervor, forcibly where necessary, enabled their success. The Safavid conquest and the accompanying conversion of most of their subjects set them at odds with the Ottoman caliphate and necessitated the importation of clerics from territories with large Shia populations, such as Lebanon.

The Safavid domain splintered as a result of Afghan, Ottoman, and Russian incursions during the eighteenth century. As Iran descended into weak tribal rule, Wahhabi forces were on the march on the Arabian Peninsula, which was mostly under the "nominal suzerainty" of the Ottoman Empire.[4] The exception was the Nejd, in central Arabia, where the Saudi-Wahhabi partnership took shape and eventually expanded to encompass nearly all of the contemporary Saudi state, as well as Qatar, Bahrain, the United Arab Emirates, and parts of northern Oman.

At their peak, Saudi forces stretched northward, raiding the wealthy shrine cities of Najaf and Karbala as well as pilgrimage caravans, and southward into Yemen. Eventually the Ottomans dispatched Egyptian troops, and by 1818 the first Saudi kingdom was routed. Its revival several years later was led by men who appreciated their limits; their internal power struggles helped abate their expansionist zeal. During this period, "Wahhabism quickly ceased being a force for endless holy war against other Muslims, and became an internal issue for the Saudi state to deal with."[5]

Although doctrinal differences sharpened the animosity between the Saudis and Iranians, the frictions have never been purely or even primarily sectarian. The two countries' rivalry has long been intertwined with the role and interests of foreign powers in the region—the Portuguese, the Dutch, the British, the Russians, and, eventually, the Americans. Outside powers initially helped extend the Safavid domain along Persia's southern flank, but over time British and Russian encroachments came at the expense of local powers. By the twentieth century, Britain had achieved predominance along both sides of the Persian Gulf.

Modern Men

While they draw upon powerful antecedents, the modern Iranian and Saudi states are shaped by the maelstrom of political, economic, ideological, and technological change underway during their emergence in the early twentieth century. The slow-motion collapse of Iran's imperial order ushered in new challenges from within—intensifying demands for state accountability—as well as from without—through European incursions that expanded to wholesale occupation during World War I. The instability generated by these historic shifts provided an opening for Reza Khan, a colonel in Iran's Russian-backed Cossack Brigade, to propel himself to power beginning in 1921.

The five years between Reza's march on Tehran to overthrow the sitting government and his formal assumption of authority honed his skill at co-opting and coercing Iran's various influential constituencies, including its religious leaders. He sought to cement his own power by establishing a centralizing, modernizing state modeled after post-Ottoman Turkey. So while he courted the clergy on his rise and emphasized religion in his 1926 coronation address,[6] Reza undertook policies as shah that undermined the religious establishment's political and economic interests.

There are parallels between Reza Shah and Abd al Aziz ibn Saud, who was proclaimed king of the third Saudi state in the same year as Reza's coronation; both waged fierce military campaigns to achieve power; both sought British assistance at crucial moments in their rise; both recognized the importance of central authority for modernizing their realms; and both benefitted immensely from the diplomatic and economic dividends of the nascent oil industry. However, the differences between the two leaders and the contexts in which they operated left an indelible impression on the states they forged and the dynamics between the two countries today.

In contrast to Reza, whose ambitions for Iran built upon a long history and a nascent constitutional framework, Ibn Saud faced more formidable obstacles. "Ottoman control was mainly symbolic";[7] central political power had never been effectively wielded; outside of the pilgrimage administration, nothing in the way of a bureaucratic state existed; and localized, mainly tribal affinities predominated. To overcome all of this, Ibn Saud had religious fervor. Wahhabi Islam generated cohesion among his tribal armies, motivating them through the protracted fighting to reclaim territory that had previously come under Saudi sway. And it was essential for legitimizing his authority, especially against rivals such as the Hashemite rulers of the Hijaz, whose resources, stature, and external allies vastly exceeded his own.

The Saudi reconquest of the Arabian Peninsula took two decades of fierce fighting and even more intense diplomacy among local power brokers, as well as those in Istanbul and London. In their 1925 seizure of Mecca and Medina, the tribal fighters known as the *ikhwan* (brotherhood) sought to destroy anything they considered idolatrous, including the tombs of the prophet Mohammad's wife and his mother as well as the destruction of the Jannat al Baqi cemetery in Medina, a revered site for Shia Muslims.

Ibn Saud's reliance on Wahhabi zeal entailed real risks; shortly after he declared himself king, the *ikhwan* rebelled against him. The bloody two-year uprising was crushed with occasional British assistance and the durable fidelity of the Wahhabi clerical establishment. As Ibn Saud routed the opposition, he "employed a tactic that was to become a hallmark of Saudi religiopolitical strategy: he turned the tables on the opposition by presenting himself as the better Muslim, publicly accusing his opponents of sectarianism, fanaticism, and of living 'against the instruction' of Islamic law."[8] This essential bargain between the new state and its religious leadership guided Saudi policy.

Tehran carefully navigated the Wahhabi rise. Logistics surrounding the *hajj* prompted early diplomatic contacts, and by 1929 the two fledgling governments had signed a treaty of friendship.[9] During the next several decades, Iran and Saudi Arabia engaged tentatively, but by necessity, their leaders mostly focused on building and resourcing their new states.

That entailed developing their nascent oil industries and the double-edged sword of great-power entanglements that came with it. Eventually, the tensions between the two states assumed a new dimension—a competition over contract terms, pricing and production policy, and markets.

America's Allies

World War II brought massive upheaval to Iran, with Reza Shah's forced abdication in favor of his twenty-two-year-old son and the severe disruption of the Allied occupation of the country. By contrast, the war spared Saudi Arabia, and as it was concluding, Ibn Saud laid the foundation of a durably consequential partnership with Washington in an extraordinary 1945 summit with President Franklin Roosevelt.

Although the young Mohammad Reza Shah was determined to secularize Iran, the sectarian divide between the two states occasionally flared. During this period, incidents surrounding the *hajj* provoked sporadic tensions: in 1943, an incident involving an Iranian pilgrim ended with his beheading and a brief rupture in diplomatic relations. Similar issues arose in 1948 and 1963—a mild premonition of the fierce ideological differences that would erupt between the two states after the Iranian Revolution.

However, the most consequential dynamics were the geopolitical threats and opportunities that emerged—the development of a new regional order along the Persian Gulf, the rise of Arab nationalism, the empowerment of family and/or clan-led states along the Gulf's southern littoral, the onset of the Cold War, and the waning of British influence and commitment to managing the region's political, economic, and security relations. While this environment presented some common threats—such as radical Arab nationalism—Saudi and Iranian interests often diverged over issues such as territorial claims and oil market policies. As a result, for much of the pre-revolutionary period, the bilateral Saudi-Iranian relationship was marked by wary cooperation and episodic tensions.

The 1968 British decision to scale back its military presence in the Persian Gulf elevated the significance of both countries in the spectrum of U.S. strategic interests. With U.S. military capabilities heavily con-

sumed by the Vietnam war, Washington repurposed the British blue-
print, which sought to devise a stable regional equilibrium by reliance on
local powers. The new U.S. security architecture for the region primarily
relied on the "twin pillars" of Riyadh and Tehran; based, however, on
capability, willingness, and personal rapport among leaders, Tehran was
the long pole in the tent.

Despite deep historical resentment of British interference in Iran, the
shah was alarmed that their departure would create an opening for his
adversaries. And while he wanted American arms, he did not welcome
a growing U.S. military footprint in the region. Nothing less than regional predominance would satisfy his ambitions. The shah did not share
the innate fiscal and foreign policy conservatism of the Saudi monarchy;
he had no meaningful theological constraints impeding direct ties with
Israel, and unlike Riyadh, he excelled at maneuvering the Cold War rivalry to his own advantage.

As a result, the U.S.-Iranian relationship shifted subtly but unmis-
takably, with Washington increasingly relying on Iran as its primary regional diplomatic partner, and the shah sensing that he had, if not the
upper hand, at least a powerful one. As Iran and its neighbors nationalized their energy resources, the associated price spikes only fueled his
ambitions to "establish Iran as a regionally preponderant and militarily
self-sufficient power."[10]

Toward this end, Mohammad Reza invested heavily in upgrading
Iran's military capabilities. "Arms dealers joked that the shah devoured
their manuals in much the same way as other men read Playboy."[11] He
was assertive across the region, occupying three strategically-located
Gulf islands, engaging in escalating skirmishes with Iraq, funding a
covert war in Iraqi Kurdistan in order to gain leverage over Iran's foremost adversary in Baghdad, and sending troops to help defeat a Marxist
insurgency in Oman.

The Saudis viewed the shah's ambitions in and around the Gulf with
considerable unease. But Riyadh was more focused on the Arab-Israeli
conflict, particularly after the 1967 war. The Saudis' top priority was an
end to the Israeli occupation of Jerusalem, and King Faisal was prepared
to use the oil weapon, reluctantly in 1967 and more seriously in 1973.

The oil embargo caused prices to quadruple, and the economic impact was far-reaching and prolonged—U.S. gross domestic product declined by 6 percent over the following two years and unemployment rates doubled. Tehran, however, opted out of the Arab oil boycott. The shah was impatient for petrodollars and he had quietly developed extensive economic and intelligence relations with Israel. Instead, he used the episode to gain market share and cement his role as Washington's key regional partner.

Despite some alignment in their strategic interests, the Saudi and Iranian monarchs never achieved a strong personal rapport. The Saudis resented the shah's arrogance and warned Washington that he would not last in power. For his part, the shah begrudged what he perceived as a double standard in Washington's approach to Tehran and Riyadh. "If you Americans are going to be so moral, you must apply a single standard to the whole world."[12]

The Revolution

Iran's revolution gathered momentum amidst dramatic developments in the American-brokered Arab-Israeli peace process. The 1978 Camp David Accords shattered Riyadh's attempt to sustain Arab unity and strained its relationship with Washington. The concurrent turmoil in Iran—a key bulwark against common adversaries such as the Soviet Union—along with a new round of civil war in Yemen compounded Saudi security dilemmas. "Power vacuums, especially in the world's most strategic area, are always dangerous," then–Crown Prince Fahd remarked to an American journalist in March 1979.[13] Convinced that Iran's upheaval was orchestrated by the pro-Soviet agitators, Fahd rebuked Washington for failing to avert the crisis.[14]

Fahd's admonition reflected more than simply the heightened external threat. The specter of a mass movement, backed by the clergy, ousting a pro-Western monarch struck too close for comfort, even if the Saudi leadership sought to dismiss the parallels. And Ayatollah Ruhollah Khomeini, the spiritual guide of the revolution and the successor state, openly challenged the religious legitimacy of Saudi rule.

Beginning in November 1979, Saudi fears were realized. Only weeks after militant Iranian students stormed the U.S. Embassy in Tehran, the Grand Mosque in Mecca, Islam's holiest site, was seized by armed Sunni extremists who denounced the royal family for corruption and its ties to Washington. The siege was forcibly ended with the help of French commandos and as many as 1,000 casualties. Even as the operation to retake the Grand Mosque was underway, Riyadh had another problem on its hands—simmering protests among Saudi Shia in the Eastern Province erupted into large-scale political demonstrations. Over several months, they launched violent protests and encouraged oilfield workers to strike. And then, on December 27, came another blow to the region's security, the Soviet invasion of Afghanistan, where the Saudis had been funding tribal opponents of the communist government.

Neither Iran's revolution nor its new Islamic regime directly instigated these events. Even among the Saudi Shia, Iran's example and messaging were powerful but not determinative. Most Shia in the kingdom did not follow Khomeini as *marja*, or source of spiritual emulation, and their grievances reflected long-standing frustration over religious restrictions, economic deprivation, and formalized discrimination in the workforce.[15] Still, the sympathetic uprisings among Shia communities across the Gulf region whet the universalist ambitions of Iran's Islamists, who aspired to topple the status quo in the broader Islamic world.

And for Riyadh and Washington, the succession of crises generated intense alarm about the stability and security of the region, ultimately strengthening their mutual interdependence. As Iran's upheaval collapsed its oil production, the Saudis stepped in to fill the gap. And they launched a massive effort to organize and fund a covert war against the Soviets in Afghanistan. Saudi clerics embraced that campaign as an obligatory holy war, or *jihad*, that drew thousands of Muslims from around the world, including a pious, well-connected Saudi named Osama bin Laden.

The Carter administration quickly appreciated that Saudi Arabia now stood as "the last remaining pro-Western bulwark in the Gulf," and embraced a more explicit commitment to Saudi security.[16] President Jimmy Carter used his January 1980 State of the Union address as a formal articulation of this commitment, in what became known as the Carter

Doctrine. In practice, the elevation of the Persian Gulf to a vital American interest and the U.S. pledge to defend Saudi Arabia translated into a two-pronged approach that has commanded bipartisan support for the past forty years, an open pipeline of advanced weapons sales to Riyadh, and an expansion of the U.S. military footprint in the Gulf.

Conclusion

The Iranian Revolution escalated and expanded the once-restrained rivalry between Riyadh and Tehran. The universalist aspirations that galvanized Iran's revolutionaries inspired a sustained investment in exporting the revolution through propaganda and proxy groups. Events at home and across the region helped persuade the Saudis that the most urgent threat to the kingdom emanated not from Egyptian-inspired leftists, but from religious radicalism. The royal family responded by doubling down on their underlying bargain with the Wahhabi clergy, pouring resources into religious institutions at home and abroad.

In the first decade after the Iranian Revolution, the animosity between Tehran and Riyadh fueled what was essentially a two-front proxy war, with the Saudis funding Saddam Hussein's war effort and Iran actively seeking to destabilize neighboring governments in the Gulf. The internationalization of the Iran-Iraq war brought the two countries considerably closer to direct military conflict and drew Washington into an undeclared but bloody naval and air war against Iran. The outcome of that conflict was disastrous for all sides.

Throughout the past forty years, Tehran and Riyadh have engaged in a violent competition across the region that has taken a significant toll on both countries. The costs beyond their borders are even steeper, including state failure and catastrophic humanitarian crisis. Iran has achieved the upper hand in this contest. Its proxies and allies are prevailing in Iraq, Syria, and Lebanon and have bogged down the Saudis and their allies in a quagmire in Yemen. Tehran is better equipped with the means for fighting the contest—more efficient and ruthless intelligence and security services. However, neither side can achieve a complete victory and neither risks falling to a proxy of the other.

While the Iranian-Saudi rivalry shows few signs of abating, the U.S.-Saudi security partnership that emerged from the crises of 1979 has come under new strain. The human and financial costs of America's "forever wars" in Iraq and Afghanistan have left little appetite among the U.S. electorate for military intervention in the Middle East. And even as the Trump administration has sought to bolster ties with Riyadh, new frictions over the Saudi-led war in Yemen and the 2018 murder of Saudi journalist Jamal Khashoggi are eroding support for the relationship among the public and across the political spectrum. Energy market dynamics, now that America ranks as the world's largest oil exporter, reinforce the challenges. Forty years after the Iranian Revolution intensified the bilateral bond, the future of the U.S.-Saudi relationship is now in doubt.

NOTES

1 Elaine Sciolino, "A nation challenged, ally's future: U.S. pondering Saudis' vulnerability," *New York Times*, November 4, 2001 (www.nytimes.com/2001/11/04/world/a-nation-challenged-ally-s-future-us-pondering-saudis-vulnerability.html)

2 Michael Crawford, *Ibn 'Abd al-Wahab* (London: Oneworld Publications, 2014).

3 See Natan J. DeLong-Bas, *Wahhabi Islam: From Revival and Reform to Global Jihad* (Oxford University Press, 2004), pp. 83–91.

4 Madawi Al-Rasheed, *A History of Saudi Arabia* (Cambridge University Press, 2002), p. 14.

5 Banafsheh Keynoush, *Saudi Arabia and Iran: Friends or Foes?* (Palgrave/Macmillan, 2016), pp. 31–32.

6 Cyrus Ghani, *Iran and the Rise of Reza Shah: From Qajar Collapse to Pahlavi Power* (I.B. Tauris, 2000), pp. 385–86; Shahrough Akhavi, *Religion and Politics in Contemporary Iran: Clergy-State Relations in the Pahlavi Period* (State University of New York Press: 1980), pp. 25–32.

7 Daryl Champion, *The Paradoxical Kingdom: Saudi Arabia and the Momentum of Reform* (Columbia University Press, 2003), p. 20.

8 Ibid., pp. 50–51.

9 Keynoush, op. cit., pp. 54–55.

10 Christian Emery, *US Foreign Policy and the Iranian Revolution: The Cold*

War Dynamics of Engagement and Strategic Alliance (Palgrave Macmillan: 2013), p. 23.

11 Ervand Abrahamian, *A History of Modern Iran* (Cambridge University Press, 2008), p. 124.

12 Andrew Scott Cooper, *The Fall of Heaven: The Pahlavis and the Final Days of Imperial Iran* (Henry Holt and Company, 2016), p. 236.

13 Arnaud De Borchgrave, "The Saudis Play Their Hand," *Newsweek* (March 26, 1979), p. 37.

14 Naif bin Hethlain, *Saudi Arabia and the US since 1962: Allies in Conflict* (SAQI, 2010), p. 122.

15 Toby Craig Jones, concludes that "although the example of Iran was indeed influential, the uprising in Saudi Arabia was not a derivative event . . . [it] reflected the convergence of external factors with specifically local grievances and objectives." Jones, *Desert Kingdom: How Oil and Water Forged Modern Saudi Arabia* (Harvard University Press, 2010), p. 186.

16 Jason H. Campbell, "The Ties that Bind: The Events of 1979 and the Escalation of U.S.-Saudi Security Relations during the Carter and Reagan Administrations," in Jeffrey R. Macris and Saul Kelly, eds., *Imperial Crossroads: The Great Powers and the Persian Gulf* (Naval Institute Press, 2012), p. 146.

20

Coexistence and Convergence in Turkish-Iranian Relations

KEMAL KIRIŞCI

The 1979 departure of Shah Mohammad Reza Pahlavi from Iran, followed by the return of Ayatollah Ruhollah Khomeini, provoked mixed feelings in Turkey. Initially, many in Turkey saw these developments as a reaction to the repression and human rights abuses perpetrated by the shah. However, once the theocratic nature of the regime became evident and Iran broke away from the Western alliance, concerns in secular Turkey emerged about Iran fomenting both Islamism and Kurdish nationalism.

In due course, Turkey learned to coexist with Iran's new regime, and during the subsequent forty years, relations between the two countries settled into a pattern of ups and downs from that of previous decades, if not centuries. The 1639 Qasr-i Shirin treaty between the Safavid and Ottoman Empires, which ended long rounds of territorial wars between them, left a legacy of coexistence and a disinclination on both sides toward escalation. After the Iranian Revolution, this tradition of mod-

168

eration evolved into pragmatism that enabled mutual tolerance between Turkey's and Iran's diametrically opposed regimes. Ironically, in recent years as Turkey's secular credentials and democracy have weakened, a degree of regime convergence around political Islam, albeit representative of two distinct branches of Islam, has followed.

The Course of Iranian-Turkish Relations Since 1979

The revolution occurred against a background of poor relations between Turkey and the shah's Iran. Turkey's policy of hosting Iranian dissidents, including Ayatollah Ruhollah Khomeini during his early exile, and the shah's active support for Kurdish separatism in Iraq in the early 1970s especially taxed the bilateral relationship. For this reason, Turkey initially did not mind the revolution, and its anti-American narrative was quite popular among the Turkish public. The left-leaning Turkish government led by Bülent Ecevit welcomed Iran's withdrawal from the Central Treaty Organization (CENTO) and sought to expand economic relations with Tehran. Ecevit sent his foreign affairs minister on an official visit in June 1979, and his reception by Khomeini seemed to signal goodwill.

However, the honeymoon soon ended. Turkey's change of government, compounded by the shock of the Iranian hostage crisis and the September 1980 military coup in Turkey, created a very different climate. The Turkish military saw Iran's increasingly theocratic regime as a threat to Turkish secularism and national security, while Tehran viewed Turkey as the "devil's servant" aspiring to undermine the revolution. Reciprocal threat perceptions and deep mistrust persisted during the 1990s and into the new millennium. For example, Iran constantly criticized Turkey for restricting women who wear hijab from accessing higher education and holding public office. In contrast, Turkey considered Tehran's enforcement of compulsory hijab as backward and unmodern. Close Israeli-Turkish cooperation, especially in the military realm, provoked Iranian anxieties, as did concerns about Turkish nationalism as a source of agitation among Iran's Azeri minority. In turn, Turkey accused Iran of supporting the secessionist Kurdistan Workers' Party (PKK) and even risked militarized confrontation by sending troops in hot pursuit of PKK militants and dispatching military aircraft to bomb their hideouts. Symbolic acts—such as the refusal of Iranian officials to visit the mausoleum of Mustafa Kemal Atatürk, the founder of the secular Turkish republic, or lower their embassy flag to half-mast on the anniversary of his death—caused deep resentment. Ankara also frequently accused Tehran of actively supporting radical Islamist groups in Turkey that were linked to the assassinations of prominent secular intellectuals.

In 1997, the Iranian ambassador's participation in an Islamist social event near Ankara triggered the military's "post-modern coup," forcing the dissolution of the then-government coalition, which included the Islamist political party, Refah (Welfare), led by Necmettin Erbakan. With the ascendance of Turkey's Islamist Justice and Development Party (AKP) in 2002, the ideological animosity between the two countries gradually diminished. Instead, rivalry over regional influences emerged as the salient fault line between Iran and Turkey. Their competition focused on post-Saddam Iraq, where Tehran succeeded in advancing Shia leaders who were deeply committed to consolidating authority over the Sunni minority, at the expense of politicians preferred by Turkey who were willing to pursue reconciliation between the two communities.

The Arab Spring further intensified the Turkish-Iranian rivalry. Initially, the upheaval seemed to be an advantage to Turkey, which enjoyed considerable influence across a changing Middle East. However, once the tide turned and advocates of reform began to retreat, Turkey's upper hand eroded and, particularly in Syria, the competition for influence shifted in favor of Iran. The Russian intervention in 2015 and the eventual defeat of the Syrian opposition consolidated Iran's influence in the country and over the regime in Damascus. The Syrian conflict established Iran and Turkey as unambiguously sectarian powers, each aspiring to defend their respective interests by arming, assisting, and advocating for the Shia and Sunni communities in the region.

Pragmatism

Despite these many frictions, a distinct strand of pragmatism runs through the Turkish-Iranian relationship, manifesting itself from a very early stage via trade and a preference for diplomacy over coercion in the form of sanctions or force. Two factors encouraged the expansion of bilateral trade after the Iranian Revolution: the September 1980 outbreak of the Iran-Iraq war, and Ankara's decision to shift toward an export-oriented development strategy. Turkish neutrality in the war facilitated a barter agreement that swapped Turkish oil imports for manufactured exports to Iran. This interdependence also deterred Iran from attacking Turkish trucks ferrying goods to Iraq and the pipeline carrying Iraqi oil to the Turkish port city of Ceyhan. Upon the war's end, trade between the two countries briefly fell but rebounded after a 1996 agreement to export Iranian natural gas to Turkey. Traditionally, Iran has been Turkey's largest source of crude oil, but this is changing with U.S. sanctions. (Until May 2019, Turkey benefited from U.S. waivers.) During the decade after 2001, bilateral trade expanded from $1.2 billion to $16 billion. Turkey ran a significant trade deficit that was offset by an ever-growing number of Iranian tourists. Lifting visa restrictions on Iranian nationals increased those numbers from less than 30,000 in 2001 to almost 1.9 million a decade later and then to 2.5 million by 2017.

Turkey's keen interest in expanding exports to and investments in Iran explains its long-standing opposition to U.S. sanctions on Iran. Turkey resisted joining early U.S. sanctions introduced after the hostage crisis and maintained this policy even at times when bilateral relations with Iran were at their worst, especially in the 1990s. Turkey played a crucial role in helping Iran circumvent sanctions during the Obama administration, through complicated gold transactions that culminated in the U.S. prosecution and sentencing of a Turkish banker and pending U.S. fines on a Turkish bank. The 2015 Iran nuclear deal came as a relief, boosting Turkish ambitions to expand business with Iran before the Trump administration withdrew from the agreement and reintroduced sanctions against Iran in 2018.

Throughout most of the post-revolutionary period, Turkish-Iranian relations have been marked by an underlying pragmatism that encouraged both sides to keep the channels of diplomacy and dialogue open even at times of tension. The most significant irritant, Iran's relationship with the PKK, was eventually resolved in 2008 when both sides agreed to cooperate against the PKK and its Iranian branch, the Kurdistan Free Life Party (PJAK). More recently, Ankara and Tehran have worked together to blunt the bid for independence by leaders of Iraqi Kurdistan. Similarly, once Turkey and its allied opposition groups began to lose ground in Syria, Iran and Turkey together with Russia began to cooperate to manage the retreat of these groups into the Idlib province of Syria and the institution of a cease-fire there. Against all odds, the cease-fire has held, and another major migration crisis into Turkey has been averted, even if the situation remains tense and the broader conflict remains far from resolved. Pragmatism was also evident in Turkey's 2010 inconclusive diplomatic effort with Brazil to resolve the impasse between Washington and Tehran over the latter's nuclear program. In this context, Turkey's decision in 2011 to accept the deployment of the NATO missile shield radar system provoked Iranian fury and threats of attack. The resulting crisis was diffused by Turkish diplomatic efforts to assuage Iranian concerns.

Convergence

Pragmatism helped both sides learn to live with two diametrically opposed regimes and even experience a degree of convergence in recent years. The process was a slow one, but by 2002 the staunchly secular Turkish president, Ahmet Sezer, not only visited Iran, including its Azeri provinces, but even delivered a lecture on Atatürk and his ideology—absolute anathema to the principles of the Iranian Revolution. This growing affinity between the two regimes gathered speed after AKP's arrival to power and was starkly illustrated in 2009 when then-president Abdullah Gül was among the first world leaders to congratulate Iranian President Mahmoud Ahmadinejad on his reelection amidst massive street protests over ballot irregularities. In contrast to a decade earlier, Ankara remained quiet about the public protests over these irregularities and the repression of the protesters. The convergence also extends to attitudes toward Israel and Palestinians. Ankara remained silent in the face of Ahmadinejad's calls for the destruction of Israel and his denials of the Holocaust. More recently, Turkey has held a much more lukewarm attitude toward the Palestinian Authority compared with the enthusiastic support extended to Hamas in Gaza, a position reminiscent of that held by Iran. This is in stark contrast to when Mahmoud Abbas and Shimon Peres were both hosted in Ankara in 2007, and then-prime minister Recep Tayyip Erdoğan pursued mediation efforts between Israel and Syria. In his current role as Turkish president, and previously as prime minister, Erdoğan has visited Iran on numerous occasions. His Islamist roots and discomfort toward secularism have made him much less inhibited by the theocratic nature of the Iranian regime, and his increasingly authoritarian approach to governance and anti-Western foreign policy has strengthened the budding partnership.

Conclusion

While the Iranian Revolution injected considerable turbulence into Iranian-Turkish relations, the two states managed to develop a relationship marked by pragmatism, consistent with their long historical legacy. Eventually a certain degree of convergence occurred in each side's world views and forms of governance. However, the legacy of secularism, even in its weakened form, and Turkey's long-standing Western vocation will constrain the degree of regime convergence. Additionally, sectarian differences between the two countries are likely to constitute an additional constraint. Lastly, independently of whatever convergence may have taken place, as two large neighbors in a particularly unstable neighborhood marked by unresolved conflicts, geopolitical rivalry is likely to persist. However, this is unlikely to undermine the realism of both sides, best manifested in the area of trade and economic cooperation.

21

Israel's Reverse Periphery Doctrine

NATAN SACHS

Iranian-Israeli hostility is actually quite odd. Tehran is well over a thousand miles from Jerusalem. The two countries do not border each other. They have no major bilateral claims toward one another. Whereas large Arab neighbors of Iran, like Iraq or Saudi Arabia, might be considered its natural competitors, Israel cannot.

Even fans of the "ancient hatreds" school of Middle East conflict would come up short. What historical memory there is of Persian-Judaic interactions is largely positive in Jewish eyes: Streets in Israel are named for Cyrus the Great, who allowed the Jews to return to Judea from their Babylonian exile in 538 BC. From the Iranian perspective, Judea never rose to compete with Persia for regional prominence, as did Greek or later Arab forces.

All else being equal, then, one might have expected cool, uncomfortable relations—or more likely, non-relations—between Israel and Iran, much like other large Muslim-majority countries, not the foreign policy-defining struggle of present. Indeed, as is often noted, this hostility between the two modern states has not always existed. It can be traced directly to one period, forty years ago: the Iranian Revolution and the birth of the Islamic Republic.

Friends Become Foes

From its inception in 1948, Israel dealt with an acute security challenge: It faced a massive, largely hostile region unified by a common religion and a common antipathy toward Israel. All four of its immediate neighbor states were Arab, as were the Palestinian Arabs, and they were backed by dozens of Arab and Muslim-majority states beyond them. Israel's natural posture was therefore to try and find fissures among its potential foes. Early in the state's existence, it did so through the "periphery doctrine," by which David Ben-Gurion, Israel's first prime minister, attempted to forge an alliance with non-Arab (yet mostly Muslim) countries in the Middle East as a counterbalance to the Arab states.[1] Chief among these non-Arab partners were Turkey and pre-revolutionary Iran, both of which then shared a common orientation toward the West and their own reasons to feel isolated in the Middle East.

Israeli-Iranian cooperation included official relations—Israel had two successive ambassadors to Tehran—and robust trade in oil, a prime concern for Israel, then under a crippling Arab boycott. The basic logic was simple: My enemy's enemy can be my friend, and Iran and Israel shared common Arab foes.

The revolution upended these relations dramatically. Not only were ties cut off, but Israel was relegated by Ayatollah Ruhollah Khomeini to the status of "Little Satan" (the "Great Satan" being the United States). For the new Iranian regime, Israel became a central focus of ideological, religion-infused vitriol. The Islamic Republic became a significant backer of any (mostly Arab) "resistance" to Israel. Iran seemingly became more Palestinian than the Palestinians. It opposed all peace negotiations between Arabs and Israelis, including the Palestine Liberation Organization's (PLO's) Oslo Accords of 1993.

A street in Tehran was named for the assassin of Egyptian President Anwar Sadat, the first Arab leader to sign a peace treaty with Israel (the

street was renamed "intifada" in 2004 in an effort to improve relations
with Egypt).[2] Iran fostered the creation of the Lebanese Hezbollah, Israel's most menacing guerilla adversary of recent years. Tehran backed
Sunni Islamist Palestinian groups, in particular the Palestinian Islamic
Jihad (PIJ) and, at times, Hamas. In Iran's fight against Israel, a seemingly endless tit-for-tat, even non-Israeli Jews were not safe. Most notably,
Argentinean prosecutors and several intelligence agencies have accused
Iran of direct involvement in the murder of eighty-five people in a suicide
bombing of the Jewish Community Center in Buenos Aires in 1994.[3]

The Threat Intensifies

Israel's approach to the Islamic Republic has been uneven. At first, despite hostile Iranian rhetoric, Israel did not see Iran as an implacable
enemy. The Islamic Republic spent much of its first decade engaged in
a brutal war with another of Israel's sworn enemies, Saddam Hussein's
Iraq. ("I wish both sides success" was the rather gruesome way Israeli
Prime Minister Menachem Begin put it.) Israel was a key player in the
Iran-Contra affair, and the possibility that some in the Iranian regime
might change its attitude toward Israel remained an option. By the 1990s,
however, as Hezbollah grew in strength and the first signs of an Iranian
nuclear program emerged, Israeli concerns heightened, leading to increasingly active diplomatic efforts and covert operations against the
Iranian programs.

While ideological considerations, anger over Israel's ties to the shah,
sympathy toward the Palestinians, and a generalized and foundational
antipathy toward the West were all important elements of the about-face,
Iran also found obvious instrumental advantages to this position. Israel
is a useful enemy for the Islamic Republic—not merely a diversion from
domestic woes, as it has been to many Middle Eastern regimes, but also
part of an Iranian attempt to play in Middle Eastern affairs. For a large,
Muslim-majority, non-Arab state committed to exporting its revolution
to Arab countries, it is useful that the main fault lines in regional affairs not be national—Arab and Persian—but rather religious: Muslim
and non-Muslim. For the major Shia power in a largely Sunni-majority

region, it is again important to draw the lines not among and between streams of Islam, as some Sunnis do, but between Muslims and others, and there is no better "other" in the Middle East than Israel.

By carrying the mantle of unwavering resistance to Israel (and the United States), Iran can, in theory, appeal to solidarity with most Arabs. Moreover, supporting the Palestinians allows Iran to expose hypocrisy and duplicity in the Arab states' positions whenever their commitment to the cause is tempered by pragmatic interests.

The result is that today, no country embodies a threat to Israelis as much as the Islamic Republic does. Iran's nuclear program appears to many Israelis to be an existential threat.[4] The nuclear question and Iran's extensive proxy operations in the Arab world have shaped Israel's foreign policy in recent years and driven much of its actions on the global stage. Iran has become a near-singular focus of Israeli leaders and planners, who identify Iran's hand in nearly every direction, often with cause.

Is Iran a useful enemy to Israeli leaders as Israel is to Iranian ones? Like all politicians, Israeli leaders do appeal at times to foreign threats to divert attention from domestic affairs, and Iran has easily filled that need. Yet when it comes to Iran, unlike Palestinian affairs, the spectrum of opinions in Israel is quite narrow—there are very few Israelis, from across the political map, who do not see the Islamic Republic's activity as a grave threat, whether they adopt the existential-threat rhetoric or not.[5] There are very few Iran doves in Israel, even if Israelis debate the means for confronting the threat.

New Alliances, Entrenched Hostilities

As a result of the major shift in Israeli-Iranian relations, Israel today has a reverse periphery doctrine. Iran has striven to forge an alignment of sorts with major Arab countries and has had remarkable success. This includes not only Egypt and Jordan, who have official peace with Israel, but even cooperation with Persian Gulf countries like Saudi Arabia, the United Arab Emirates, and Oman.[6] Limited in scope and entailing no embassies, these relations are far less developed or overt than the relations Israel had with the shah's Iran. Yet, the logic is the same as it was in the 1950s, but in reverse: My enemy's enemy can be my friend, and these Arab states and Israel share a common overriding foe in Iran. (They also share a common, though far less severe, hostility toward Recep Tayyip Erdoğan's Turkey, Israel's other main "peripheral" partner of old.)

The reverse periphery doctrine has been a boon to Israel in important ways. It now finds itself in one camp with major Arab players, limiting the short-term damage of the continued Israeli-Palestinian conflict (though not alleviating, and perhaps worsening, its long-term consequences) and allowing Israel to engage with world powers from a position of regional strength.

The benefits come with a very heavy price, however. The Iranians have proven themselves to be formidable foes. Israeli planners often express grudging respect for their Iranian enemies—a respect they, frankly, do not always exhibit toward their Arab adversaries, with the possible exception of Iranian-backed Hezbollah. The Iranian Quds Force and its commander, Qassem Soleimani, have exhibited tenacious opportunism, going after any opening they can find to advance and disengaging temporarily when they cannot. Israeli successes against Iranian forces in Syria have come with the knowledge that Iran will strike back.[7] The Iranians have also shown an ability to create long-term threats to Israel and the patience to see them through, as with the creation, cultivation, and armament of Hezbollah. Iran as an enemy may help unite part of the Middle East, but it is not necessarily the enemy you want.

Moreover, the Israeli-Palestinian conflict has gradually transformed from a national conflict to a religious one, in some part due to Iranian proxy activity. Iran's casting of the struggle in Islamic terms instead of Arab terms is only one factor in this transformation, and organizations supported by Iran had a dramatic impact on the prospects of Israeli-Palestinian peace. Hamas and PIJ's efforts to derail the Oslo process in the 1990s were a key factor in its failure. The rise of Hamas more generally—largely independent of Iran, but with its intermittent support—eventually led to the bifurcation of the Palestinian territories between the West Bank and the Gaza Strip. For decades, Israel feared Arab nationalism—Gamal Abdel Nasser, Saddam Hussein, the PLO— but like many others, it underappreciated the menace of religiously inspired conflict with either Iran or with Sunni Islamist parties. Religious conflict in any form often proves far more impervious to pragmatic solutions, and therefore more dangerous, than national conflict.

The last forty years have produced deep hostilities between Israel and Iran. That these hostilities serve Iranian interests does not make them any less severe or real, as the damage wrought by hostilities in Lebanon, Israel, Gaza, and elsewhere makes clear. Still, it is instructive to view the ways by which structural and instrumental considerations can shape conflict. Past is not necessarily prologue, but the warm relations Israel enjoyed with Iran under the shah indicate that the present levels of hostility are not inevitable. Forty years ago, a domestic revolution in Iran transformed the Middle East as far as the Mediterranean. Domestic change in Iran could transform it again.

NOTES

1 Yossi Alpher, *Periphery: Israel's Search for Middle East Allies* (Lanham, MD: Rowman & Littlefield, 2015).

2 Associated Press, "Ties with Egypt to Be Restored, Iran Says," *Los Angeles Times*, January 7, 2004 (www.latimes.com/archives/la-xpm-2004-jan-07-fg-ties7 -story.html).

3 Dexter Filkins, "Death of a Prosecutor," *The New Yorker*, July 13, 2015 (www.newyorker.com/magazine/2015/07/20/death-of-a-prosecutor).

4 Peter Hirschberg, "Netanyahu: It's 1938 and Iran Is Germany; Ahmadinejad Is Preparing Another Holocaust," *Haaretz*, November 14, 2006 (www.haaretz. com/1.4931862).

5 Natan Sachs, "Israel and Iran's Role in the Middle East," testimony before the Committee on Foreign Affairs, U.S. House of Representatives, July 16, 2004 (www.brookings.edu/testimonies/israel-and-irans-role-in-the-middle-east/).

6 Raphael Ahren, "PM Justifies Tacit Support for Saudi Arabia Despite 'Horrific' Khashoggi Murder," *Times of Israel*, December 13, 2018 (www.times ofisrael.com/pm-justifies-tacit-support-for-saudi-arabia-despite-horrific-khashoggi-murder/); "In First, 'Hatikva' Anthem Played at UAE Contest as Israeli Judoka Wins Gold," *Times of Israel*, October 28, 2018 (www.timesofisrael. com/in-first-hatikva-anthem-played-at-uae-contest-after-israeli-judoka-wins-gold/); "Israel's Prime Minister Visits Oman, an Arab Monarchy—and Is Welcomed," *The Economist*, November 3, 2018 (www.economist.com/middle-

east-and-africa/2018/11/03/israels-prime-minister-visits-oman-an-arab-mon
archy-and-is-welcomed).

7 Dror Michman and Yael Mizrahi-Arnaud, "Will Iran Attack Israel Over
the Syrian Conflict? It's Only a Matter of Time," Brookings *Order from Chaos*,
April 18, 2018 (www.brookings.edu/blog/order-from-chaos/2018/04/18/will-
iran-attack-israel-over-the-syrian-conflict-its-only-a-matter-of-time/).

22

Emboldened and Then Constrained
Repercussions of Iran's Revolution for Sunni Islamists

SHADI HAMID *and* **SHARAN GREWAL**

The Iranian Revolution was the first Islamist revolution of the modern era, so it is no surprise that it would still loom large forty years later—not just for Iran or for Shia Muslims, but for Sunni Islamists as well. The revolution's legacy on Sunni Islamists has been mixed. At first, the Islamic Revolution emboldened Sunni Islamist groups, galvanizing their followers into thinking that revolution could be possible elsewhere. But Sunni Islamists soon soured on the Iranian experience due to ideological disagreements, sectarian animus, and strategic considerations.

In hundreds of interviews over the years with members and officials of Muslim Brotherhood branches and affiliates across the region, we have never once heard Iran mentioned as a model to be emulated. Despite this, the legacy of the Iranian Revolution continues to color how the West views mainstream Islamist groups like the Brotherhood. For these groups, the revolution has become a constraint and a burden. This was not always the case. How and why did it change?

Islamists Emboldened

However radical Ayatollah Ruhollah Khomeini and other Shia clerics were, they sought to avoid alienating Sunnis. More importantly, being Islamists themselves, they saw movements like the Muslim Brotherhood as potential allies to be courted. The Sunni-Shia divide mattered, but sectarian frictions were not as acute as they are today. The revolution itself was part of a broader cross-sectarian religious revival throughout the region. Shared ideology around the centrality of Islam's role in politics took precedence over sect. In other words, Sunni Islamists had more in common with Shia Islamists than they did with Sunni secularists. When Khomeini declared that "Islam was political or nothing else," he was saying something that Sunni Islamists had themselves long understood.

Khomeini's political theology, which diverged from the views of the traditional Shia religious establishment, argued that direct clerical engagement in politics did not require waiting until the return of the Imam. None other than Sayyid Qutb—in many ways the Egyptian Muslim Brotherhood's last true revolutionary—had developed something of a following in Iran, with much of his work being translated and disseminated in Farsi. As Yusuf Ünal notes, "Qutb was an influential figure among Iranian revolutionaries," with his ideas playing "an instrumental role in shaping the discourse of Islamism in pre-revolutionary Iran."[1]

Ironically, it was Rached Ghannouchi of Tunisia's Ennahda Party, perhaps the most "progressive" of today's Islamist leaders, who was initially most sympathetic to the aims of the Iranian Revolution. During his time as a student in Paris, he participated in the Islamic students' association, which was headed by an Iranian student who introduced him to the work of Mehdi Bazargan, an opposition leader who served as Iran's first post-revolutionary prime minister in February 1979. In his biography of Ghannouchi, Azzam Tamimi writes that "for Ghannouchi, the arrangement reflected a high degree of tolerance, for no one objected to the Shiism of the Iranian student or considered it an impediment to his election as head of a society, the rest of whose members were all Sunnis."[2]

Ghannouchi recalled in 1995:

As we readied to accept the notion that conflicts other than the ideological existed along the political and social fronts, the Iranian Revolution came to give us a new set of Islamic discourses. It enabled us to Islamize some leftist social concepts and to accommodate the social conflict within an Islamic context.[3]

Disillusionment

The flirtation did not last long, with Sunni Islamists, almost across the board, souring on the Iranian experiment.[4] The leftism that Ghannouchi points to quickly became obscured by the Islamic Republic's intensifying authoritarianism and intolerance of any opposition. By 1984, according to Tamimi, Ghannouchi was criticizing the ayatollahs "for portraying themselves as if they were the possessors of absolute truth, as if they alone understood the message of Islam, and as if their revolution was the only legitimate method of change."[5]

During the 1980s, an important shift was taking place among mainstream Islamist movements, as Shadi Hamid discusses in *Temptations of Power*.[6] With a religious revival spreading across the region, they decided to take advantage of their growing popularity by entering parliamentary politics (to the extent that regimes allowed them). The alliance the Egyptian Muslim Brotherhood formed with the secular Wafd Party won fifty-eight seats in the 1984 parliamentary elections, up until then the best-ever result for the Egyptian opposition. It helped that the 1984 and 1987 elections were the most competitive Egypt had seen up until then (although far from free and fair). Jordan's "transition" seemed to hold even more promise. In 1984, the Jordanian Muslim Brotherhood contested elections on the university, municipal, and national levels, exceeding expectations in each. The "Islamic trend" swept the elections for the University of Jordan's student union, while on the national level, for the first time since 1967, reasonably free by-elections were held for eight vacated parliamentary seats, with the Brotherhood winning two of them by comfortable margins.

With Sunni Islamist movements calling for gradual democratization through elections, Iran's authoritarianism and its model of revolution-

ary change was becoming inconvenient. Khomeini's seizure of power
through regime overthrow was quite different from trying to win a few
parliamentary seats here and there. From a public relations standpoint,
hailing Iran as an inspiration would have also amplified already substantial fears that the Brotherhood's true aim was total revolution rather than
gradual reform.

Geopolitical developments would also play a role in entrenching a gap
between Sunni and Shia Islamists. Immediately after the Islamic Revolution, relations between the Iranian and Syrian regimes remained tense
for several years. However, when revolutionary Iran solidified its alliance
with a Syrian regime that was waging war against Islamists at home,
Muslim Brotherhood affiliates across the region increasingly looked at
Iran with suspicion. The Syrian Muslim Brotherhood, bearing most of
the brunt of Hafez al-Assad's repression, shifted its criticism of the Assad
regime in a more explicitly anti-Shia direction. (Previously, Sunni Islamists did not see the Assad family's Alawi sect as Shia per se, and even
most Twelver Shia clerics did not consider Alawis to be true Shia.)

The distance with Iran would only grow as Sunni Islamists learned
a strategic lesson from the 1990s and 2000s: Winning elections was not
enough to assume power. Just as important for Sunni Islamists was reas-
suring the West that they would not follow the Iranian model or pursue
"one man, one vote, one time."[7] In 1992, when the Islamic Salvation Front
(FIS) was on the verge of winning parliamentary elections in Algeria,
the military—supported by the United States—canceled the election
and dissolved the party, sparking a decade-long civil war.[8] In 2006, after
Hamas swept Gaza's parliamentary elections, the United States and its
Western allies refused to recognize Hamas's victory and instead imposed
sanctions on Gaza. It was yet another reminder of what an important
determinant the United States was in whether Islamists would actually
be allowed to take office.

To neutralize American opposition to their electoral participation,
Islamists elsewhere in the region put renewed emphasis on persuading
Western audiences that they did not want an Iranian-style revolution. As
Brotherhood member of parliament Magdy Ashour remarked in 2007:
"We would like to change the idea people have of us in the West. . . .

We do not want a country like Iran, which thinks that it is ruling with a divine mandate."[9] Even during the throes of the 2011 Egyptian uprising, for instance, prominent Muslim Brotherhood leaders took the time to pen multiple op-eds in major Western newspapers to this effect. The then-relatively unknown Brotherhood functionary Mohammed Morsi, who would later become Egypt's president, wrote that "this is Egypt's revolution, not ours," while his colleagues Essam al-Erian and Abdel Moneim Abou al-Fotouh insisted that the Brotherhood wanted democracy and gradual reform, not an Islamic revolution.[10][11][12] Similarly, when Ghannouchi returned from exile in March 2011, Ennahda reportedly "instructed its supporters to not come to the airport to meet him upon his return for fear of creating images reminiscent of Khomeini's return to Iran."[13]

Tensions between Sunni Islamists and the Islamic Republic intensified as Iran and its Lebanese proxy, Hezbollah, backed Bashar al-Assad during Syria's civil war. Brotherhood leader Gamal Heshmat condemned "Iran's expansionist project in the region," while al-Erian reportedly threatened that the Arab Spring could come to Iran.[14][15] In June 2013, the Brotherhood-linked preacher Yusuf al-Qaradawi condemned Iran and Hezbollah—in English, the "party of God"—by calling the latter the "party of the devil."[16]

Still Constrained

Despite this criticism of Iran, Sunni Islamist movements remain tainted and constrained by its legacy. Top U.S. policymakers continue to paint all Islamists, Sunni and Shia, with one broad brush. "They are all swimming in the same sea," claimed former secretary of defense James Mattis.[17] Dennis Ross advised the United States "not [to] reach out to Islamists," a label under which he lumped ISIS, the Muslim Brotherhood, Ennahda, and Iran. "What the Islamists all have in common is that they subordinate national identities to an Islamic identity. . . . Their creed is not compatible with pluralism and democracy."[18]

It has been forty years since the Iranian Revolution began, and over the course of this period, attitudes toward the Iranian experiment with

Islamic governance have both run the gamut and run their course. Sunni Islamists have been souring on the Iranian Revolution for different reasons and in different ways. But despite their criticism of Iran, Islamist groups are still widely associated with the Islamic Revolution and accused of harboring secret intentions of following Iran's path. Four decades after Iran's revolution, Islamists are still constrained by a legacy they cannot quite seem to shake.

NOTES

1 Yusuf Ünal, "Sayyid Quṭb in Iran: Translating the Islamist Ideologue in the Islamic Republic," *Journal of Islamic and Muslim Studies*, vol. 1, no. 2, November 2016, pp. 35–60.

2 Azzam S. Tamimi, *Rachid Ghannouchi: A Democrat Within Islamism* (Oxford University Press, 2001).

3 Ibid.

4 Toby Matthiesen, "The Iranian Revolution and Sunni Political Islam," Project on Middle East Political Science, December 21, 2017 (https://pomeps.org/2017/12/21/the-iranian-revolution-and-sunni-political-islam/).

5 Tamimi, op. cit.

6 Shadi Hamid, *Temptations of Power: Islamists and Illiberal Democracy in a New Middle East* (Oxford University Press, 2014).

7 Edward P. Djerejian, "The U.S. and the Middle East in a Changing World," U.S. Department of State Dispatch, vol. 3, no. 23, June 8, 1992, pp. 444–47.

8 K. A. Beyoghlow, "America and Political Islam: Clash of Cultures or Clash of Interests by Fawaz A. Gerges. Cambridge University Press, 1999." *American Political Science Review* vol. 95, no. 1 (2001), pp. 255–56, https://www.cambridge.org/core/journals/american-political-science-review/article/america-and-political-islam-clash-of-cultures-or-clash-of-interests-by-fawaz-a-gerges-new-york-cambridge-university-press-1999-282p-5995-cloth-1895-paper/91E9702DAEC44D571451465DC9D9EF01.

9 James Traub, "Islamic Democrats?" *New York Times,* April 29, 2007 (www.nytimes.com/2007/04/29/magazine/29Brotherhood.t.html).

10 Mohammad Mursi, "This Is Egypt's Revolution, Not Ours," *The Guardian*, February 8, 2011 (www.theguardian.com/commentisfree/2011/feb/08/egypt-revolution-muslim-brotherhood-democracy).

11 Essam el-Errian, "What the Muslim Brothers Want," *NYT,* February 9, 2011 (www.nytimes.com/2011/02/10/opinion/10erian.html?_r=1).

12 Abdel Moneim Abou al-Fotouh, "Democracy Supporters Should Not Fear the Muslim Brotherhood," *Washington Post*, February 10, 2011 (www.washingtonpost.com/wp-dyn/content/article/2011/02/09/AR2011020906334.html?noredirect=on).

13 Marc Lynch, "Tunisia's New al-Nahda," *Foreign Policy,* June 29, 2011 (https://foreignpolicy.com/2011/06/29/tunisias-new-al-nahda/).

14 Zvi Bar'el, "Muslim Brotherhood Lawmaker: Arab Spring Headed to Iran," *Haaretz,* February 28, 2012 (www.haaretz.com/1.5191774).

15 Ikhwanweb: The Muslim Brotherhood's Official English website, "Gamal Heshmat: Muslim Brotherhood Against Iran Expansionism," May 5, 2015 (www.ikhwanweb.com/article.php?id=32119).

16 Reuters, "Leading Sunni Muslim Cleric Calls for 'Jihad' in Syria," June 1, 2013 (www.reuters.com/article/us-syria-crisis-qaradawi-idUSBRE9500CQ20130601).

17 "Mattis: Political Islam Is Not in America's Best Interest," Counter Jihad Video, March 2, 2017 (www.youtube.com/watch?v=7GkXJ_lb2z8).

18 Dennis B. Ross, "Islamists Are Not Our Friends," *New York Times,* September 11, 2014 (www.nytimes.com/2014/09/12/opinion/islamists-are-not-our-friends.html).

23

In Pakistan, Another Embassy Under Siege

MADIHA AFZAL

On November 21, 1979, a few hundred student protesters from the Quaid-i-Azam University in Islamabad stormed the U.S. embassy in that city, setting it on fire. They took one embassy employee hostage, and their aerial fire killed a 20-year-old Marine. About 140 people assembled in the embassy's vault for five hours while they waited for the Pakistani Army to disperse the rioters. It later emerged that the students were part of the Jamaat-e-Islami Islamist party, which had been emboldened under Pakistan's military dictator General Muhammad Zia-ul-Haq, who took power in a coup in 1977.

This incident is described in the first chapter of Steve Coll's Pulitzer prize-winning book *Ghost Wars*, but it has otherwise largely fallen out of the collective consciousness of even those who closely follow the U.S.-Pakistan relationship, dwarfed by the other events that took place that year in the region: the Iranian Revolution, the Iranian hostage crisis, the Soviet invasion of Afghanistan.[1] But the incident had direct links with the Iranian Revolution and the hostage crisis, and was also an indicator of the rising influence of the Jamaat in Pakistan and of Zia-ul-Haq's coming Islamization.

Brothers in Arms

The siege on the U.S. embassy in Islamabad came a day after an attack by Islamist militants on the Grand Mosque in Mecca. Iran's new supreme leader, Ayatollah Ruhollah Khomeini, publicly blamed America and Israel for the attack. Pakistani newspapers carried that accusation as news. Anti-American sentiment in Pakistan was running particularly high because the Carter administration had cut off aid earlier that year over Pakistan's construction of a uranium enrichment facility. Cue the Iranian Revolution and then the hostage crisis, and Jamaat-affiliated students, always anti-American, were particularly emboldened. The Mecca mosque attack was the last straw.

In the end, the Pakistani Army dispersed the rioters. The attack cost $20 million in damages; the protesters returned the hostage unharmed. Two of the attackers were killed in firing from the Pakistani side. That night, Zia-ul-Haq told the country that no Americans or Israelis were involved in the Mecca attack. He also gently scolded the attackers in Islamabad, saying that while he understood "the anger and grief over this incident were quite natural," this was not the way to react.

Khomeini praised the rioting in Islamabad. He declared it was a "great joy for us to learn of the uprising in Pakistan against the U.S.A. It is good news for our oppressed nation. Borders should not separate hearts."

Zia-ul-Haq pacified the U.S. government, expressing great regret over the loss of American life. The Soviet invasion of Afghanistan the following month, and Zia-ul-Haq's signing on as a party with America and Saudi Arabia to train *mujahideen* for the war meant the beginning of a decade-long alliance between America and Pakistan; ironically, some of the Jamaat's madrassas helped train the *mujahideen*, and some of those fighters were Jamaat members.

An Emboldened Islamization

From 1977 to 1989, Zia-ul-Haq engaged in a multifaceted Islamization of Pakistan and used the Jamaat-e-Islami to help him, especially in the early years. Though his reasons for this Islamization were political—he relied on Islam for legitimacy, as did many of Pakistan's leaders—he was no doubt encouraged by the Islamic Revolution in Iran. And though Pakistan did not become a theocracy like Iran—there was no centrally imposed, sectarian version of religion—in that decade Zia-ul-Haq successfully "*sharia*-tized" aspects of Pakistan's laws, emboldened its Islamist parties, and Islamized its curricula. His changes have proven all but impossible to reverse.

In 1979, Zia-ul-Haq enforced *Hudood* laws—with *sharia*-like legislation—that in particular served as a blow to the status of women. The laws criminalized adultery and introduced draconian punishments such as stoning to death for adultery and chopping off hands for theft. That same year, he created "*shariat* benches" in the provincial high courts to rule on the repugnancy of Pakistan's laws to the Quran and Sunnah (the body of Islamic practice based on the Prophet Muhammad's teachings). In 1980, Zia-ul-Haq also established the Federal Shariat Court, which could issue rulings that were mandatory.

In 1981, Zia-ul-Haq's University Grants Commission issued the following guidance to Pakistan Studies textbook authors: "To guide students towards the ultimate goal of Pakistan—the creation of a completely Islamized State." The first chapter of these social studies textbooks was now titled the "Ideology of Pakistan," which the textbooks said was Islam. It was the Jamaat that coined the term "ideology of Pakistan."

In 1984, Zia-ul-Haq engaged in a referendum to extend his rule. He framed it a referendum on Islam, asking Pakistanis:

Do you endorse the process initiated by General Muhammad Zia-ul-Haq, the President of Pakistan, for bringing the laws of Pakistan in conformity with the injunctions of Islam as laid down in the Holy Quran and Sunnah of the Holy Prophet (PBUH) and for the preservation of the Islamic ideology of Pakistan, for the continuation and consolidation of that process, and for the smooth and orderly transfer of power to the elected representatives of the people?

His government claimed that 98.5 percent of those who voted said yes.

And in 1986, Zia-ul-Haq amended Pakistan's blasphemy laws to make offenses against the Prophet Muhammad punishable by death, setting in motion decades of violence over the issue. More than a thousand Pakistanis have been accused of blasphemy since the mid-1980s, and at least a few dozen killed in vigilante killings.

Zia-ul-Haq's Islamization and the Iranian Revolution also helped stoke Sunni-Shia sectarian tensions in Pakistan in the 1980s. Zia-ul-Haq's *shariat* benches were staffed with Sunni judges who favored Sunni legal interpretations; the madrassas that mushroomed in the 1980s, with Saudi aid, were Sunni. Meanwhile the man Zia-ul-Haq had deposed, Prime Minister Zulfiqar Ali Bhutto, was Shia. In 1979, Zia-ul-Haq had him hanged. All this stung Pakistan's 20 percent Shia minority; they were also emboldened by the revolution in Iran. The stage was set for Sunni-Shia conflict.

Ultimately, it was the most immediate and visible effect of the Iranian Revolution in Pakistan, the November 1979 embassy siege in Islamabad, that had the shortest-term impact on Pakistan and on U.S.-Pakistan relations. It was Iran's more subtle effect on Zia-ul-Haq, on the Jamaat-e-Islami, and on Sunni-Shia sectarian tensions that transformed its eastern neighbor, and defines it still.

NOTES

1 Steve Coll, *Ghost Wars: The Secret History of the CIA, Afghanistan, and Bin Laden, from the Soviet Invasion to September 10, 2001* (New York: Penguin Books, 2004).

24

Bad Judgment and a Chain of Blunders
Soviet Responses to the Iranian Revolution

PAVEL BAEV

The Soviet leadership was surprised by the Iranian Revolution to an even greater degree than the Carter administration in the United States, even if the interests of the Soviet Union were less directly affected. There was no shortage of information, but the problem was that the spectacular collapse of the shah's state contradicted the three main Soviet perspectives on developments within Iran. The first one portrayed Mohammad Reza Pahlavi's regime as the main regional ally of the United States and assessed Iran's military capabilities as superior to any external and domestic challenges. The second perspective focused on the leftist opposition—primarily the Tudeh (or "masses") Party—and exaggerated the strength of shah's intelligence service, SAVAK. The third perspective depicted the Islamic movement as archaic and dismissed Ayatollah Ruhollah Khomeini as a marginal figure. None of these readings of the Iranian Revolution produced a useful interpretation of the events, and the misinformed recommendations resulted in a chain of blunders that contributed to the collapse of the Soviet Union just twelve years after the Iranian metamorphosis.[1]

The misconceptions were developed by three different bureaucracies: the first by the military intelligence (GRU) and further by the influential General Staff; the second by the even more influential KGB;[2] and the third by the international department of the Central Committee of the Communist Party.[3] The interplay between these institutions and their perspectives was distorted by the political crisis in Afghanistan, which had an entirely different character than the Iranian turmoil but occurred simultaneously—and from Moscow's view on the world, threatened the same southern periphery of the Soviet Union.[4]

The time of troubles in Afghanistan started in April 1978, when a group of "progressive" officers organized a coup against President Mohammed Daoud Khan and murdered most of his family. Moscow had maintained close ties with Daoud Khan's regime and didn't instigate the coup, but had to accept a *fait accompli*—and justified it as the "April revolution."[5] Soviet relations with the government of Nur Muhammad Taraki were further upgraded, and that turn of events reinforced the general perception of the army as the dominant political force (with a propensity to internalize communist ideas) in the wider Middle East.

The failure of the shah's army and SAVAK to suppress the unrest spreading from Qom to Tabriz to Abadan and to Tehran stunned the Soviet authorities, and before a coherent interpretation was developed, the situation in Afghanistan spun out of control. On September 14, 1979, soon after returning from a trip to Moscow, Taraki was assassinated by his rival Hafizullah Amin, who sought to establish an even more brutally dictatorial regime. Decison making in the Kremlin on restoring order in Kabul, which had come to be seen as an important ally, was agonizingly incoherent, but one of the key considerations was the assumption that U.S. attention was preoccupied with the hostage crisis in Tehran, dragging on after November 4, 1979. There were also persistent—and entirely misplaced—concerns in Moscow that Washington would organize another coup in Iran, perhaps in combination with a military intervention.

The very narrow circle of elderly decisionmakers in the Politburo had reason to believe that the Soviet military intervention in Afghanistan, described as "brotherly help" and the performance of "international duty," would be criticized but effectively accepted by the United States and Western Europe because of their deepening worries about the violent mess in Iran.[6] The Kremlin certainly got it wrong and was astounded not only by the ostracism in the West, but also by the fierce condemnation from revolutionary Iran, where the Soviet Union was defined as the "Lesser Satan." A stronger distraction from the gradually escalating hostilities in Afghanistan was needed, and the outbreak of the Iran-Iraq war in September 1980 provided just that. Moscow declared "neutrality" in that war but served as the main supplier of arms to Iraq in hopes of mollifying key Arab states, which had been alienated by the invasion into Afghanistan. It is obvious in retrospect that the strategy of covering one mistake with another blunder was doomed to be a mega-failure, and in this fashion, the debacle in Afghanistan became a major driver of the collapse of the "indestructible" Soviet Union.

The geopolitical gain for the Soviet Union from the breakdown of the alliance between Iran and the United States was negated by the severe deterioration of the Soviet position caused by the mismanaged Afghan war. For Moscow, the security threat from the "old" Iran was familiar and manageable, but the new challenges from Islamic fundamentalism and insurgency were incomprehensible and insuppressible. Soviet military command had to concentrate far greater effort than it wanted on waging this peripheral war. As far as Iran was concerned, Soviet top brass were shocked by the collapse of shah's army, but they found the capacity of the chaos-consumed Iran to regroup and repel Iraq's aggression astounding. For the KGB, the post-revolutionary extermination of the Tudeh Party and other prospective Soviet allies within Iran was shocking, and the spread of the Islamic networks and influence appeared deeply disturbing. The Politburo elders and the dogmatic party-ideological apparatus were unable to comprehend the sustained public mobilization in Iran for the Islamic cause and to explain away the rising resistance in Afghanistan.

The Soviet Union, as it happened, had no long-term perspective, and the Russian state has successfully made peace and even entered into an alliance of sorts with Iran's Islamic Republic, which is no longer its neighbor. This rapprochement has brought Russia much trouble, as is increasingly obvious in Syria. However, the "strategic partnership" has not erased the fundamental incompatibility between Russia's opportunistic policy of asserting its "great power" status and Iran's ideological policy of advancing the cause of the still-spirited Islamic Revolution.

NOTES

1 One useful Russian analysis is Dmitry Asinovsky, "The Soviet Union and the Iranian Revolution," *Russia in Global Affairs*, October 29, 2018 (https://eng.globalaffairs.ru/number/The-Soviet-Union-and-the-Iranian-Revolution-19809).

2 Leonid Shebarshin, the KGB resident in Iran in 1978–1983, wrote remarkably frank memoirs and admitted that adherence to dogmas of Marxism-Leninism distorted the understanding of the Iranian Revolution; see Shebarshin, *Ruka Moskvy: Zapiski Nachalnika Sovetskoi Razvedki (The Hand of Moscow: Memoirs of the Head of the Soviet Intelligence)*, (Moscow, Russia: Tsentr-100, 1992).

3 Rostislav Ulyanovsky, who was in charge of the Iranian file in this department, presented his assessments in the instructive article "The Iranian Revolution and Its characteristics," *Kommunist*, in Russian, October 1982.

4 I am grateful to Mikhail Krutikhin for sharing his firsthand impressions from the Tehran streets and reflections on the official interpretations; see also his "A New Revolution in Iran is Far Away", *Snob.ru*, in Russian, January 11, 2018 (https://snob.ru/entry/156469).

5 One of the best accounts of this confusion is Odd Arne Westead, "Prelude to Invasion: The Soviet Union and the Afghan Communists, 1978–1979," *International History Review* vol. 16, no. 1, 1994, pp. 49–69.

6 That fateful decision is examined in Artemy Kalinovsky, "Decision-Making and the Soviet War in Afghanistan: From Intervention to Withdrawal," *Journal of Cold War Studies* vol. 11, no. 4, 2009, pp. 46–73.

APPENDIX A

Iranian Revolution Timeline of Events

SUZANNE MALONEY *and* KEIAN RAZIPOUR

Storm Clouds Gather

January–July 1977: Journalists, intellectuals, lawyers, and political activists publish a series of open letters criticizing the accumulation of power at the hands of the shah.

October 1977: A ten-night poetry festival organized by the Iranian writers' association at the Goethe Institute in Tehran attracts thousands of participants for lectures criticizing the government.

October 23, 1977: Mostafa Khomeini, the eldest son of exiled cleric Ayatollah Ruhollah Khomeini, dies of unknown causes at age 47 in Najaf, Iraq. The elder Khomeini has lived in exile since 1963, when he was arrested for leading protests against the shah's modernization program.

November 15–16, 1977: During a visit to Washington, the shah's welcome at the White House is disrupted by protesting Iranian students (as well as the tear gas used by police to quash the protests).

December 31, 1977: On a brief visit to Iran, President Jimmy Carter toasts the shah, describing Iran as "an island of stability in one of the most troubled areas of the world."

A Spark Ignites

January 6, 1978: Iranian newspaper *Ettela'at* publishes a front-page editorial disparaging Ayatollah Ruhollah Khomeini, reportedly written by the royal court at the directive of the shah.

January 9, 1978: The main bazaar in Qom, where Iran's largest seminaries are based, closes to protest the defamation of Khomeini. Several thousand protestors attack symbols of the monarchy; security forces kill at least five people.

February 18, 1978: Consistent with Shia tradition, mourning ceremonies are held in cities across Iran on the fortieth day following the death of the Qom protestors. A student protestor is killed in Tabriz, provoking riots and further violence.

March–May 1978: The cycle of protests, repression, violence, and mourning continues in three dozen Iranian cities.

June 7, 1978: The shah replaces General Nematollah Nassiri, the head of SAVAK; one of his successor's first moves is to order the release of 300 detained clerics.

July 20, 1978: Protests erupt in Mashhad after the death of a cleric in a road accident; a number of people are killed in the upheaval there and elsewhere.

August 9–10, 1978: The arrest of a cleric provokes riots in Isfahan, which quickly spread to Shiraz, Qazvin, Tabriz, Abadan, and Ahwaz. The Shiraz Art Festival is canceled and an estimated 100 are killed. Martial law is declared in Isfahan.

A Revolution Erupts

August 19, 1978: 477 Iranians die in a deliberately set fire at Cinema Rex in Abadan. The opposition blames SAVAK; after the revolution, an Islamist confesses and is prosecuted for the arson.

August 27, 1978: Prime Minister Jamshid Amouzegar resigns; his successor, Jafar Sharif-Emami, undertakes reforms intended to assuage rising public dissatisfaction.

September 8, 1978: On the morning after the shah declares martial law, security forces fire on a large protest in Tehran's Jaleh Square. At least 100 are killed and the event becomes known as "Black Friday."

October 3, 1978: At the shah's behest, the Iraqi government deports Khomeini. After he is denied entry to Kuwait, Khomeini travels to France and settles in Neauphle-le-Chateau, a Parisian suburb, where he benefits from far greater media access and attention.

November 6, 1978: Days after protests swell in Tehran on a religious holiday, efforts to broker a national unity government with the opposition collapse thanks to Khomeini's defiance. Prime Minister Sharif-Emami resigns and is succeeded by General Gholamreza Azhari. The shah broadcasts on national television a promise not to repeat past mistakes and to make amends, saying, "I heard the voice of your revolution. . . . As shah of Iran as well as an Iranian citizen, I cannot but approve your revolution."

December 6, 1978: Only a week after he publicly reaffirmed U.S. support for and "confidence in" the shah, President Jimmy Carter publicly hedges in press statements, noting that, "We personally prefer that the shah maintain a major role, but that is a decision for the Iranian people to make."

December 10–11, 1978: Millions of Iranians protest all over the country demanding the removal of the shah and return of Ayatollah Ruhollah Khomeini.

December 29, 1978: The shah appoints Shapour Bakhtiar as prime minister. A long-time nationalist politician and vocal critic of the shah, he is confirmed by the parliament two weeks later.

January 12, 1979: In Paris, Ayatollah Khomeini forms the Revolutionary Council to coordinate the transition.

The Interregnum

January 16, 1979: The shah and his family leave Iran for Egypt, ostensibly for "vacation." As he departs, the shah tells Prime Minister Bakhtiar, "I give Iran into your care, yours and God's."

February 1, 1979: Khomeini returns to Iran and is greeted by millions of people in the streets of Tehran.

February 4, 1979: Khomeini appoints Mehdi Bazargan as the prime minister of an interim government. Bakhtiar insists that he remains the head of the only legitimate Iranian government.

February 10, 1979: Bakhtiar announces a countrywide curfew and martial law. Khomeini orders his followers to ignore the curfew and rise up in national revolution.

February 11, 1979: The armed forces declare neutrality, and any remnants of the shah's government collapse. Bakhtiar quickly flees Iran for France, where he is assassinated in 1991 by Iranian agents.

The Provisional Government

February 14, 1979: The U.S. embassy in Tehran is attacked by crowds; embassy staff initially surrender, but the protestors are ousted on the order of Iran's acting foreign minister, Ibrahim Yazdi.

March 8, 1979: Tens of thousands of Iranian women protest in Tehran on International Women's Day to oppose mandatory veiling.

March 30–31, 1979: Iranians participate in a national referendum on whether Iran should become an "Islamic republic"; the motion (which offers no alternatives) receives near-unanimous support.

May 5, 1979: The Islamic Revolutionary Guard Corps is established by a decree issued by Khomeini.

August 3, 1979: Iranians vote in nation-wide elections for the Assembly of Experts, a clergy-dominated body empowered to finalize the draft constitution. Due to boycotts by leftist, nationalist, and some Islamist factions, voter turnout falls far below the March referendum.

October 14, 1979: The Assembly of Experts approves the new constitution, enshrining Khomeini's innovative doctrine of *velayat-e faqih*, which accords ultimate authority to a religious leader.

October 22, 1979: Shah Mohammad Reza Pahlavi is allowed to enter the United States for medical treatment. Khomeini condemns the United States for allowing the deposed shah entry into the country.

The Hostage Crisis

November 4, 1979: Student protestors overrun the U.S. embassy in Tehran, seizing its personnel as hostages.

November 6, 1979: Senior figures in Iran's provisional government resign in protest, ceding uncontested authority of the new state to Khomeini and the Revolutionary Council.

November 7, 1979: U.S. president Jimmy Carter sends emissaries with a personal note to Iran to negotiate the release of the hostages, but they are refused entry.

November 14, 1979: The United States freezes all the property and assets of the government of Iran and the Central Bank of Iran.

November 19–20, 1979: Thirteen female and African American hostages are released in a unilateral Iranian gesture.

December 2–3, 1979: Iran's new constitution is overwhelmingly approved in a popular referendum that draws participation by 75 percent of the electorate.

December 4, 1979: The United Nations Security Council passes a resolution calling for Iran to release the hostages.

December 15, 1979: The shah leaves the United States for Panama.

January 25, 1980: Abolhassan Bani-Sadr is elected as the Islamic Republic's first president; within 18 months, he was impeached and fled the country.

March 14, 1980: Iranians vote in parliamentary elections, with a second round held in May.

April 7, 1980: The United States formally severs diplomatic relations with Iran.

April 25, 1980: Operation Eagle Claw, the U.S. embassy hostage rescue mission, fails after sandstorms cause the crash of one of the helicopters and the death of eight U.S. soldiers.

April 28, 1980: U.S. Secretary of State Cyrus Vance announces his resignation, submitted to President Carter four days before the launch of the rescue operation.

July 9, 1980: Iranian authorities discover a coup plot and launch a new purge of the military.

July 27, 1980: Shah Mohammad Reza Pahlavi dies in Cairo, Egypt.

September 12, 1980: In a speech, Ayatollah Khomeini outlines Iran's preconditions for an agreement to free the hostages.

September 22, 1980: Iraq invades Iran, setting off an eight-year conflict that results in hundreds of thousands of casualties on both sides.

January 20, 1981: All remaining U.S. hostages are released after 444 days, after Tehran and Washington conclude the Algiers Accords. The agreement unfreezes Iranian assets, lifts other U.S. sanctions on Iran, and establishes a tribunal to adjudicate billions of dollars of financial claims between the two countries.

APPENDIX B

What to Read to Understand the 1979 Iranian Revolution

SUZANNE MALONEY, ELIORA KATZ, *and* KEIAN RAZIPOUR

Iran's revolution has inspired countless books, articles, films, and commentary. To mark the fortieth anniversary of that momentous event, we have compiled some recommendations on further reading for anyone interested in a deeper understanding of the establishment of the Islamic Republic and its legacy.

Shaul Bakhash, *The Reign of the Ayatollahs: Iran and the Islamic Revolution* (London: Tauris, 1985). Journalism is often said to be the first draft of history. This is especially true when the journalist also happens to be a distinguished historian. Bakhash brings his keen eye for narrative and detail from his time as editor and news analyst for Kayhan newspaper before the revolution, as well as the context of his deep expertise in Iran's history. Few books written in the immediate aftermath of epic events can stand the test of time. *The Reign of the Ayatollahs* is a notable exception.

Darioush Bayandor, *The Shah, the Islamic Revolution and the United States* (New York: Palgrave Macmillan, 2019). Meticulous and comprehensive, this newly released study of the 1979 revolution is a very worthy addition to an already copious literature on Iran. With the distance of history and expanding archival access that offers new insights into American efforts to engage with Ayatollah Ruhollah Khomeini on the eve of the monarchy's collapse, Bayandor provides a gripping chronicle of the forces that gave rise to a populist revolution and a theocratic post-revolutionary government.

David Burnett, *44 Days: Iran and the Remaking of the World* (Washington, D.C.: National Geographic Society, 2009). It is impossible to understand the Iranian Revolution without visuals, and this book offers a stunning portrayal of the revolution through the lens of an American photojournalist who was in Iran at the time the conflict began to take root. The book documents the revolution through photos that capture the chaos and drama of Iran in 1978–1979. Burnett includes several eyewitness accounts describing the last days of the Iranian monarchy and the first days of Khomeini's rule.

Peter Chelkowski and Hamid Dabashi, *Staging a Revolution: The Art of Persuasion in the Islamic Republic of Iran* (London: Booth-Clibborn, 2002). Imagery played a crucial role in helping to galvanize the mobilization against the shah, and Chelkowski and Dabashi explain how the revolution built upon an ideological reconfiguration and how symbolism was deployed to mobilize opposition to the shah and define the new era. The book's vivid reproduction of the artworks of the revolution—posters, paintings, murals, cartoons, leaflets, movies, and even banknotes and stamps—might lead the reader to presume this is merely a magnificent coffee-table book, except that the images are accompanied by detailed text that is equally rich with analysis and informed commentary.

Andrew Scott Cooper, *The Fall of Heaven: The Pahlavis and the Final Days of Imperial Iran* (New York: Henry Holt and Company, 2016).

In writing this book, Cooper benefited from cooperation with Farah Pahlavi, the queen who was especially influential during the final years of the monarchy. So it comes as no surprise that the end result is a much more sympathetic interpretation of the shah than mainstream literature has offered to date. And yet his intimate portrayal of the royal family's life within the palace walls as their world crumbled around them remains well worth the read. (Pair this with the front row seat provided by Gholam Reza Afkhami's masterful biography of the shah or the judicious perspective offered by Abbas Milani's account.[1, 2])

Oriana Fallaci, "The Shah of Iran: An Interview with Mohammad Reza Pahlevi" (*The New Republic*, December 1, 1973)[3]; "An Interview with Khomeini" (*New York Times*, October 7, 1979)[4]; "Everybody Wants to Be Boss" (*New York Times*, October 28, 1979)[5]. Italian journalist Orianna Fallaci lived an exceptionally colorful life, in which her pioneering work as a political correspondent unfortunately became overshadowed by the anti-Muslim polemics she wrote in her later years. But at the height of her career, Fallaci utilized her devastating capacity as an interviewer in grilling some of the world's most powerful leaders. A trio of conversations with key Iranians—the shah, Ayatollah Khomeini, and Iran's first post-revolutionary prime minister, Mehdi Bazargan—make for captivating and informative reads.

Joseph Kraft, "Letter from Tehran" (*The New Yorker*, December 18, 1978)[6]. Kraft was said to be a confidante of the Iranian establishment, hardly an unusual status since the Pahlavi elite openly courted opinion makers in the West. His firsthand account of his conversations with a wide range of Iranians—the shah, opposition leaders, influential clerics, academics, and government officials—just as the maelstrom of the revolution overtook the monarchy is poignant both for its prescience and its misplaced expectations. The piece concludes with the expectation of compromise along with the caveat that "the moment is not going to last very long."

Charles Kurzman, *The Unthinkable Revolution in Iran* (Harvard University Press, 2004). The Iranian Revolution has confounded experts from a variety of disciplines and backgrounds. What precipitated the revolution, and what enabled this movement to succeed where so many others have failed? Kurzman, a sociologist who has conducted research in Iran and among Iranian emigres, examines the traditional theories around revolutions, which in turn emphasize economic, political, cultural, organizational, and military factors, and finds no single explanation sufficient. Instead, he concludes: "So long as revolution remained 'unthinkable,' it remained undoable. It could come to pass only when large numbers of people began to 'think the unthinkable.'"

Abbas Milani, *The Persian Sphinx: Amir Abbas Hoveyda and the Riddle of the Iranian Revolution* (London: I.B. Tauris, 2000). This is not strictly a book about the revolution, but it begins and concludes in the prisons of the nascent theocracy, where the man who had served the monarchy as prime minister for nearly thirteen years spent his final days. In compelling fashion, Milani recounts Hoveyda's life in the service of the shah—who nonetheless detained him in hopes of assuaging public anger as the revolution reached its frenzied peak—and his death at the hands of the revolution's infamous tribunals, where his final words were, "It wasn't supposed to end like this."

Roy Mottahedeh, *The Mantle of the Prophet: Religion and Politics in Iran* (Oxford: Oneworld Publications, 2002). As Suzanne Maloney wrote almost a decade ago, "Iran scholars are a fractious bunch, but one book commands nearly universal respect. Roy Mottahedeh's *The Mantle of the Prophet*, they agree, offers an unparalleled perspective on the revolution and its antecedents as seen through the eyes of an archetypical cleric."[7] In this work of historical fiction, Mottahedeh elegantly threads together the historical and cultural antecedents that shaped the revolution.

Azar Nafisi, *Reading Lolita in Tehran* (New York: Random House, 2004). In this tour de force, Azar Nafisi invites the reader into her home for an intimate look into the psychosocial fallout of the revolution through the eyes of Iranian women. Nafisi illustrates the harrowing ways daily lives were altered during the Iranian cultural revolution. The memoir follows a reading group she held at her home for seven of her former students and the parallels they drew between great works of literature and their own experiences, including being beaten and incarcerated for sins like "bad hijab." From the first major protest of the post-revolutionary era to today's social media campaigns, Iranian women have played crucial roles in contesting Iran's revolution, and this book provides key insights for understanding how and why.

Nate Penn, "444 Days in the Dark: An Oral History of the Iran Hostage Crisis" (*GQ*, November 3, 2009)[8]. For many in the United States and elsewhere around the world, the foremost memories of Iran's revolution transpired six months in its aftermath, with the November 1979 seizure of the U.S. embassy in Tehran by a radical student group. The 444-day standoff that followed completed the bitter rupture of the bilateral relationship, facilitated the clerics' consolidation of control over the post-revolutionary order, torpedoed President Jimmy Carter's reelection prospects, and left an enduring legacy of the Islamic Republic's spurning of international norms and law. This *GQ* article draws on interviews with over fifty Americans and Iranians who were in some way involved with or affected by the siege, including former hostages, their captors, government officials and experts. (If you come away eager for more details on the U.S. response, there is no better resource than *American Hostages in Iran: The Conduct of a Crisis*, by Warren Christopher and others.)[9]

Marjane Satrapi, *Persepolis: The Story of a Childhood* (New York: Pantheon Books, 2003). This graphic novel features stark black-and-white drawings and sharp dialogue, as Marjane Satrapi draws on her personal experiences growing up in Iran during the revolution to detail its immediate impact on the daily lives of ordinary Iranians. Satrapi gives us the view of these historic events from the perspective of a rebellious young girl. Satrapi's two *Persepolis* novels were eventually translated into an award-winning film.

Gary Sick, *All Fall Down: America's Tragic Encounter with Iran* (New York: Random House, 1985). For an episode that had such dramatic impact on U.S. politics and security, there are relatively few thorough accounts of how the U.S. government approached the crisis as it unfolded. (Robert Jervis's *Why Intelligence Fails* convincingly addresses one dimension of the puzzle.[10]) From his vantage as a chief National Security Council official on Iran during the revolution and the hostage crisis, Sick provides a dispassionate play-by-play of the policy process within the Carter administration during this tumultuous period.

Theda Skocpol, "Rentier State and Shi'a Society in the Iranian Revolution" (*Theory and Society 11*, no. 3, 1982, pp. 265–83). Renowned political scientist Theda Skocpol is the author of, among many other works, an authoritative tome on social revolutions. That book focused on the structural causes of revolutions, arguing that international pressures exacerbate state weaknesses and produce new strains on the regime's agricultural base, thus provoking peasant uprisings. Revolutions are not made, she asserts—they come. Unfortunately, the book's original publication coincided with the Iranian Revolution, whose patterns directly contradicted Skocpol's arguments. In this piece, she addresses the challenges to her broader theory of revolutions and highlights Iran's rentier economy and the symbolic and organizational opportunities afforded by Shia Islam as distinguishing factors.

NOTES

1 Gholam Reza Afkhami, *The Life and Times of the Shah* (Berkeley: University of California Press, 2009).

2 Abbas Milani, *The Shah* (New York: Palgrave Macmillan, 2011).

3 Oriana Fallaci, "The Shah of Iran: An Interview with Mohammad Reza Pahlevi," *The New Republic*, December 1, 1973 (https://newrepublic.com/article/92745/shah-iran-mohammad-reza-pahlevi-oriana-fallaci).

4 Fallaci, "An Interview with Khomeini," *New York Times*, October 7, 1979 (www.nytimes.com/1979/10/07/archives/an-interview-with-khomeini.html).

5 Fallaci, "Everybody Wants to Be Boss," *New York Times*, October 28, 1979 (www.nytimes.com/1979/10/28/archives/everybody-wants-to-be-boss-an-interview-with-mehdi-bazargan-prime.html).

6 Joseph Kraft, "Letter from Tehran," *The New Yorker*, December 18, 1978 (www.newyorker.com/magazine/1978/12/18/letter-from-iran).

7 Suzanne Maloney, "What to Read on Iranian Politics," *Foreign Affairs*, June 12, 2009 (www.foreignaffairs.com/articles/2009-06-12/what-read-iranian-politics).

8 Nate Penn, "444 Days in the Dark: An Oral History of the Iran Hostage Crisis," *GQ*, November 3, 2009 (www.gq.com/story/iran-hostage-crisis-tehran-embassy-oral-history).

9 Warren Christopher and others (eds.), *American Hostages in Iran: The Conduct of a Crisis* (Yale University Press, 1985).

10 Robert Jervis, *Why Intelligence Fails: Lessons from the Iranian Revolution and the Iraq War* (Cornell University Press, 2010).

Contributors

MADIHA AFZAL is the David M. Rubenstein Fellow in the Foreign Policy program at the Brookings Institution. She previously worked as an assistant professor of public policy at the University of Maryland, College Park, and has consulted for various organizations, including the World Bank and UK's Department for International Development (DFID). She has written for Pakistani and international publications and is the author of *Pakistan Under Siege: Extremism, Society, and the State*, as well as several book chapters and reports.

RANJ ALAALDIN is a visiting fellow at the Brookings Doha Center and co-director of the Proxy Wars Initiative. He was previously a visiting scholar at Columbia University and led election-monitoring and fact-finding teams in Iraq as well as Libya. He is writing a book on Shia militias in Iraq and Syria, and has published extensively with academic and policy journals. He holds a PhD from the London School of Economics and Political Science.

SCOTT R. ANDERSON is a fellow in Governance Studies at the Brookings Institution, a senior fellow in the National Security Law Program at

Columbia Law School, and a senior editor and counsel for *Lawfare*. He previously served as an attorney-advisor for the U.S. State Department and as the legal advisor for the U.S. embassy in Iraq.

PAVEL BAEV is a nonresident senior fellow in the Center on the United States and Europe at Brookings, senior associate fellow at the Institut Francais des Relations Internationales (IFRI), and has a full-time position as a research professor at the Peace Research Institute Oslo (PRIO). He previously worked with the Institute of Europe in Moscow and in various research and editorial positions at PRIO. He has published several books and numerous articles on the Russian military, energy interests in Russian foreign policy, Russian-European relations, and peacekeeping and conflict management in Europe, the Caucasus, and Central Asia.

DANIEL BYMAN is a senior fellow at the Brookings Center for Middle East Policy, vice dean for undergraduate affairs at Georgetown University's Walsh School of Foreign Service, and a professor in its Security Studies Program. Previously, Byman served as a staff member with the 9/11 Commission and the Joint 9/11 Inquiry staff of the House and Senate intelligence committees, and at the RAND Corporation and for the U.S. government. He is the author of numerous books and articles on counterterrorism, state sponsorship of terrorism, and conflict and terrorism in the Middle East.

ALI FATHOLLAH-NEJAD is a visiting fellow at the Brookings Doha Center. He has taught in the doctoral program of Qatar University's Gulf Studies Center. Previously, he was a post-doctoral associate with the Harvard Kennedy School's Iran Project. Fathollah-Nejad researches and publishes widely on Iran, the Middle East, the post-unipolar world order, and right-wing populism in the West.

VANDA FELBAB-BROWN is a senior fellow in the Foreign Policy program at Brookings. Felbab-Brown has written extensively on international and internal conflicts, and on nontraditional security threats including insurgency, terrorism, organized crime, urban violence, and illicit economies. She has published numerous books, policy reports, and articles, and her fieldwork and research have covered, among others, Afghanistan, South Asia, the Andean region, Mexico, Morocco, Iraq, and various regions of Africa.

JEFFREY FELTMAN is the John C. Whitehead Visiting Fellow in the Foreign Policy program at the Brookings Institution. As the United Nations under-secretary-general for political affairs, he was the chief foreign policy advisor to both Secretary-General Ban Ki-moon and Secretary-General Antonio Guterres. Previously, Feltman was a U.S. Foreign Services Officer for over twenty-six years, with tours in Erbil, Baghdad, Jerusalem, Tel Aviv, Tunis, Amman, Budapest, and Port-au-Prince. He also served as the U.S. ambassador to Lebanon and as the assistant secretary of state for Near Eastern Affairs with the rank of career minister.

SHARAN GREWAL is an assistant professor in the Government Department at the College of William & Mary and a visiting fellow at Brookings. He previously served as a Brookings postdoctoral research fellow and at the U.S. State Department. His research on democratization, security studies, and political Islam in the Arab world, especially Egypt, Tunisia, and Algeria, has been published in a number of academic and policy journals and media outlets.

SAMANTHA GROSS is a fellow in the Cross-Brookings Initiative on Energy and Climate. She has more than twenty years of experience in energy and environmental affairs, including as director of the Office of International Climate and Clean Energy at the U.S. Department of Energy; as a visiting fellow at the King Abdullah Petroleum Studies and Research Center; as director of integrated research at IHS CERA; and in other government and private sector positions. She has authored numerous papers on energy and environment issues.

SHADI HAMID is a senior fellow at the Brookings Center for Middle East Policy and a contributing writer at *The Atlantic*. He is the author of *Islamic Exceptionalism: How the Struggle Over Islam is Reshaping the*

World and co-editor of *Rethinking Political Islam*. Hamid previously served as director of research at the Brookings Doha Center.

KATE HEWITT is a contractor with the National Nuclear Security Administration (NNSA). She was previously a research assistant at the Brookings Institution and a Herbert Scoville Peace Fellow, conducting research for the Brookings Arms Control and Nonproliferation Initiative.

ELAINE C. KAMARCK is a senior fellow in Governance Studies at the Brookings Institution as well as director of the Brookings Center for Effective Public Management. Kamarck is also a lecturer in public policy at the Harvard Kennedy School of Government. She is the author of *Primary Politics: Everything You Need to Know about How America Nominates Its Presidential Candidates* and *Why Presidents Fail and How They Can Succeed Again* and has published extensively on American electoral politics and government innovation and reform in the United States, OECD nations, and developing countries.

ELIORA KATZ is a research assistant in the Center for Middle East Policy at the Brookings Institution. She was previously a Robert L. Bartley Fellow on the editorial page of the *Wall Street Journal*.

KEMAL KIRIŞCI is the Turkish Industry and Business Association senior fellow in the Brookings Center on the United States and Europe and director of its Turkey Project. Previously, he was a professor of international relations and held the Jean Monnet chair in European Integration in the department of Political Science and International Relations at Boğaziçi University in Istanbul. He is the author of several books on Turkey and has published extensively in academic journals and media on Turkish foreign policy, European-Turkish relations, and immigration. His most recent book, *Turkey and the West: Fault Lines in a Troubled Alliance*, was published by the Brookings Institution Press in 2017.

SUZANNE MALONEY is deputy director of the Brookings Foreign Policy program and a senior fellow in the Brookings Center for Middle East

Policy. The author of several books on Iran, she has advised Republican and Democratic administrations on Iran and the broader Middle East, and previously served as Middle East advisor to ExxonMobil Corporation.

RICHARD NEPHEW is a nonresident senior fellow with the Brookings Arms Control and Nonproliferation Initiative and a senior research scholar and program director at the Center on Global Energy Policy at Columbia University. He is the author of a book, *The Art of Sanctions*, and previously served in a variety of positions related to Iran, sanctions and nonproliferation at the U.S. State Department, the National Security Council, and the Department of Energy.

KENNETH M. POLLACK is a resident scholar at the American Enterprise Institute (AEI). He previously served as senior fellow, director of research, and director of the Brookings Center for Middle East Policy. He began his career as a Persian Gulf military analyst at the Central Intelligence Agency (CIA) and served twice on the National Security Council. Pollack has authored ten books, including *Armies of Sand: The Past, Present, and Future of Arab Military Effectiveness*, and numerous articles.

BRADLEY S. PORTER is a project manager within the Brookings Institution's Security and Strategy Team. He conducts and manages research and events on issues of subnational threats and transnational networks. He has provided and managed research support for seven Brookings books.

ITAMAR RABINOVICH is a Brookings distinguished fellow, a member of the Brookings International Advisory Board, and professor emeritus at Tel Aviv University, where he previously served as president. Rabinovich served as Israel's ambassador to the United States and chief negotiator with Syria. He has been appointed to the boards of several charitable and research institutions, and he is the author of numerous books and other academic works.

KEIAN RAZIPOUR previously held internships at the Brookings Center for Middle East Policy, with the Project on Middle East Democracy, and for several offices on Capitol Hill, including those of Representative Ted Lieu and Senator Dianne Feinstein.

BRUCE RIEDEL is a senior fellow in the Brookings Center for Middle East Policy. During thirty years at the CIA, he served as a senior advisor on South Asia and the Middle East on the National Security Council to four U.S. presidents. He was also deputy assistant secretary of defense for the Near East and South Asia and a senior advisor at NATO in Brussels. He is the author of seven books, is a contributor to three others, and has published numerous articles. He is a recipient of the Intelligence Medal of Merit and the Distinguished Intelligence Career Medal.

NATAN SACHS is a fellow in and director of the Brookings Center for Middle East Policy. He was previously a Hewlett Fellow at Stanford's Center on Democracy, Development, and the Rule of Law, and has taught at Georgetown University. His forthcoming book examines Israeli grand strategy and its domestic origins.

DJAVAD SALEHI-ISFAHANI is a professor of economics at Virginia Tech. He is a nonresident senior fellow at the Global Economy and Development program at the Brookings Institution and a research fellow at the Economic Research Forum (ERF) in Cairo. His research on energy economics, demographic economics, and the economics of the Middle East has been published in numerous academic and policy journals, and he is the coauthor of two books and editor of several others.

STROBE TALBOTT is a distinguished fellow in the Foreign Policy program at the Brookings Institution. He previously served as Brookings president for fifteen years; as founding director of the Yale Center for the Study of Globalization; and in the U.S. State Department as ambassador-at-large, special adviser to the secretary of state for the new independent states of the former Soviet Union, and then as deputy secretary of state for seven years. Before his government service, Talbott spent twenty-one years with *Time* magazine as a reporter, Washington bureau chief, editor-at-large, and foreign affairs columnist.

TAMARA COFMAN WITTES is a senior fellow in the Brookings Center for Middle East Policy. Wittes previously served as director of the Center for Middle East Policy and as deputy assistant secretary of state for Near Eastern Affairs, where she oversaw the Middle East Partnership Initiative and served as deputy special coordinator for Middle East transitions. Her previous book examined U.S. democracy promotion in the Arab world, and her current research assesses U.S. ties to autocratic allies.

Index

abaya, 61. *See also* hijab
Abbas, Mahmoud, 173
Abou al-Fotouh, Abdel Moneim, 185
absolutist rhetoric, 32
activism, 36–37, 41, 53, 60. *See also* protests and demonstrations
activism, women's rights, 13, 51–62, 71; Alinejad and, 51–52, 53–56, 58, 59, 60–61; criminal charges, 53–54; gradualism approach, 57–58; "Stealthy Freedom" anti-hijab activism campaign, 51, 54, 56, 59, 60; through social media, 51–52, 53, 54, 58–60. *See also* hijab; women
addiction, 41–46, 152
Afghanistan: drug smuggling and, 42, 45; poppy cultivation and opium production in, 40–41, 43, 45–46; Soviet invasion of, 164, 193–194; U.S. military action in, 4, 83, 84
age: birth rates after revolution, 36; youth and job access, 10, 11–12, 23; youth population, 10, 11–12, 60

âghâzâdeh (regime affiliates), 11
Ahmadinejad, Mahmoud, 19, 24, 34, 45, 172
AKP (Islamist Justice and Development Party, Turkey), 170, 172
Alaska, 117
alcohol use and abuse, 41, 44
Algeria, 106, 184
Algerian elections (1991), 94
Algiers Accords, 99, 106–108
Alinejad, Masih, 51–52, 53–56, 58, 59, 60–61
Amin, Hafizullah, 193
anti-American sentiment. *See* U.S.-Iran relations, anti-American sentiment
anti-American sentiment, in Pakistan, 189
Aoun, Michel, 149–151, 153
Arab-Israeli conflict: U.S. involvement, 163. *See also* Israel-Palestine conflict
Arab Spring, 126, 170
arms deals, 72, 82, 130
Arslan, Talal, 150

Ashour, Magdy, 184–185
al-Assad, Bashar, 125–127, 132, 147, 185
al-Assad, Hafez, 123, 184
Astana Forum (Russia, Iran, and Turkey), 124
Atatürk, Mustafa Kemal, 170, 172
Australia, 97–98
Austria, 97
authoritarianism, 13, 14, 57, 59
"Axis of Evil" speech, 83–84
Azerbaijan, 147
al-Aziz, Tariq, 138

Baath Party, 137, 138, 139
Bahrain, 126
Baqri, Mohammed Hussain, 128
Bassil, Gebran, 152, 149149
bast (sanctuary as form of political protest), 36
Bayat, Asef, 11–12
Bazargan, Mehdi, 31–32, 35, 182
Begin, Menachem, 176
Ben-Gurion, David, 175
Bhutto, Zulfiqar Ali, 191
bin Laden, Osama, 164
black swan national security crisis, 76
blasphemy laws (Pakistan), 191
Bolton, John, 100
bombings: in Lebanon, 143–144; suicide bombings, 144, 146, 147, 176
brain drain, 12
Brelis, Dean, 4
Britain, 70, 158–159, 161–162
Browers, Michelle, 139
Buenos Aires Jewish Community Center suicide bombings, 147, 176
Bulgaria, 147
Bureau of Human Rights and Humanitarian Affairs (U.S. State Department), 92
Bush, George H. W., 82
Bush, George W., 83–84, 91
Bush, H. W. administration, 94

Bush, Laura, 61
Bush, W. administration, 109

Camp David Accords (1978), 163
Canada, 98
cannabis, 45, 46
Carswell, Robert, 98
Carter, Jimmy, 76; gasoline shortages and, 116–117; hostage crisis and, 6, 74, 88–91, 96–97, 117; human rights policy, 5, 92–93; presidential campaign, 1980, 74, 89–91, 117; shah and, 73, 75, 81, 89, 93
Carter administration: Pakistan and, 189; Saudi Arabia and, 164–165; U.S.-Iran relations during, 75, 81
Carter Doctrine, 164–165
Central Committee of the Communist Party (Soviet Union), 193
Central Intelligence Agency (CIA), 5–6, 43, 50–51, 70–71, 132, 142
Central Treaty Organization (CENTO), 169
chador, 52, 56, 57–58. *See also* hijab
China, 13–14, 41, 71, 97, 100
Christians, in Lebanese government, 145, 149–151, 153
clean water, 9, 20
clerical rule, 31, 74, 136, 182
Clinton, Bill, 82
Clinton, Hillary, 61
Clinton administration, 82–83
Cold War, 71
Coll, Steve, 188
communism, 136–137
confessional system (Lebanon), 144–145, 151
Constitutional Revolution (1905), 70
Contra fighters, 82; Iran-Contra scandal, 51, 82, 130, 146, 176
counterrevolutionary efforts, 81
Crawford, Michael, 157
crime. *See* legal issues and criminal offenses

crude oil, 97, 115–119, 171. *See also* oil
Cuba, 97
Cyprus, 147

Davis, Richard J., 98
Dawa Party (Iraq), 136–137, 138
death penalty, for drug-related offenses, 42, 43, 45
demonstrations. *See* protests and demonstrations
Denmark, 98
deregulation, 10, 116–117
Derian, Patricia, 92
"Dictatorships and Double Standards" (Kirkpatrick article), 93
diplomacy, hijab and, 61
disarmament requirements of Taif Agreement, 148
dissidents, 6, 13, 60, 82, 169
drug policy, 40–46
drug smuggling, 42, 45, 46

Ecevit, Bülent, 169
economic sanctions. *See* sanctions
economy, Afghanistan, 45–46
economy, Iran, 9–12, 18–26; Algiers Accords claims and, 107; cost-benefit analysis of leaders, 99–100, 101; frozen assets, 96–97, 98, 104, 106, 107, 108; GDP, compared with Turkey, 21; growth rates, 19, 22, 23, 25, 26, 71–73; jobs and employment and, 10, 11–12, 23, 24–25; oil effects on growth, 19, 21–24, 26, 73; poppy cultivation and drug policy's effects on, 41, 42, 43; populism and, 19–23; poverty and, 9–10, 20, 22–23; pragmatism and, 18–19, 32; Rouhani's campaign plan and, 84; Turkish trade and, 171, 173; U.S. energy and military trade, impact on, 72; U.S. sanctions, during hostage crisis, 96–101, 104, 105; urban-rural policy shift, 19–20, 25

economy, Turkey, 21, 24
economy, U.S., 90, 163
education, 9, 20, 23–25, 71, 72
Egypt, 6–7, 95, 125, 177, 183, 185
Eizenstat, Stu, 89
elections: of Ahmadinejad, 172; Algerian (1991), 94; candidacy requirements, 13; Carter's 1980 presidential campaign, 74, 89–91, 117; hijab issue, for political candidates, 56, 57–58; of Khatami, 57, 82, 83; in Lebanon, 148, 149; protests over, 35, 37–38, 172; reform movement adopts, 31, 33–34; of Rouhani, 28, 57–58, 84; Sunni Islamist movements and, 183–185; women's right to vote in, 71
electricity, 9, 20
embargo, oil, 70, 97–98, 162–163
embassies. *See under U.S. embassy*
embassy, Iranian (in U.S.), 109
embassy seizure. *See* U.S. embassy seizure and hostage crisis (November 1979)
employment. *See* jobs and employment
Ennahda Party, 182
Erbakan, Necmettin, 170
Erdoğan, Recep Tayyip, 124, 173
al-Erian, Essam, 185
executions, 12
Executive Order 12170 (asset freeze), 96, 97

Facebook, women's activism through, 51
Fahd, Prince of Saudi Arabia, 163
Faisal, King of Saudi Arabia, 156, 162
family law, 52, 71
family planning, 21
Fathollah-Nejad, Ali, 36
Felbab-Brown, Vanda, 46
Feltman, Jeffrey, 154
Feltman, Mary, 154
FIS (Islamic Salvation Front), 184

France, 98, 131

freedom and democracy goals of Iranian Revolution, 8, 12–15

Freedom's Unsteady March: America's Role in Building Arab Democracy (Wittes), 94

Free Patriotic Movement (FPM, Lebanon), 149–150, 151, 152

frozen assets, 96–97, 98, 104, 106, 107, 108

fundamentalism. *See* radicalism and radicalist groups; terrorism

futures contracts, on crude oil, 118–119

gasoline shortages, price controls and, 116–117

Gaza, 184

Gemayel, Bashir, 145

gender. *See* activism, women's rights; men; women

Ghannouchi, Rached, 182–183, 185

Ghost Wars (Coll), 188

Girls of Revolution Street, 53–54, 55, 61

global gender gap, 53

Goldwater-Nichols Department of Defense Reorganization Act (1986), 91

gradualism, 28, 30, 57–58

Grand Mosque seizure (1979), 164

Great Britain, 70, 159, 161–162

Great Famine (1870–1872), 41

gross domestic product (GDP): Iran and Turkey, compared, 21; oil revenue and, 26

Guardian Council, 13

Gül, Abdullah, 172

hajj, 161

al-Hakim, Muhsin, 136, 137

Hamas, 131, 173, 176, 178, 184

Hama uprising (1982), 130

hard-liners, 13, 34, 65n43, 83, 85

Hariri, Rafiq, 147

Hariri, Saad, 150

Health Ministry (Lebanon), 152

health services, 9, 20–21, 41–42, 46

Hernandez, Rick, 89–90

heroin production, exports, and use, 42, 43–45, 46; opium production, exports, and use, 41–45

Hezbollah, 130, 143–155; Aoun provides Christian cover to, 149–151, 153; al-Assad and, 125–127, 147, 185; attacks by, 130, 144, 146, 147; current state of, 151–153; drug-related accusations against, 46; FPM and, 149–150, 151, 152; historical origins of, 144–146; Israel and, 146, 148, 149, 151, 152, 176, 178; as Lebanese actor, 147–148; manifesto (1985), 151; as strategic asset for Iranian influence, 147; suicide bombings and, 144, 146, 147; Syria and, 147, 151–152. *See also* Lebanon; Shia Muslims; terrorism

hijab, 51–62, 169; criminal charges for protesting, 51, 52, 53–54, 56; Iranian mandate extended beyond citizens, 61; protests of, 51, 52–55, 56, 58–60; in Saudia Arabia, 61; as symbol of women's coercion, 55–57. *See also* activism, women's rights

Hitchens, Christopher, 76

Holf, Fred, 147

Hosseini, Narges, 53, 54

hostage crisis. *See* U.S. embassy seizure and hostage crisis (November 1979)

housing, 9–10

Hoveyda, Amir Abbas, 73–74

al-Huda, Bint, 138

Hudood laws, 190–191

Human Development Index (HDI), Iran's rating, 9; Turkey, compared, 21

human rights policy: Carter administration, 5, 92–93; U.S. foreign policy debates, 92–95

Hussein, Saddam: decision to invade Iran, 130; Israel and, 176; Khomeini and, 139, 141; mistakes of, 140–142; Mujahideen and, 51; U.S. removal of, 83, 124

ibn Abd al Wahhab, Muhammad, 157
Ibn Saud, Abd al Aziz, 159–161
ICJ (International Court of Justice), 104–106, 108–109, 110–111
"ideology of Pakistan" (term), 190
ikhwan (brotherhood, tribal fighters), 160
income inequality, 10–11, 24
India, 13–14
infant and maternal mortality rates, 21
infrastructure and social development, 18–26, 35, 36, 71; basic services expansion, 9, 20; education and unemployment failures in, 23–25; to eliminate rural-urban divide, 9, 19–22, 25; HDI, 9, 21; social justice goal of Iranian Revolution, 8, 9–12
International Court of Justice (ICJ), 104–106, 108–109, 110–111
International Emergency Economic Powers Act (IEEPA, 1977), 96
international law. *See* legal issues and criminal offenses
International Monetary Fund (IMF), 19
Iran. *See* economy, Iran; infrastructure and social development; Islamic Republic; Saudi Arabia-Iran relations; U.S.-Iran relations
Iran-Contra scandal, 51, 82, 130, 146, 176
Iran Human Rights Documentation Center, 37
Iranian Army, 128
Iranian embassy, in U.S., 109
Iranian nuclear deal (JCPOA). *See* Joint Comprehensive Plan of Action (JCPOA)
Iranian Quds Force, 178
Iranian Revolution, goals of, 8–15

Iranian Revolutionary Guards, in Lebanon, 146, 153
Iranian-Saudi rivalry. *See* Saudi Arabia-Iran relations
Iran-Iraq War (1980-1988), 19, 123, 140, 142, 146, 165; as distraction from Soviet Union-Afghanistan hostilities, 194; number of casualties, 12; Turkey and, 171; U.S. arms deals in, 82, 130
#IranRegimeChange, 30
Iran's intelligence service, 131
Iran's Political Economy since the Revolution (Maloney), 98
Iran-United States Claims Tribunal (IUSCT), 107–109
Iraq: "Axis of Evil" and, 83; Communist Party, 136–137; Dawa Party, 136–137, 138; drug smuggling and, 46; "first Islamic Revolution" and, 135–139; Hussein and, 51, 83, 124, 130, 139, 140–142, 176; impact of Iranian Revolution on, 140–142; Iran-Lebanon land bridge through, 128; Khomeini deported to, 71–72; Shia Muslims in, 130, 136–138, 139; terrorism in, 130; U.S. invasion of (2003), 83, 84, 124, 139, 166
Iraqi Communist Party, 136–137
Iraq-Iran relations. *See* Iran-Iraq War (1980-1988)
Iraq War. *See* Iran-Iraq War (1980-1988)
Islam. *See* Shia Muslims; Sunni Muslims
Islambouli, Khalid, 7
Islamic economic development strategy, 18
Islamic Liberation Front of Bahrain, 130
Islamic Republic: economic growth, 19, 22, 23, 25; hardliners of, 13, 34, 83, 85; Iranian public opinion, 8, 9; political system established, 13

Islamic Republic, change predictions for, 27–38; debates, 29–31; gradualism and, 28, 30; moderates/reformers and, 33–35; opponents of change, 34–35; protests as pressure for change, 27–28, 30, 35, 37–38; stability assumptions, 29, 30–31; supporters of change, 33–35

Islamic Republic, hijab enforcement by. *See* hijab

Islamic Republic, socioeconomic development by. *See* infrastructure and social development

Islamic Republic, U.S. and. *See* U.S.-Iran relations

Islamic Revolutionary Guard Corps (IRGC), 131, 153

Islamic Salvation Front (FIS), 184

Islamic State (ISIS), 32, 127, 132

Islamism, 12, 93, 127, 132, 168, 182

Islamist Justice and Development Party (AKP, Turkey), 170, 172

Israel, 125–126, 127; Hezbollah and, 146, 148, 149, 151, 152, 176, 178; Iran and, historical origins of hostility, 174–179; Iranian cooperation with, 175; Islamic Republic and, 175, 176, 177; Khomeini and, 175, 189; occupation in Lebanon, 146, 148; periphery doctrine, 175, 177–178; PLO conflicts, 145; Turkey and, 169, 175

Israeli raid on Entebbe (1976), 90

Israel-Palestine conflict, 90, 124, 145–146, 153, 172–173; Iran's role in, 131, 175–177, 178

Italy, 98

IUSCT (Iran-United States Claims Tribunal), 107–109

Jamaat-e-Islami Islamist party (Pakistan), 188–191

Japan, 97

jihadism, 129, 131, 164

jobs and employment, 10, 11–12, 23, 24–25; unemployment, 10, 23, 24–25, 163

Joint Comprehensive Plan of Action (JCPOA), 84–85, 100–101; hopes for, 36, 85; U.S. withdrawal from, 17, 27, 28, 29, 109, 110

Joint Special Operations Command, 132

Jordan, 177, 183

journalism: Alinejad and, 51–52, 53–56, 58, 59, 60–61; imprisoned journalists, 13; protests over press restrictions, 35

Kar, Mehrangiz, 58

Kennedy, Ted, 89, 90

Kerry, John, 84–86

KGB, 193, 194

Khalkhali, Sadegh, 43

Khamenei, Ali, 54, 55, 85, 86, 154

Khan, Mohammed Daoud, 193

Khandan, Reza, 54

Khatami, Mohammad, 35, 45, 57, 82, 83

Khomeini, Ruhollah: anti-American sentiment of, 74, 86, 189; Bazargan and, 31–32; Carter administration peace efforts, 75; charismatic religious activism of, 129; clerical rule vision of, 31; deported to Iraq, 71–72; drug policy by, 42; exile of, 4, 44, 71–72, 135–136, 137, 140, 169; hostage crisis and, 32, 74, 89, 103; Hussein and, 139, 141; Israel and, 175, 189; on Saudi leadership's religious legitimacy, 163; seizure of power, 184; Shia perspective on, 164; Soviet perspective on, 192; Sunni Muslims and, 182; Turkish perspective on, 168; *velayat-e faqih* developed by, 136, 137

Khosravi, Shahram, 10

Ki-moon, Ban, 154

Kirkpatrick, Jeane, 93
Kurdish nationalism, 138, 168–169
Kurdistan Free Life Party (PJAK), 172
Kurdistan Workers' Party (PKK),
    169–170, 171–172
Kuwait, 130

labor. *See* jobs and employment
land reform, 19, 71
law. *See* legal issues and criminal of-
    fenses
Lebanese Armed Forces (LAF), 152
Lebanon, 125, 126–128; Aoun presi-
    dency, 149–151, 153; civil war, 144,
    145, 146; commemorations of U.S.
    lives lost in, 143–144; Health Min-
    istry, 152; Iranian Revolutionary
    Guards establish training camps in,
    146, 153; Israeli forces in, 146, 148;
    religious-political government of,
    144–145, 151; Shia Muslims in, 46,
    123, 144, 145, 149, 151, 153; Sunni
    Muslims in, 145, 150, 151, 153; U.S.
    embassy in, 143–144; U.S. involve-
    ment, 130, 143–144, 146, 152–154.
    See also Hezbollah
legal issues and criminal offenses: death
    penalty, 42, 43, 45; drug policy and,
    42, 44–45; hijab-related offenses,
    51, 52, 53–54, 56; ICJ and, 104–106,
    108–109, 110–111; international
    law, U.S.-Iran relations and, 104,
    110–111; IUSCT adjudication in,
    107–109; journalists imprisoned,
    13; legal reform initiatives, 57–58;
    self-expression, 56–57; vigilante
    violence, 56, 191
Libya, 131
literacy rates, 9, 11
living conditions, 9–10

Maloney, Suzanne, 98
Marcos, Ferdinand, 94

marijuana, 45, 46
Maronite Christians, 145, 149–151, 153
martial law, shah declares, 5
Mattis, James, 185
May, Theresa, 61
McSally, Martha, 61
men: education and, 9; laws favoring,
    55
Merkel, Angela, 61
methadone, 43, 45
Mexico, 97, 117
middle class, 11, 22–23, 71
Middle East region. *See* power shifts
    in Middle East region; U.S.-Middle
    East involvement; U.S-Middle East
    involvement; *specific country*
militant groups, 129, 130, 131, 132–133,
    189
military, Iranian, 128; under shah, 81,
    140, 142, 193, 194
military, Iraqi, 142
military, Lebanese, 125
military, Pakistani, 188, 189
military, Soviet, 43–44
military, U.S. *See* U.S-Middle East
    involvement, military engagement
Mirzakhani, Maryam, 56
Moaveni, Azadeh, 53
moderates, 13, 31, 33–35, 74, 93
modernity and modernization, 70–71;
    shah and, 9, 52, 71, 72–73, 156.
    See also infrastructure and social
    development
Mogherini, Federica, 62
morality police, 56
Morsi, Mohammed, 125, 185
Mossadegh, Mohammad, coup to over-
    throw (1953), 50–51, 70, 83
Movahed, Vida, 53, 54
Mubarak, Hosni, 95, 125
Mujahideen-e Khalq (left-wing terrorist
    group), 30, 43, 51, 189
Multinational Force (Lebanon), 145

Musawi, Abbas, 148
Muslim Brotherhood, 182, 183, 184–185
Myanmar, 44

Nakash, Yitzhak, 135
narcotics, drug policy and, 40–46
Nasrallah, Hassan, 148–151, 152, 154–155
Nasser, Gamal Abdel, 178
nationalism, 12, 115, 139; Arab, 161, 178–179; Kurdish, 138, 168; Turkish, 169
naval base plans of Iran, in Syria, 127–128
"netback" oil pricing structure, 119
New York Mercantile Exchange (NYMEX), 118–119
New York Times, 72, 118
Nixon, Richard, 3
Nixon Doctrine, 3
North Korea, 83
North Sea, 117
Norway, 98, 117
nuclear deal (2015). *See* Joint Comprehensive Plan of Action (JCPOA)
nuclear issues, 101, 125, 127, 172, 176, 177. *See also* Joint Comprehensive Plan of Action (JCPOA)

Obama, Barack, 84–86, 100, 101
Obama, Michelle, 61
Obama administration, 51, 84–86, 95
oil, crude, 97, 115–119, 171
oil booms, 10, 19, 23–24, 71
oil embargo, 70, 97–98, 162–163
oil exports: dependence on, 21–22; economic effects of, 21–22, 24; effects on domestic distribution, 24; sanctions and, 22–23, 97, 98, 171; by U.S., 166
oil market, 75; futures contracts role in, 118–119; Israel and, 175; nationalized controls, 162; panic buying effects on, 115–116; price fluctuations, 19, 24, 72–73, 115–119, 163; spot market

development, 117–119; Turkey and, 171; U.S. regulations, 116–117
oil production: fluctuations, 19, 115–119, 164; oil shocks, 115–119; OPEC and, 117–119; in Saudi Arabia, 119, 159, 161, 164
oil rents, 11, 23–24
oil revenue: effects on economic growth, 19, 21–24, 26, 73; populism and, 19, 23
oil sanctions, 22–23, 97, 98, 171
Oman, 177
OPEC production cuts, 117–119
Operation Eagle Claw, 89–91, 132
Operation Neptune Spear, 91
opium production, exports and use, 41–45; heroin production, exports, and use, 42, 43–45, 46

Pahlavi, Mohammad Reza: Carter and, 73, 75, 81, 89, 93; death of, 6, 75, 99; economic growth under, 21–22; exile of, 4, 6, 81; exiles Khomeini, 140; goals of, 3–4, 124, 162; hijab prohibited by, 52; infrastructure development and, 9, 71; Israel and, 179; Kurdish separatism supported by, 169; land reform policy, 19, 71; medical issues, 6, 103; military focus of, 162; oil embargo and, 70, 163; opium production policy by, 41–42; overthrow of, 69, 73–76, 81, 88, 94, 140–141, 168; Persepolis festivities, 3–4; Saudi Arabia and, 163; secularist and modernist policies of, 9, 52, 71, 72–73, 156; Soviet perspective on, 192; Talbott interviews, 5–6; Turkey and, 168, 169; U.S. backing of, 70–71, 72, 77, 162, 163; U.S. public opinion on, 88, 93–94; "White Revolution," 71
Pahlavi, Reza Shah, 52, 159–161
Pakistan, 43, 45, 131, 188–191
Pakistani Army, 188, 189

Palestine, 146, 175

Palestine-Israel conflict. *See* Israel-Palestine conflict

Palestine Liberation Organization (PLO), 145, 175, 178

Palestinian Authority, 173

Palestinian Islamic Jihad (PIJ), 176, 178

Paris Peace Conference, 70

Peres, Shimon, 173

periphery and reverse periphery doctrine, 175, 177–178

PJAK (Kurdistan Free Life Party), 172

PKK (Kurdistan Workers' Party), 169–170, 171–172

Poland, 97

political prisoners, executions of, 12

political system, establishment of Islamic Republic, 13

Pompeo, Mike, 50

poppy cultivation, 40–46

population of Iran, 9; birth rates after revolution, 36; oil revenue and, 19; youth in, 10, 11–12, 23, 60

populism, economic policy and, 19–23

Portugal, 97

poverty rate, 9–10, 20, 22–23

power shifts in Middle East region, 34–35, 69–70, 123–128, 135, 170, 179; Arab-Israeli conflict, 124, 174–177; British involvement, 70, 158–159, 161–162; democratization and, 14–15; Iran's hegemonic goals, 123, 124, 151; Islamic state's rise, 32; Obama administration and, 85; oil production's effects on, 161–162, 166; Soviet involvement, 70, 192–195; Sunni-Shiite conflict, 89, 135, 157, 176–177; terrorism and, 131–132, 152, 153; Trump administration and, 110–111, 166; as unanticipated, 73; U.S. military engagement and, 70, 76–77, 161–162, 163, 165, 166. *See also* Hezbollah; Iraq; Saudi Arabia-Iran relations; U.S.-Iran relations

pragmatism: economic strategy determined by, 18–19, 32; Turkey-Iran relations and, 169–173

President Carter: The White House Years (Eizenstat), 89

price of oil. *See* oil market

prison. *See* legal issues and criminal offenses

protests and demonstrations: in 2009, 35, 37–38, 51, 58; in 2017-2018, 27–28, 30, 37–38; *bast* as form of, 36; election-related, 35, 37–38, 172; factions cooperate and organize for, 73; of Hezbollah, 154; of hijab, 51, 52–55, 56, 58–60; in Iraq, 138–139; in Pakistan, 188–189; against press restrictions, 35; *Safar* Intifada (1977), 139; in Saudi Arabia, 164; in Syria, 126. *See also* U.S. embassy seizure and hostage crisis (November 1979)

purchasing power parity (PPP), 22

Qaddafi, Muammar, 131

al Qaeda, 131

al-Qaradawi, Yusuf, 185

al-Qasim al-Khoei, Abu, 137

Qasr-i Shirin treaty (1639), 169

quietist tradition, 137

Qutb, Sayyid, 182

radicalism, hostage crisis and. *See* U.S. embassy seizure and hostage crisis (November 1979)

radicalism and radicalist groups: attacks on Americans in Iran, 73; ISIS, 32, 127, 132; Kurdish nationalism, 138, 168–169; Muslim Brotherhood, 182, 183, 184–185; power of, 74; recruitment, 132; Revolutionary Council and, 32; Soviet response, 194; threat of emerging, 93, 115, 161, 165; Trump and, 91; in Turkey, 170. *See also* Hezbollah; terrorism

Raein, Parvis, 4

Rafsanjani, Ali Akbar Hashemi, 19, 32

Raghfar, Hossein, 10

Ramazani, Ruhollah, 14

Reagan, Ronald, 81–82, 90, 91, 94, 117

Reagan administration, 81–82, 101, 146

reform movement, 32, 33–35, 36, 71, 83;
    elections and, 31, 33–34; gradualism
    in, 28, 30, 57–58

religion: Christians, in Lebanese gov-
    ernment, 145, 149–151, 153. *See also*
    Shia Muslims; Sunni Muslims

religious radicalism. *See* radicalism and
    radicalist groups

reparations, U.S. claims for, 105–106

republican political system, 13

Revolutionary Council, 32, 104

Revolution Street, 53

Reza Khan (Reza Shah), 52, 159–161

Rice, Condoleezza, 61

Riedel, Bruce, 76

Roosevelt, Franklin Delano, 161

Rose Garden strategy, 89

Ross, Dennis, 185

Rouhani, Hassan, 12, 19, 85; election of,
    28, 57–58, 84

Rouhani government, 26

rural-urban divide, 9, 19–22, 25. *See
    also* infrastructure and social devel-
    opment

Rushdie, Salman, 34

Russia, 13–14, 70, 124, 127, 172. *See also*
    Soviet Union

Sadat, Anwar, 6, 130, 175–176

Sadjadpour, Karim, 85, 126

Sadr, Musa, 145–146

al-Sadr, Mohammad Baqir, 136, 138

Safar Intifada protests (1977), 139

Safavid Empire, 158–159

Salehi-Isfahani, Djavad, 10

sanctions, 10, 108–109, 110, 184; Hez-
    bollah and, 147, 152; as hostage crisis

response, 96–101, 104, 105; interna-
    tional response, 97–98, 100, 105, 171;
    oil and, 22–23, 97, 98, 171

Satanic Verses, The (Rushdie), 34

Saudi Arabia: drug smuggling and,
    46; hijab in, 61; oil market and, 119,
    159, 161, 164; Shia Muslims in, 164;
    Sunni Muslims in, 157; terrorism
    and, 129, 130, 131–132; U.S. rela-
    tions, 61, 70, 132, 157, 158, 161–165,
    166

Saudi Arabia-Iran relations, 126,
    131–132, 156–166; current state of,
    165–166; during Iranian Revolu-
    tion, 163–165; Iraq and, 130; Israel
    and, 177; Obama on, 85; origins of,
    156–159; Reza Shah and Ibn Saud,
    influences compared, 159–161; role
    of foreign powers in, 130, 158–159,
    161–165, 166, 177; U.S. and, 157,
    158, 161–165, 166; Wahhabism in,
    157–158, 160

SAVAK (secret police), 5, 192, 193

sectarianism. *See* Sunni-Shia divide

secularism: in Iran, 9, 52, 71, 72–73,
    156, 161; in Turkey, 168–169, 170,
    172, 173

September 11, 2001, 132

Sezer, Ahmet, 172

shah. *See* Pahlavi, Mohammad Reza

Shahroudi, Mahmoud Hashemi, 27

Shajarizadeh, Shaparak, 53–54

sharia law, 160, 190

al Shaykh family (Wahhab's descen-
    dants), 158

Shia Muslims, 125, 126; Christian al-
    liance, 149; in Iraq, 130, 136–138,
    139; in Lebanese government, 145,
    149, 151, 153; in Lebanon, 46, 123,
    144, 145, 149, 151, 153; mobiliza-
    tion efforts, 135, 145–146; political
    emergence of, 135–137; in Saudi
    Arabia, 164; in Turkey, 170; *velayat-*

e faqih (rule of the jurist) and, 136, 137; Wahhabism ideology objects to practices of, 157–158. *See also* Hezbollah; Sunni Muslims

Siniora, Fouad, 154

Sistani, Ali, 136, 137

slums, 10

social class: composition changes in, 22–23; income inequality and, 10–11, 24; middle class, 11, 22–23, 71

social development. *See* infrastructure and social development

socialism, 12, 18

social justice goal of Iranian Revolution, 8, 9–12. *See also* infrastructure and social development

social media, women's activism through, 51–52, 53, 54, 58–60. *See also* activism, women's rights

Society Against Opium and Alcohol, 41

socioeconomic issues. *See* economy, Iran; infrastructure and social development

Soleimani, Qassem, 178

Sotoudeh, Nasrin, 54

Soviet Union, 43–44, 192–195; invades Afghanistan, 164, 193–194; Russia, 13–14, 70, 124, 127, 172; vetoes U.S. sanctions on Iran, 97, 100, 105

spot market development, 117–119

stability, Iran's apparent pre-revolution, 73–74

state sponsorship, 131

"Stealthy Freedom" anti-hijab activism campaign, 51, 54, 56, 59, 60

student movements, 4, 13, 37, 83, 182–183. *See also* U.S. embassy seizure and hostage crisis (November 1979)

Sudan, 131

suicide bombings, 144, 146, 147, 176. *See also* terrorism

Sullivan, William, 6

Sunni Muslims, 127, 135; Iranian Revolution's impact on, 181–186; Islamist movements, 183–185; jihadism and, 129, 131; in Lebanese government, 145, 151, 153; in Lebanon, 145, 150, 151, 153; in Saudi Arabia, 157; in Turkey, 170

Sunni-Shia divide, 127, 182, 184, 191; regional power shifts and, 89, 135, 157, 176–177

Sweden, 61, 97

Syria, 126–128, 131, 170; civil war, 123, 126, 127, 132, 185; drug smuggling and, 46; Hama uprising (1982), 130; Hezbollah and, 147, 151–152; Muslim Brotherhood in, 184; Turkey and, 172; U.S. involvement, 127, 151, 153

Taif Agreement (Lebanon, 1989), 145, 148, 150

Talbott, Strobe, 4, 5–6

Taliban, 83

Tamimi, Azzam, 182–183

Taraki, Nur Muhammad, 193

tawhid (oneness) doctrine, 157

Temptations of Power (Hamid), 183

terrorism, 129–133; Saudi Arabia and, 129, 130, 131–132; suicide bombings, 144, 146, 147, 176; U.S. and, 84, 108, 127, 132, 152–153, 185. *See also* Hezbollah; radicalism and radicalist groups

theocratic political system, 13

"Tie a Yellow Ribbon 'Round the Ole Oak Tree" (Tony Orlando and Dawn), 89

Time magazine, 4

tourism, 61, 72

trade bans. *See* sanctions

traditionalism, 72. *See also* modernity and modernization

Trans-Alaska Pipeline, 117

Treaty of Amity, Economic Relations, and Consular Rights (1955), 105, 108, 109

Trump, Donald, 91

Trump, Melania, 61

Trump administration, 60–61, 110–111, 128, 166; Hezbollah and, 152–153; JCPOA and, 17, 28, 29; sanctions use in, 100, 108–109, 110

Tudeh Party, 192, 194

Tunisia, 182

Turkey, 168–173; economy, 21, 24; Israel and, 169, 175; opium in, 42, 43; secularism in, 168–169, 170, 172, 173; U.S. and, 43, 169, 171

Ünal, Yusuf, 182

unemployment rates, 10, 23, 24–25, 163

United Arab Emirates, 177

United Kingdom, 70, 98, 130, 159, 161–162; Britain, 70, 158–159, 161–162

United Nations Security Council, 97, 105, 110

United States: drug use and trade in, 43, 44, 46; gasoline crisis, 116–117; human rights foreign policy, 5, 92–95; Hussein removal, 83, 124; JCPOA, withdrawal from, 17, 27, 28, 29, 109, 110; military reform, 91–92; oil exports by, 166; Pakistan relations, 188–191; public opinion on shah in, 88, 93–94; Saudi Arabia relations, 61, 70, 132, 157, 158, 161–165, 166; shah backed by, 70–71, 72, 77, 162, 163. *See also* U.S.-Iran relations; U.S.-Middle East involvement

United States, sanctions by. *See* sanctions

U.S. Department of Energy, oil shocks and, 116

U.S. embassy, Lebanon, 130, 143–144

U.S. embassy, Pakistan, 188–191

U.S. embassy seizure (February 1979), 74

U.S. embassy seizure and hostage crisis (November 1979), 103–106; Carter and, 6, 74, 88–91, 96–97, 117; CIA response, 142; contributing factors, 6, 37; hostages released, 90, 99, 106; ICJ proceedings, 104–106; Iranian government response, 103–104, 110; Khomeini and, 32, 74, 89, 103; lasting political impact, 37, 74, 81, 88–91, 99–101; Operation Eagle Claw response, 89–91, 132; Rose Garden strategy, 89; U.S. economic sanctions response, 96–101, 104, 105

U.S.-Iran relations: Algiers Accords arbitrations, 99, 106–108; arms deals, 72, 82, 130; Carter administration and, 75, 81; criticism of, 50–51; international legal disputes in, 104, 110–111; IUSCT adjudication in, 107–109; JCPOA and, 84–85, 100–101, 109, 110; modernity's role in, 70–71, 72–73; Pompeo on, 50; Saudi Arabia and, 157, 158, 161–165, 166; Soviet Union and, 194; Trump administration and, 28, 29. *See also* sanctions

U.S.-Iran relations, anti-American sentiment: "Axis of Evil" speech fuels, 83–84; of Iran's leaders, 74, 75, 77, 82–83, 86, 93–94, 189; museum, in former U.S. embassy, 109; regional impact of, 76; terrorism and, 84, 130; Turkey and, 169

U.S.-Iran relations, rapprochement efforts, 80–87; Bush, George H. W. administration, 82; Bush, George W. administration, 83–84; Carter administration, 81; Clinton administration, 82–83; criticism of, 101; Obama administration, 84–86; Reagan administration, 81–82

U.S.-Iran relations, revolution's impact on, 69–77, 129; abruptness of transformation and, 73–74, 75; blame-placing narratives and, 75–76, 93; historical context, 70–72; lasting effects of, 69–70, 76–77, 157; modernity's role in, 72–73

U.S.-Middle East involvement, 4–5, 10, 13; Arab-Israeli peace process, 163; Iraq, 124, 141; Lebanon, 130, 143–144, 146, 152–154; Pakistan, 188, 189, 191; Saudi Arabia, 61, 70, 132, 157, 161, 163–164, 165, 166; Syria, 127, 151, 153; terrorism and, 84, 108, 127, 132, 152–153, 185; Turkey, 43, 169, 171. *See also* Joint Comprehensive Plan of Action (JCPOA); sanctions; U.S.-Iran relations

U.S.-Middle East involvement, military engagement: in Afghanistan, 44, 83, 84, 166; in Iraq, 83, 84, 124, 139, 166; Operation Eagle Claw, 89–91, 132; regional power shifts and, 70, 76–77, 161–162, 163, 165, 166; in Syria, 151

U.S. State Department, Bureau of Human Rights and Humanitarian Affairs, 92

urbanization, 9, 11

urban-rural policy shift, 19–20, 25

Vance, Cyrus, 81

veiling, compulsory. *See* hijab

velayat-e faqih (rule of the jurist, Iran's governance framework), 136, 137

Velayati, Ali Akbar, 126

Vienna Convention on Consular Relations (VCCR), 105–106, 109

Vienna Convention on Diplomatic Relations (VCDR), 105–106, 109

Voice of America (VOA) television

voting rights, 71

Wafd Party, 183

Wahhabism, 157–158, 160

weapons, arms deals, 72, 82, 130

West Germany, 98

"White Revolution," 71

Wind in My Hair, The (Alinejad), 51

women, 13, 50–62, 71; education and, 9; *Hudood* laws and, 190; social exclusion of, 24. *See also* activism, women's rights; hijab

working-class poor, 10

World Bank, 19

World Wars, 70

Yemen, 126, 128, 131, 147

youth: as disproportionate demographic, 60; job access for, 10, 11–12, 23

Zarif, Mohammad Javad, 85

Zia-ul-Haq, Muhammad, 188–191

Zibakalam, Sadegh, 8